Critical Small Schools

Beyond Privatization in New York City Urban Educational Reform

Critical Small Schools

Beyond Privatization in New York City Urban Educational Reform

Edited by

Maria Hantzopoulos
Vassar College

Alia R. Tyner-Mullings
The New Community College at CUNY

Information Age Publishing, Inc.
Charlotte, North Carolina • www.infoagepub.com

Library of Congress Cataloging-in-Publication Data

Critical small schools : beyond privatization in New York City urban educational reform / edited by Maria Hantzopoulos and Alia R. Tyner.
p. cm.
Includes bibliographical references.
ISBN 978-1-61735-683-4 (pbk.) -- ISBN 978-1-61735-684-1 (hardcover) -- ISBN 978-1-61735-685-8 (ebook)
1. Small schools--New York (State)--New York--Case studies. 2. Education, Urban--New York (State)--New York--Case studies. 3. School improvement programs--New York (State)--New York--Case studies. I. Hantzopoulos, Maria. II. Tyner, Alia R.
LB3012.5.C75 2011
371.009173'2097471--dc23

2011043686

Cover art by Christina Kemp

Printed in the United States of America

Dedication

This volume is dedicated to all of the students and
teachers in public schools, both in New York City and across the country.

CONTENTS

FOREWORD

Critical Small Schools— Windows On Educational Justice in a Neoliberal Blizzard

Michelle Fine

REFLECTING BACK ON 30 YEARS OF CRITICAL RESEARCH AND ORGANIZING AND TEACHING ...

In New York and Philadelphia, as in California and Chicago and throughout the country, small schools in the 1980s and early 1990s were designed and constructed with a rich sense of justice and democracy; a place where educators, parents, community and youth would come together to build knowledge, capacity and community power. The educational imagination was wide open. In New York, the District for Alternative Schools encouraged creative, "out of the box" thinking, led by educators who insisted that children of poverty deserve the same education as children of elites. The Diamond Foundation released a request for proposals (RFP) for innovative small schools in New York City, in which proposals had to be submitted jointly by a group of educators and a community-based organization. Two hours south, the Philadelphia Schools Collaborative enjoyed a substantial grant from the Pew Charitable Trusts to redesign big schools into teacher-led, community engaged, inquiry based, detracked small schools. Both cities were dotted with thrilling new ideas for

Critical Small Schools: Beyond Privatization in
New York City Urban Educational Reform, pp. ix–xvii
Copyright © 2012 by Information Age Publishing
All rights of reproduction in any form reserved.

how to organize time, critical pedagogy, assessment, teacher development, and collaborations with community groups. We had successfully decoupled building and school; there could be multiple small schools in a building—and not necessarily at the same grade levels. Interested in critical reflection on policy and practice, the small schools movements of the 80s and 90s launched their own internal and external evaluations of student work, graduation rates, teacher engagement, parent involvement and community relations. We were engaged in a radical movement for educational justice; held ourselves deeply accountable to communities, students, educators, and reinvigorating a Deweyian and Freirian vision of schooling linked with democracy and community development.

And then the winds of neoliberalism swept aggressively through urban America. In New York, in particular, philanthropy joined with mayoral control in a campaign to move small schools to scale. This was a heady and confusing time—was this good news or not? It soon became clear that the small schools movement was being coopted and commodified; Xeroxed and distributed across the city, with most of the key radical commitments of participation, equity, inquiry and dignity "left behind." Lifting only the numeric essence of small out from deep community moorings, the "move to scale" ripped the idea of small from the roots of participation, mistaking size as the point, rather than just a vehicle for justice. Suddenly our sweet radical experiment was mainstream, and deformed. In Chicago, Pauline Lipman writes that small schools were the front line of gentrification; in Milwaukee, a way to undermine teachers' unions and professionalism; in New York, a strategy that produced competing, overcrowded and underresourced small schools fighting with each other within the same building; and throughout the country, small became the chrysalis for hatching charters, the sac for drip fed privatization into the public school system.

There was a gathering in Chicago in 2004 called by the editors of *Rethinking Schools*—a critical meeting of educators, organizers and writers, to discuss how small schools were becoming a technology of dispossession by mayors, philanthropy and "reformers" dedicated to diminishing the power and influence of educators, community, parents and youth. In 2005, we produced a special volume of *Rethinking Schools* on small schools. Sobered by what I learned from friends and colleagues around the country, "Michelle, they are forcing small schools down our throats, using them for gentrification; teachers have no say—and handing out your articles!!" I wrote an essay, "Not in our name."

So thank you Maria and Alia for crafting a volume that re-members the small schools movement as a movement of justice, for relationships, of democracy, dignity, equity and inquiry—always reaching for what could be, even if we fall short.

* * *

I admit I am a fool for small schools. In the beginning these were smart, thrilling, politically engaged collectives of educators, parents and youth designing practices and settings for inquiry, democracy, antiracist and critical pedagogy to be woven into the fabric, papered to the walls, stitched into the soul of all who entered the doors. Reading this volume is like falling in love with an old lover, after years of estrangement. I was reminded of Lillian Hellman's (1973/2000) writing on *Pentimento*:

> Old paint, on a canvas, as it ages, sometimes becomes transparent. When that happens it is possible, in some pictures, to see the original lines: a tree will show through a woman's dress, a child makes way for a dog, a large boat is no longer on an open sea. That is called pentimento because the painter "repented," changed his mind. Perhaps it would be as well to say that the old conception, replaced by a later choice, is a way of seeing and then seeing again. (p. 3)

Like Hellman's pentimento, *Critical Small Schools* creates a translucent gauze over the contemporary small schools to induce a conversation between then and now; between Hellman's dog at play with the child who came before; the boats sailing on a water-less landscape. These chapters lift up the filaments of justice and commitment that were the life blood of the early small schools movement, and remind us of how these commitments have aged over time, weathered the neoliberal storm, bearing the scars of centralization and privatization and yet standing as strong relentless evidence of the power of deeply relational, highly participatory, actively accountable and always reflexive spaces for teaching and learning.

In the early days, issues of democracy, equity, intentionality and inquiry were fundamental to the design of schools, and the conversations held across schools. In District 4, Deborah Meier and the other directors of small schools sat around tables to make sure that there was an equitable distribution of experienced educators, special needs students, English language learners, resources and opportunities. And then on Friday afternoons, we held Loft Talks, where secondary small school educators, with me and bottles of wine, gathered to weave a critical and safe-ish community of practice, and laughter, desire and disappointment. High on the fumes of new schools and the experimental libratory energy of "what could be," we knew well what policies and practices we did not want to reproduce: tracking, suspensions, standardized testing, segregation. But, as Debbie Meier liked to say, "We were building the boat as we were sailing." When a hard wave hit, it was easy to revert to the traditional—if problematic—habits of education: track, punish, test, suspend, segregate. And so together, we built a counterhegemonic basket of linked bodies and a bit of wine, to invent practices for what could be, to be carried into schools the very next day and discussed critically, together, at our next gathering.

Since 2002, when mayoral control was implemented, the painter—in Hellman's language—or the mayor, indeed changed his mind about the soul of small schools. Like tearing beautiful flowers from their stems, the rich commitments of small schools were yanked from their social justice roots, their neighborhoods, their teachers, their communities of practice. New York City now has scores of small schools, but only a core remains *critical.* Thanks to the delicate harvesting of examples by Maria Hantzopoulos and Alia Tyner-Mullings, this volume allows us to "see, and see again," that these commitments have not been fully erased from the canvas.

Critical Small Schools: Beyond Privatization in New York City Urban Educational Reform reminds us that *small school* is neither an adjective nor a noun; it is an aspiration, a desire. Like democracy, small schools embody a vision of what must be: messy work, undertaken through collective participation, spiked with vibrant questions, in a deep and restless community, with strong commitments, fueled by raw vulnerabilities and generations of wisdom. Always aware that small schools have not fully slayed the dragons of racism, xenophobia and the scars of poverty, the volume speaks about the real challenges of education in neoliberal America and interrupts the white noise of privatization, charters, testing, centralization and Racing to the Top. This book is a powerful testament to what Debbie Meier called the "power of ideas" over time, sustained, cultivated and negotiating in the difficult air of the twenty-first century. At the same time, this book is a time capsule for educators coming up, to remember that public schools must be the capillaries of democracy, that parents are a gift, educators are intellectuals and activists and students are full of wonder—even as the toxic rains fall.

Let me end with a thought experiment. What if the chapters of *Critical Small Schools* were analyzed as the raw public evidence of the small schools movement? What if we imagined, for a moment, *participatory accountability*, engaged by what Maria Elena Torre would call a contact zone of multiple constituencies who value public schools as the capillaries of democracy? Participatory collectives of policymakers, educators, parents, advocates and youth could be invited to review this archive of evidence and then reflect on the accomplishments, struggles and remaining structural challenges of the critical small schools movement. The point of such an exercise would be to support, transform, critique and revise, nurture and develop schools as resources in community life—rather than discipline and punish, humiliate and close, exile parents/community/youth and re-open schools with selective admissions for the "deserving." We might invent a rubric, a set of grounding, non-negotiable principles that we know to be foundational to critical small schools; and then identify what structural or policy conditions get in the way, and what challenges still remain. We might create a rubric like the one below (Table 1), and then read chapters deeply to consider what is, and what could be.

Table 1.   Rubic

Essential Elements of Critical Small Schools	Exemplars	Structural and Policy Impediments	Ongoing Challenges
Sustained relationships among educators, youth and parents/community	Jessica Schiller, "City Prep staff took the relationship building aspect of NCSI very seriously in this test driven climate" Lesley Bartlett and Jill Koyama, "Close relationships were enjoyed by all, not only the most high achieving students ... trust, safety, cultural belonging ... a tight identification as a *familia*...."	Reliance on **short term educators,** e.g. TFA or teaching fellows not expected to stay in the system **Teacher Turnover** and **School Closings** **Disproportionate teacher placement** of new/inexperienced/long term subs in low income communities without support	Relationships among teachers, with students and families are always precarious and particularly fragile in communities marked by structural instabilities and histories of racism, especially in the midst of a recession Relationships are difficult to sustain and disrupted by high rates of teacher turnover, school closings, structural 'insecurity' induced by policies that disrespect teachers or pit teachers against each other or against students "Going to scale" often disrupts sustained relationships; there must be a deeply participatory process of replication that takes seriously place, context and history, supported by respectful seeding, mentoring and flexible adaptation of key principles of practice (Feldman)

Table continues on next page.

Table 1. Rubic Continued

Essential Elements of Critical Small Schools	Exemplars	Structural and Policy Impediments	Ongoing Challenges
Authentic student-inquiry as teaching, learning and assessment	Liza Bearman and Nora Ahmed, "interdisciplinary, real world connected- and project based education... integrates students' interests and voices into the curricula, shift teachers' roles from deliverers of knowledge to facilitators of learning..." Martha Foote, With freedom from high-stakes testing and the high accountability "Consortium students, despite their disadvantages upon entering high school, stay in school, learn to think deeply and critically, and graduate prepared for college where they earn solid GPAs and persist into the second year... They can write, discuss, present and develop and support their theses."	Over-reliance on **high-stakes testing** Limited access to the Consortium testing variance The insistence on **4 year graduation rates** as a measure of school success As Rosa Rivera-McCutchen explains, "What can one school realistically accomplish in four years when over 60% of kids are entering at below grade level in literacy and numeracy? Unless NCLB and local Department of Education policy mandates begin to de-emphasize traditional four-year graduation rates as a benchmark for accountability, critical small schools may be forced to make educational trade-offs at the expense of students." The **uneven distribution of experienced and passionate staff who want to be in the communities where these schools are located**	Students arrive at high school severely underprepared to engage in rigorous academic work. Low expectations are sometimes misinterpreted as caring. Rosa Rivera-McCutchen, "With the absence of explicit conversations about race and class dynamics, teachers in schools like Bridges run the risk of falsely conflating caring with high expectations. Furthermore, given that small schools in urban communities will often inevitably face high turnover, it is crucial that they develop protocols and procedures that will institutionalize strong practice. Without a solid academic infrastructure that guides their work in the absence of a veteran staff, small schools run the risk of reproducing the failures of the large schools they replaced."

Table continues on next page.

Table 1. Rubic Continued

Essential Elements of Critical Small Schools	Exemplars	Structural and Policy Impediments	Ongoing Challenges
Commitments to Equity, College Readiness and Public Conversations about Educational Justice	Alia Tyner-Mullings "The school proved to be a space within which students who are overwhelmingly underserved by the urban public school system could be educated and prepared for productive participation in life outside of school. It contributed to a dialogue on urban education and was at the forefront of a social movement to address some of the inequalities inherent in the educational system."	Selective admissions to charters and new small schools in gentrifying communities Class based/privatized college access structures Janice Bloom writes, "there is little question that access to higher education continues to be stratified across race and class lines.... Schools serving working class students need to create structures that replicate the dominant cultural and social capital available to middle class students in their college search and application process."	College access— Structuring process to facilitate access Supporting students to engage with the full range of college experiences, including lectures and even bad teaching! Sustaining strong commitments to democracy, voice and social change when the contexts of higher education are orthogonal to democratic and authentic practice; as Hantzopoulos tells us, "many former students described difficulty negotiating their 'Prep ideals' with external realities, those that work in these organizations and have experiences with them may have models for how to respond to challenges they may face beyond their democratic critical small schools."

Table continues on next page.

Table 1.   Rubic Continued

Essential Elements of Critical Small Schools	Exemplars	Structural and Policy Impediments	Ongoing Challenges
Participatory Democracy by communities of color and local schools	Maria Hantzopoulos provides a detailed sketch of how, at Humanities Prep, school governance, pedagogy, curriculum and assessments are organized to be both participatory and democratic for faculty and students: "encourage[ing] democratic participation, 'collective' critical consciousness, and a commitment to social change. It also helps socialize students academically, giving them a platform from which to think about the world differently and imagine different alternatives for the future. As a result, many of the practices at Prep ... are informative for the broader critical small schools movement." Anthony De Jesús offers a compelling narrative on El Puente Academy for Peace and Justice where the educational project within the walls of the Academy is infused with respect for the history, struggles and dreams of the Latino community to which the school is accountable. De Jesús allows us to bear witness to **participatory democracy by communities of color and local schools.**	Critical small schools aim to be democratic institutions in a severely "un-democratic" system, such that all of the **structures and enactments of participation need to be relentlessly protected from larger forces that encourage privatization, hierarchy, ranking, punishing, excluding and silencing of educators, communities and youth** When schools are controlled by corporate minded, centralized control (e.g. Mayor's offices), community and local culture are severely marginalized. As accountability regimes become more omnipresent and educational governance more centralized and corporatized, educators, parents, community and youth voice is silenced, and trivialized. We see the need for organizing and schools in which there is active participation by communities of color.	Students, once they leave Prep, reflect on the effects of being 'sheltered' from the larger world in which undemocratic principles prevail. Thus: "a closer look at the experiences of current students and alumni indicates that they also **encountered barriers to their sense of "voice" and their agency to affect change** when confronted with external "realities" within and beyond the school." Anthony De Jesús ends by telling readers: "policy makers and school reformers must consider the ways in which they structure opportunities at every level for communities to be involved in the schooling of their own. That is, of course, if they care to do so." Evidence suggests that communities and educators must **organize collaboratively and demand deep local participation and voice,** because it seems clear that current regimes are unwilling to 'care to do so.'"

What if *Critical Small Schools* were the evaluation rubric through which collectives of educators, parents, youth and policymakers could assess schools' relationships, pedagogical/curricular/assessment-based commitments to inquiry, structures of participation and intentionality toward equity? What if evaluation and accountability were not moments of newspaper displayed ridicule but instead local, public invitations to dialogue about goals and challenges, complex contradictions and weighty disappointments of small schools trying to counter the corrosive effects of racism and poverty? What if this volume were celebrated by the Mayor as a documentation of the incredible courage and accomplishments of the small schools movement in New York which has, over the past 25 years, achieved the unimaginable?

I will end with the words of coeditor and author Alia Tyner-Mullings, a stunning young scholar who reflects the passions and commitments of so many critical small school educators—ever reflexive, passionately dedicated and therefore never quite satisfied:

> While, clearly, the recent proliferation of critical small schools has not produced large scale economic equality or equivalent social mobility for low income and minority students, the emergence of these schools and their alternatives to traditional educational goals continues to reduce the disparities in educational access and to create individuals who can comprehend and compete in the quickly globalizing world around them.

And, as you will read in the words of Janice Bloom, "Willie Rivera deserves no less."

Thank you, Maria and Alia for allowing us to "see and see again, the original lines" of the small schools movement—sketching images of educational justice even or especially in very dark times.

REFERENCE

Hellman, L. (2000). *Pentimento: A book of portraits*. New York, NY: Bay Back Books. (Original work published 1973)

PREFACE

In the fall of 1998, Maria Hantzopoulos and Alia R. Tyner-Mullings, the coeditors of this volume, met as teachers at Humanities Preparatory Academy (Prep). The school was in its second year—recently developed from a program within a larger, traditional New York City public school. Teachers came to the school from a variety of backgrounds and experiences to turn the program into a small school with an emphasis on democratic processes, strong community, project-based assessment, and a commitment to social justice and equity. Maria had just finished a professional development internship at the Beacon School through Teachers College, and had also spent 3 years as one of the coordinators of the leadership development program at ASPIRA of New York. Alia arrived at the school having previously graduated from a similar high school, Central Park East Secondary School (CPESS), and, after college, was seeking an environment that had been akin to her own experiences. Together, with several other teachers and under the guidance of the founders, we helped build the foundation for this school and others to create an alternative educational environment for public school students that emphasized the aforementioned methods and values. It was exciting for us to be part of such a collaborative and innovative work environment, in which teachers' and students' ideas about education were valued and of central importance.

During our time at Prep, we expanded our knowledge of what it meant to be part of a reemerging small school movement that was dedicated to rethinking how schools were organized and how students were educated. Through teacher-centric professional development and activist networks like the New York Performance Standards Consortium and the Coalition of Essential Schools, we met with other educators and youth workers that were committed to sharing innovative structures and practices that distinguished their schools from others that were just small in size. While many

Critical Small Schools: Beyond Privatization in
New York City Urban Educational Reform, pp. xix–xxiv
Copyright © 2012 by Information Age Publishing
All rights of reproduction in any form reserved.

of the schools had different missions and student populations, they all shared a strong allegiance to the principles of a movement embedded in democratic participation, complex forms of assessment, social justice and equity (Ayers, Klonsky, & Lyon, 2000; Fine, 2005; Hantzopoulos, 2009). Moreover, most of the schools were dedicated to ensuring high levels of student achievement, particularly for those frequently marginalized from school, often working class and youth of color (Apple & Bean, 1995/2007; Ayers, Klonsky, & Lyon, 2000; Fine, 2005; Harber, 1996; Nieto, 2000; Powell, 2002). In New York City, many of these schools were historically referred to as alternative schools, though other programs that did not reflect the same principles were also under this category (Tyner-Mullings, 2008).

As the small schools movement proliferated rapidly through the early 2000s, the distinction between these earlier schools and many of the newer, small schools needed to be made more clearly, particularly as many of the latter schools were opening and were not maintaining the vision of the original movement (Fine, 2005; Hantzopoulos, 2009, Tyner-Mullings, 2008). When Maria was discussing this shifting phenomenon in relationship to her dissertation with one of her colleagues, Monisha Bajaj, at Teachers College, the term "critical small schools" emerged from their conversation as a potential way to classify this distinction, since up until then, "small schools" was the nomenclature for all schools that were smaller in size (Hantzopoulos, 2008, 2009). When Alia and Maria met to discuss the overlap in their research in the summer of 2008, we realized that there were many commonalities in our approaches, particularly in relationship to the shifting tides of the original small schools movement. More importantly, we had also recognized that our own work at Prep and our previous teaching and learning experiences propelled us to conduct research in "critical small schools" for our dissertations, and we had come to the conclusion that the stories and data unearthed from our research and data needed to be told.

It soon became apparent that we were not alone in this endeavor; many authors in this volume besides us were also once K-12 teachers, youth workers and advocates in and for "critical small schools." Like us, many of these "teacher-scholars-activists" were driven by the desire to make meaning of these complex and unique experiences, with a deeper understanding of how some students thrived in these environments, how others struggled, and in general, how to move forward as a movement that was never simply about smallness, but about equity, social justice and high achievement for all. This volume was thus born out of this desire, fulfilling a need to document and understand the promise of such schools, as well as embrace their struggles and re-imagine possibilities for continual and reflective reform.

Situated in the current climate of neoliberal discourses about standards-based and marketized reform, the case studies in this volume demonstrate how educational sites might be counternarratives to increasing standardization and privatization in education through their commitment to developing schools with unique, democratic missions and identities and innovative progressive teaching methods for all students. This is especially relevant as recent controversies over the effectiveness of small schools have left the movement in a precarious position. Critics have cautioned that public small schools are too costly, lacking rigor in math and science, and most despairingly, too exclusive by prohibiting admission to English Language Learners, special education students, and recent immigrants (Bloomfield, 2005; Ravitch, 2005; New York Immigration Coalition and Advocates for Children, 2006). These are valid and important critiques. However the problem with lumping all small schools together— mainstream and critical—is that these criticisms obscure the significant data that many small schools are effective in engaging students who have been marginalized and underserved by the public school system as many of the schools in *Critical Small Schools* demonstrate.

This volume, therefore, views the critical small schools movement as one that is vibrant, ever-evolving, dynamic and in constant flux. We hope that as new educational trends and fads come and go, people will turn to this volume to obtain keen insight into the challenges and possibilities of comprehensive school reform. Therefore, we hope that it will be widely read in courses on educational policy, urban educational reform, schoolwide practices, teacher education and social justice education. *Critical Small Schools* is also an important resource in urban studies, sociology of education, and courses on structural and institutional inequalities in education. It offers important studies of the promise, limitations, and struggle that these small high schools face at a time when the broader small schools movement has been subject to both praise and controversy among city, state and national policymakers.

ACKNOWLEDGMENTS

The editors are deeply appreciative of the many people that made this volume possible. First, we are grateful to the contributors of this volume who submitted drafts, responded to feedback, and worked with us diligently in making this a complete and comprehensive whole. We are also grateful to all of the schools in this volume, named and anonymous, that opened their doors to the researchers so that we could strive to tell their stories in the most authentic and accurate manner. We are especially appreciative of Christina Kemp, a teacher at Prep, who created the artwork for the cover. Special mention goes to Christine Cruz, Sarah Marco, and Amanda Cheung the three research assistants from Vassar College that provided feedback, suggestions, and copy-editing throughout this process. We also would like to thank Michelle Fine for capturing the essence of the volume in her foreword and for her unwavering support. Finally, we would like to appreciate our editors at Information Age Press for their attention to detail, patience, and advice.

Maria Hantzopoulos' Acknowledgments

I am deeply indebted to many people that contributed feedback and input during the various stages of this project and am grateful for their friendship and guidance. In particular, I acknowledge my writing group from Vassar College: Colette Cann, Erin McCloskey, and Eréndira Rueda, all of whom provided sage counsel, advice, and technical support throughout the work on this volume. I am also appreciative of many people with whom I had informal conversations about this project, specifically Monisha Bajaj, Roozbeh Shirazi, and Zeena Zakharia. They served as friends and critical colleagues, offering advice and an ear when needed. It has also been an incredible experience to work on this whole volume with coeditor Alia Tyner-Mullings. I feel lucky to have had the opportunity to work with someone who is so thorough, thoughtful, intelligent, and fun. I look forward to even more collaborative projects together. I am also deeply indebted to the community of people that helped care for my children as I worked on this project. In particular, I am grateful for the wonderful teachers at my daughter's old daycare, the Vassar Infant/Toddler Center, and her current preschool, Les Enfants, as well to Margarita Vlachos and Doina Maldarescu, for their attentive and loving care.

I would also like to thank my family for their incessant love and support, including my parents, Peter and Chris, and all of my siblings. I also owe so much to my incredible husband, Johnny Farraj, whose love, patience, and amazing home-cooked food sustained me during this enduring and arduous process. Finally, I acknowledge my daughter, Dalia, an amazing force and source of love and determination, and my newborn son, Ziyad, who literally helped kick this manuscript out of me. I could not have achieved this without them.

Alia R. Tyner-Mullings' Acknowledgments

I would like to add special appreciation for Nikisha Williams and Angelique Harris, my writing group and friends, who worked closely with me through many iterations of this project—editing, providing advice and taking time out of their busy schedules to help me with mine. I would also like to offer thanks to my family and friends. My parents, Jarvis

Tyner, Lydia Bassett, Manning Marable and Leith Mullings all encouraged me in many ways. I particularly thank my mother, whose help has been invaluable, encouraging me to do my best work and using her own experience to improve mine; and my stepfather, who helped to read and edit drafts of this contribution in several forms. I thank my brothers, Michael and Colby Tyner—especially Michael who read my work and participated in discussions with me about critical small schools—and my friends, Johanna Cepin, Ivonne Garcia, Enrique Figueroa, Gerald Blankson, Daniel Mani and Jacques Montemoiño who always know when to leave me alone, when to drag me out and when to offer help. I would like to echo my coeditor's thoughts about this experience of collaboration with her. Working with Maria Hantzopoulos through this process has been a pleasure and I also anticipate several future endeavors that we can complete together.

REFERENCES

Apple, M. W., & Beane, J. A. (Eds.). (1995). *Democratic Schools*. Alexandria, VA: Association for Supervision and Curriculum Development. (Original work published 1970)

Ayers, W., Klonsky, M., & Lyon, G. (2000). *A simple justice*. New York, NY: Teacher's College

Bloomfield, D. (2005). Come clean on small schools. *Education Week*. Retrieved on January 20, 2005 from http://www.edweek.org

Fine, M. (2005). Not in our name. *Rethinking schools, 19*(4), 1-6.

Hantzopoulos, M. (2008). Sizing up small: An ethnographic case study of a critical small high School (Unpublished doctoral dissertation). Teachers College, Columbia University, New York, NY.

Hantzopoulos, M. (2009). Transformative teaching in restrictive times: Engaging teacher participation in small school reform during an era of standardization. In F. Vavrus & L. Bartlett (Eds.), *Comparatively knowing: Vertical case study research in comparative and development education* (pp. 111-126). New York, NY: Palgrave.

Harber, C. (1996). *Small schools and democratic practice*. Nottingham, England: Education Heuristics Press.

New York Immigration Coalition and Advocates for Children (2006). *So many schools, so few options: How Mayor Bloomberg's small school reforms deny full access to immigrant students*. Retrieved on September 13, 2007 from www.thenyic.org

Nieto, S. (2000). A gesture towards justice: Small schools and the promise of equal education. In W. Ayers, M. Klonsky & G. Lyon (Eds.), *A simple justice*. (pp. 13-19). New York, NY: Teachers College Press.

Powell, L. (2002, June). *Small schools and the issue of race*. New York, NY: Bank Street College of Education Occasional Paper Series.

Tyner-Mullings, A. (2008) *Finding space: Educational reforms in practice in an urban public school* (Unpublished doctoral dissertation). CUNY Graduate Center, New York, NY.

Ravitch, D. (2005, November 6). Downsize high schools? Not too Far. *Washington Post*, B07.

INTRODUCTION

Forging a Homegrown Movement— The Case for Critical Small Schools in New York City

Maria Hantzopoulos and Alia R. Tyner-Mullings

THE SMALL SCHOOLS MOVEMENT: ORIGINS, DEVELOPMENT, AND EXPANSION[1]

The "critical small schools" featured in this volume were not created in a vacuum. As Fine (2005) emphatically states in her *Rethinking Schools* article about reclaiming the original purpose of small schools, it is absolutely essential to unmask the democratic and community-based roots of the movement so that current successful small schools are not seen as isolated anomalies, but rather part of a larger, collective of students, educators and activists that have organized for educational justice.

The basis for the original small schools movement began several decades ago out of a system that was relatively resistant to change. Historically, there had been a tradition of small schools in the United States, but they fell out of fashion in the late 1950s under the vision of James Bryant Conant who transformed curriculum to reflect advances in technology, research and science. Believing that schools were too small and could not meet the diversified needs of their growing student bodies, Conant pushed for the creation of large comprehensive high schools, which

Critical Small Schools: Beyond Privatization in
New York City Urban Educational Reform, pp. xxv–xliv
Copyright © 2012 by Information Age Publishing
All rights of reproduction in any form reserved.

involved consolidating rural school districts and constructing new ones in the cities and suburbs (Barker & Gump, 1964; Ravitch, 2000; Tyack & Cuban, 1995).

New York high schools fell into this category of "comprehensive schools" and suffered from many of the problems these types of schools faced: namely the lack of support for struggling students, sense of alienation in a depersonalized environment, concerns over safety and violence, and low achievement and high dropout rates for students. Situated within the "sick" bureaucracy (Ballantine, 2001; Ravitch, 1974; Rogers, 1968) of the New York City Board of Education,[2] many aspects of the school system were often left unsupervised as each department or office was so detached from others. The distance from The Board of Education headquarters in downtown Brooklyn to many low-income and underserved neighborhoods was also metaphorical, far enough that students often did not feel the benefits of the system, although they were often affected by its failings.

Both the centralization (and the attendant inability to supervise all parts of the system) and decentralization (creating spaces that allowed new ideas to develop) of the New York City Board of Education laid the groundwork for the launch of an innovative public school in New York City, Central Park East One (CPE1) elementary school. Basic to the creation of this school was the view that schools could make changes in the lives of children, despite external social forces. In addition, this type of school had the potential to promote larger systemic changes—to build the foundation for what would become a social movement to spread small, alternative and critical schools. Subsequently, in 1974, Deborah Meier opened CPE1 to a largely poor student body of color in East Harlem. The district (District 4) was considered one of the struggling districts in the city—populated by low-income and mostly students of color—with high dropout rates, absenteeism and violence along with low levels of mathematic ability and literacy (Fliegel, 1993).

Shortly before CPE1 reached its 10 year mark, *A Nation at Risk* was published. This report, commissioned by the U.S. Department of Education, generated fervent debate nationwide about the failing nature of American public schooling. The statistics from that report seemed to indicate a decrease in academic achievement and test scores, suggesting that 40% of American students were not ready for college or work (Bernard & Mondale, 2001). The public "scandalization" (Steiner-Khamsi, 2003) of the U.S. educational system justified the eventual introduction of standards-based reform, and thus began a public discourse about accountability and testing in schools. The findings of *A Nation at Risk* were not completely unexpected. In the early 1980s, a series of reports lamented the purported decline of public schools. In particular, these studies noted lowered teacher expectations of students, increased credit offerings for "non-academic" coursework, the decline of SAT scores, and diminished vocabulary among students (Ravitch, 2000). While more students than ever were attending higher education, many cautioned that opening the doors of college to unprepared students was a sham of democratization. For proponents of standards-based reforms, real democracy in education would have required that the public schools make sure that every high school graduate gained the literacy, numeracy, and other skills necessary for technical occupations and higher education (Ravitch, 2000). Thus, from the beginning, standards-based reform warned of an eroding American democracy that was grounded in the failure of public schools.

The Nation at Risk findings that schools were insufficiently responding to the changes in the nation's economy had huge implications for educational policy though the consequences were not immediately wholly manifest (National Commission on Excellence in Education, 1983). Couched in language of equity and opportunity, the document asserted that:

> All, regardless of race or class or economic status, are entitled to a fair chance and to the tools for developing their individual powers of mind and spirit to the utmost. This promise means that all children by virtue of their own efforts, competently guided, can hope to attain the mature and informed judgment needed to secure gainful employment. (p. 11)

In order to achieve this promise, the Commission recommended that all high school students study "the new basics" that emphasized a commitment to high academic standards. While many educators and educational historians challenged the findings that schools were steadily declining (Ayers, 2000b; Bernard & Mondale, 2001; Meier, 2000; Tyack & Cuban, 1995), state after state eventually began adopting policies that mandated curriculum, standards and testing. According to education historian Diane Ravitch (2010), the emphasis on testing diluted an authentic standards-movement that could have emerged from these findings.

In the year following the publication of *A Nation at Risk,* Theodore Sizer (1984), former headmaster of the elite Phillips Academy, wrote *Horace's Compromise,* which presented a radical rethinking of the structure of the American high school. Sizer (1984, 1992, 1996) believed that schools and classes needed to be smaller and that teachers, instead of bureaucratic overseers, needed to run schools. This move contrasted to teacher accountability models that were embedded within the emerging, though not yet fully realized, high-stakes standards-based reform initiatives. Sizer subsequently created the Coalition of Essential Schools (CES), a national education reform organization dedicated to transforming American public education so that not only "every child in every neighborhood, regardless of race or class, attends a small, intellectually challenging, personalized school," but also that these types of schools become the norm of American public education (Coalition of Essential Schools, n.d.). In this sense, Sizer and many of his followers saw standards as something that arose from the ground-up rather than imposed from the top-down.

Meanwhile, CPE1 in New York City had become a success, attributed to its personalized, community-oriented philosophy that was built on teacher and student trust (Bensman, 2000). The success of CPE1 paved the way for a movement of small school creation, particularly among high schools, as they were increasingly seen as not meeting the needs of students. On the elementary school's tenth anniversary, Sizer approached Deborah Meier to ask her to expand CPE1 using the principles he laid out in Horace's Compromise. Central Park East Secondary School was created by committee over the next year (Meier, personal communication, March 3, 2007) and opened in 1985 as a seventh grade with Meier as its principal. Its first graduating class was in 1991.

CPESS helped to create the 10 common principals that all current CES schools use in their school's structure. These common principles serve as a guide to creating schools that strive to nurture students to reach their fullest potential. Those in CES schools believe that to change the public school system, there needed to exist a large number of individual small schools that were fully committed to enacting these principles, so that these schools could both serve as models to other schools and demonstrations to the public that it is possible to reimagine education. The principles were created to achieve this. They call for concepts like personalized instruction to address individual needs and interests; small schools and classrooms, where teachers and student know each other well and work in an atmosphere of trust and high expectations; multiple assessments based on the performance of authentic tasks; democratic and equitable school policies and practice; and close partnerships with the school's community (see Coalition of Essential Schools, n.d.). When CES expanded to create a Small Schools Network (see Feldman & O'Dwyer, this volume; Hantzopoulos, 2009), they explicitly viewed the principles as guidelines for the schools rather than confining rules. For instance, CES sees school reform as "an inescapably local phenomenon, the outcome of groups of people working together, building a shared vision and drawing on the community's strengths, history, and local flavor" (Coalition of Essential Schools, n.d). These principles stand in complete contradistinction to the ones underwriting the standards-based reform movement, which informs "mainstream" small schools movement.

With reform platforms like that of CES and other community-based endeavors, the 1980s spawned a "quiet revolution" (Fine, 2005) of small schools that emerged throughout the United States, particularly in urban centers of New York, Chicago, Boston and Cincinnati. In most instances, students, teachers, parents, and community members were intimately included in their creation (Apple & Beane, 1995/2007; Ayers, Klonsky, & Lyon, 2000; Clinchy, 2002; Fine, 2000, 2005; Fine & Somerville, 1998). Many of these schools were not affiliated with CES, yet were equally committed to providing personalized and meaningful education as well as fashioning unique, democratic, and rigorous pockets of schools, particularly for historically minoritized young people (Fine, 2005). Attempting to reclaim the public sphere, small schools were seen as reinvigorating public education with anti-racist practices and agendas (Fine, 2005; Fine & Powell, 2001; Powell, 2000). They were also deeply embedded with democratic principles that encouraged all parties to actively shape and direct their education (Apple & Beane, 1995/2007). In New York City, some of these earlier schools besides Central Park East Secondary School were El Puente Academy for Peace and Justice in Brooklyn, the Urban Academy Laboratory High School in Manhattan, International High School in Queens, University Heights in the Bronx, and the Satellite Academies that were in several boroughs. All of these small schools were committed to project-based assessment, even at a time when state graduation requirements were not dependent on Regents examinations.

From the late 1990s and into the twenty-first century, the once "quiet revolution" transformed into one that became increasingly popular, vociferous, and ultimately co-opted. As mentioned earlier, there was suddenly a rapid expansion of small schools that took root in urban centers across the nation. Initially resting upon an overall vision that attempted to engage local actors in rectifying the dropout crisis and transforming American public education, the movement snowballed into something much larger and gained mainstream political support, particularly in New York City. While the Annenburg Institute backed some of the earlier small schools, the momentum for creating more of them intensified when other organizations and foundations, like the Bill and Melinda Gates Foundation, began to funnel money into the creation of smaller learning communities. This reform was viewed by some as one of the main ways to reform American public education and a means to redress increasing dropout rates in high schools, particularly among African-American and Latino youth (The Bill and Melinda Gates Foundation, n.d.). Coupled with the backing of Mayor Michael Bloomberg and now former schools' Chancellor Joel Klein, this funding contributed to a rapid proliferation of small schools in New York City. For example, in partnership with the NYC Department of Education (DOE), local educational and community organizations launched more than 200 small schools between 2001 AND 2008 (see Gootman, 2006; O'Day, Bitter, & Talbert, 2011).

Yet, initial supporters of small schools were skeptical about their rapid growth. In part, this had to do with other neoliberal educational reforms that rose in tandem with the small schools movement. In particular, the emphases on high-stakes standardized testing, and accountability for schools and teachers measured through the students' performances on these examinations, undermined the goals of the original small schools. Despite these paradoxical trajectories and visions, the small schools movement became viewed as a singular panacea for educational reform, particularly in New York City. Yet, the turn toward standardization changed the shape and direction of the original small schools movement, as it partly (though not entirely) became co-opted by both the national and local neoliberal educational programs that emphasized standards-based reform over student project and inquiry-based learning. This resulted in many of the original small schools redefining themselves in response to this pressure, abandoning original visions of school pedagogy and practice to prepare students for these tests. Many of the new small schools opening were "big schools in drag" (Fine, 2005, p 1), meaning that they were reproducing some of the same structures and pedagogies they were meant to replace.

It is partially out of these debates and discussions that this book was developed. There was a space in the education literature on small schools that missed the difference between the various types of small schools and the debates surrounding standardized tests, school size, and urban educational reform. Our definition of these schools as critical small schools is intended to addresses this gap. Early on in the small schools movement, the commitment to defining effective learning communities *beyond* small-ness was an essential feature and their distinct missions, structures, curricula and pedagogies continues to be what makes them interesting sources of research. Moreover, as an urban center, New York is often cited as an ideal site in which the small schools movement has burgeoned, yet it is also referred to as one of the states with the most rigorous and confining graduation requirements.[3] It is important to note that many of these original small schools in New York City united in 1997 to form the New York Performance Standards Consortium, an organization that opposes high-stakes tests in favor of project-based assessment (see Performance Assessment, n.d.).

Critics of the proliferation of the small schools movement were not only cautious about the de-emphasis on effective pedagogies, structures and assessments, but also questioned both the hierarchical ways in which the new schools were being created and the influx of money from the private sector. During the exponential growth of small schools, NYC transitioned to mayoral control. Many of the newer small schools were thereby imposed upon communities and did not have the requisite community-based support. Moreover, there has since been a shift in educational policy towards the funding and support of all small schools. Despite substantial research that attributes the success of many public small schools that serve working class and of color populations to the innovative pedagogies and relationships that transpire in them,[4] some major funders of small schools, like the Bill and Melinda Gates Foundation have redirected their monetary support towards other initiatives. According to their foundation, which contributed over 2 billion dollars to the creation of new small schools nationwide, those schools that did not radically alter their school culture (including changing their hiring practices and curriculum) fell short in transforming educational opportunities for American high school students. Rather than encouraging schools to make changes in school aspects beyond a simple shift in size, the foundation has used this analysis to abandon the public small schools project, announcing in January of 2009 that they would reallocate their educational resources away from this initiative to the sole creation of more charters. Similarly, New York City politicians like Mayor Bloomberg and former Chancellor Klein, who touted public small schools as part of their educational and political agenda, eventually explicitly shifted their focus towards the creation of small *charter* schools, requesting that the state cap on charters be lifted so that the city can have more of them.[5]

While these moves also support the educational platform propagated by the federal government, critics claim that these shifts represent a blatant move away from public schooling to privately funded schools. In New York City, this contested terrain of reform has become a fierce battleground as the creation of these charter schools come at a cost. Many existing small and large public high schools have been deemed failures and slated for closure, providing a physical space for the creation of charters. Yet, the students who had been served by those existing schools are often pushed out and into overcrowded and underfunded ones. Further, the controversy surrounding these closures centers on the ways in which "failure" has been determined, as well as the ways in which parents, communities, teachers, and the students themselves have been excluded from the decision-making process.

At this pivotal moment in educational reform, *Critical Small Schools* challenges this new direction that steers successful school development away from public education. Although we wholeheartedly agree with the Gates' analysis that school culture is an essential and fundamental feature of educational reform, we emphatically disagree that abandoning the creation of effective and innovative small public schools is the answer. While many small schools have not fulfilled their promise of developing college-ready students, we partially attribute this to a misguided emphasis on *size only* in a political context that privileges neoliberal and standardized educational policies over innovative school cultural reform (see Fine, 2005; Hantzopoulos, 2009; Klonsky & Klonsky, 2008). This has resulted in recent years to a bifurcation of the small schools movement; on one end are the small schools which have embraced the democratic, participatory and self-governing nature of the original movement, while on the other end are schools that have simply reduced their size without rethinking school structures and practices.

As such, we find it imperative to distinguish the "critical" small schools featured and researched in this volume from schools that are simply small. By documenting the practices, successes and challenges that take place in these particular schools, we also show (1) how the neoliberal direction of the small schools movement has undermined the goals of the original small schools movement and (2) how the current emphasis on charter schools and teacher preparation alone is misdirected. This volume presents some of the most current research on critical small, public schools, many of which have narrowed the achievement gap through their high graduation **and** college acceptance rates. While smallness is an essential feature in the design of these schools, it is certainly not the only one and this volume offers research and insight into the other elements that contribute to these schools' successes and shortcomings, critically examining the current state of the small schools movement. Moreover, the research presented not only provides insight into how schools can re-socialize students academically, but also sheds light on how schools work for the greater public good by being responsive to the communities that they serve. We acknowledge that every site is fraught with some tension, and the case studies presented here not only provide insight into intellectually vibrant and democratic learning communities, but also acknowledge that these concepts are not static and continually necessitate reflection and renewal.

CRITICAL SMALL SCHOOLS

Our volume presents important and current empirical research about the effectiveness and limitations of both the new small schools that continue to emerge and the older ones that grow toward maturity and expand, particularly for students who have been historically marginalized from schooling in the United States. The chapters in this volume are concerned with "critical small schools" because they use innovative approaches to assessment, curriculum, pedagogy, and/or school structure. These types of schools are not merely small schools; nor are they necessarily schools for individuals who cannot function in traditional school environments. Rather, they are small schools established with a specific mission: to create a particular educational environment, one that is democratic and humane, and driven by students' and teachers' passions and interests. They are committed to providing equitable, intellectually rigorous, and socially just spaces for youth, so that young people can realize their fullest potential and truly have an opportunity to pursue their dreams.

While the schools presented in this volume have different missions and visions, many of them share some common practices that help define their criticality. This has included the replacement or supplementing of the state required standardized high-stakes Regents exams with project-based or performance-based assessment tasks (PBATs) (see Bearman & Ahmed; Bloom; De Jesús; Feldman & O'Dwyer; Foote; Hantzopoulos; Rivera-McCutchen; Tyner-Mullings). In these schools, such as Prep, Baldwin, CPESS, Bridges, and El Puente, students complete collections of work in order to demonstrate their understanding of 4 to 14 different subject areas. Students are also required to present or discuss these projects with teachers, other students and/or outside evaluators in order to prove their proficiency in the topic. Performance-based assessments work well in these schools because they complement the schools' use of theme or inquiry-based learning, where students explore a topic in depth, emerging with significantly more than the superficial fact attainment which test preparation often produces (see Bearman & Ahmed; De Jesús; Foote; Hantzopoulos, Tyner-Mullings). Students can connect more deeply to these projects because of the connections many of these schools attempt to make with the students' culture and their communities (see Bartlett & Koyama; De Jesús; Hantzopoulos; Shiller; Tyner-Mullings). While not all of the schools have the state-issued variance for the PBATS, critical small schools endeavor to create opportunities for authentic engagement and assessment, despite the pressures of the high-stakes standardized exams.

Critical small schools also often emphasize the importance of the relationships shared by the individuals within the school. The teachers and administrators of these schools strive to create a community that students, throughout these chapters, often refer to as a "family" (see Bartlett & Koyama; De Jesús; Hantzopoulos; Rivera-McCutchen; Shiller; Tyner-Mullings) and breaking down the walls built between teachers and students. Much of this happens through the use of an advisory system. While some of the specifics differ at the different sites, most of the schools in our volume included a "class" of no more than 15 students who come together once a day as a way to maintain close ties with each other and their teacher. The "advisor" is responsible for knowing where their students are in their work and charting their process through school. Each advisor is responsible to and for their advisees and can act as an early warning system for any problems the student may face (see Bloom; Shiller).

Additionally, critical small schools create spaces and venues for student-centered, democratic learning. This learning also goes beyond the traditionally academic and often involved intentional structures like community activism and service (see De Jesús; Hantzopoulos; Tyner-Mullings), peer mediation and restorative justice (see De Jesús; Hantzopoulos) and town meetings (see Feldman & O'Dwyer; Hantzopoulos). For many of these schools, this connection to democratic learning and education comes out of the community-based approach to the creation of the school, as several of the schools were created by organizations that have been staples of the community for many years.

Finally, while we acknowledge that critical small schools provide many possibilities for students and teachers, we also realize that there are many challenges to enacting their programs for the teachers as well as current and former students. This volume examines some of the issues related to launching and maintaining small schools (see Feldman & O'Dwyer; Rivera-McCutchen; Shiller) as well as the myriad of student's experiences transitioning into and surviving beyond the school sites (see Bloom; Hantzopoulos; Rivera-McCutchen; Tyner-Mullings).

Overall, the schools in this volume are also important case studies of urban educational reform. While the word "urban" often has come to represent underserved Black and Brown students and under resourced schools, we refocus the discourses about public schools from the dominant deficit model to include larger ideas about social justice, democracy, community and family. The case studies in this volume view students, schools and their communities as primary to the educational experience (Fine, 2005), and demonstrate how "urban" sites are full of possibility, potential and success. Further, this book complicates the singular assumptions of what is considered stereotypically urban; instead, we examine the diverse populations found in these urban centers. While we find that the term urban can mask the complexity of the populations in areas such as New York City, the schools in this volume include students who are Black, Hispanic, White and Asian as well as those that identify as members of other groups. This does not deny that many of these schools serve students that are mostly of color; yet, in some examples, we also show the possibilities of urban educational reform when intentional desegregated spaces are created, not in an attempt to be "color-blind," but rather, as Fine, Weis, and Powell (1997) suggest, to render a space in which multiracial youth relations flourish under the conditions of community, analysis of difference, and investment in democracy.

SUMMARY OF CHAPTERS

Given the distinction between critical small schools and mainstream schools that are simply small, the chapters in this book present empirical research that distinguishes the constitutions and essential features of small schools, investigating their successes and challenges. Each section provides readers with a glimpse of the many ways that critical small schools operate: what their goals are, how they achieve them, what challenges they face, where they fall short and where they succeed. While smallness is a key component in the designs of these schools, we show which other factors, circumstances and influences contribute to their success. In this sense, small is *not* all.

We have divided the volume into three sections: (1) Creating and maintaining critical small schools: Challenges and possibilities; (2) Inside the Learning Communities: the culture, practices, and form of critical small schools; and (3) Beyond the sphere of schooling: Students navigating post-secondary transitions, reviewed in more detail below. While many of the themes in the sections overlap, we have organized the volume in this way so that readers can easily identify key areas that they would like to explore further. We have also included brief introductions to each section, with questions for further exploration.

Part I: Creating and Maintaining the Visions of Critical Small Schools: Challenges and Possibilities

Jessica T. Shiller's chapter profiles a small Bronx high school, City Prep, that opened under The New Century Schools Initiative (NCSI) funded by the Gates Foundation. Claiming that small size would create a personalized environment that would then lead to improved academic achievement, NCSI built upon an earlier wave of small schools that existed in the city. However, by starting hundreds of schools at once and privileging test score gains above all else, Shiller shows how NCSI reformers overlooked the supports small schools need to build strong relationships between teachers and students. Despite this, the staff at City Prep made relationship-building a priority, strengthening its school culture and students' attachment to school. As such, the processes at City Prep serve as an example of what is possible even in a climate that prioritizes improvements in data as the main indicator of a successful school, shedding light on important considerations during the pivotal start-up phase of school creation.

In her chapter, Rosa L. Rivera-McCutchen, provides an illustrative example for how critical small schools, can "maintain [their] educational vision[s]" over time. One of the earlier small schools, Bridges Institute emerged from the restructuring of a failing comprehensive high school in the Bronx as part of the Coalition Campus Schools Project, a larger small school reform initiative in New York City in 1994. In particular, she explores how Bridges was influenced by the interaction between its unique educational processes and the challenges it confronted beyond its start-up years, by examining the "core of educational practice" (Elmore, 1996) there, and the extent to which that core has been instrumental in sustaining the school's vision of small school reform. Through ethnographic interviews with school founders, veteran and novice staff, and school alumni, she describes how administrators in this school built a solid school foundation through the hiring of veteran teachers that believed in the core practices of authentic assessment and high expectations. Because of this decision, when leadership and political climate changed, and the teachers felt the mission of the school was in jeopardy, they took ownership over the school until they found someone who understood how the school should be run. Through this process, they also created structures to maintain their institutional memory. Within the broader context of small school reform, the lessons about maintaining ones' vision is incredibly timely. Understanding the evolution of Bridges and the role of its community and policy contexts in its conceptual stages reveals important lessons that can inform small school reformers and advocates as we look forward to the newest generation of small schools.

Jay Feldman and Anne O'Dwyer examine the birth and early years of a new small high school, James Baldwin School (Baldwin) in Manhattan. Created through a unique process of seeding, replication and mentoring, Baldwin used their relationships with their mentor school, Humanities Preparatory Academy (Prep) and the Coalition of Essential Schools (CES) to create a school which students ranked highly on engaging them academically and socially—as compared to their previous "noncritical" schools. In particular, the process of opening Baldwin involved some teachers and students from Prep becoming some of the founding members of Baldwin as well as including many of the key organizational and classroom practices of Prep in the Baldwin design. Through comprehensive surveys and interviews, students and teachers were asked to discuss the effectiveness of this approach to school creation. By comparing Baldwin surveys with a national sample of student surveys from other start-up high schools, this chapter sheds light on the possibilities of school mentoring as an effective way to increase student achievement and engagement in school as well as enhancing the creation of new critical small schools.

Part II: Inside the Learning Communities: The Culture, Practices, and Form of Critical Small Schools

Anthony De Jesús' chapter features El Puente Academy for Peace and Justice, one of the older critical small New York City high schools, founded and operated by a Latino/a community-based organization in Brooklyn. Using in-depth interviewing, participant observation, and document review, this chapter describes the experiences of students at this school and analyzes these student perspectives within a framework of critical care advanced by scholars in recent years (Antrop-Gonzalez & De Jesús, 2006; Bajaj, 2009). Unlike many small schools established by neoliberal school reform organizations, and private philanthropy, El Puente Academy for Peace and Justice's founders sought to address the educational needs of Latino students as they defined them and created progressive formal and informal curriculum and pedagogical practices as a result. Students interviewed experienced these structures as transformative and linked their increased academic engagement to authentic caring and reciprocal relationships with adults characterized by the provision of academic and interpersonal support (Antrop-Gonzalez & De Jesús, 2006; Stanton-Salazar, 2001). The implications of these student perspectives for school reform in New York City and the U.S. underscore the primacy of communities of color in the creation of small high schools that reflect their social, cultural and political interests. As a result, De Jesús' research suggests that policy makers and school reformers must consider the ways in which they structure opportunities at every level for communities to be involved in the schooling of their own.

Lesley Bartlett and Jill P. Koyama present an important case study of Gregorio Luperón High School, a culturally additive, bilingual newcomer high school for Latino immigrant youth in New York City. In particular, they explore how the school uses additive linguistic and cultural practices to achieve an 85% graduation rate with a population often left behind or ignored in schools (including in the mainstream small schools movement). The chapter briefly examines the "subtractive" circumstances that influence the education of immigrant youth, including the heightened poverty in which they often live, the federal, state and local educational and language policies to which they are subject, the social structures that influence youth development and the constrained economic and educational opportunities they face should they succeed in graduating. Based upon 5 years of careful qualitative research, the core of the chapter describes how Luperón's instructional and assessment policies build additive linguistic and cultural practices. Rather than subordinating the students' language and culture, Luperón uses it to educate students in their own language and to help them to learn more about themselves and their communities. Additionally, the chapter details the school culture, the school's de facto language policy and use, and other educational features that prove to be culturally responsive. In presenting these materials, this chapter suggests how critical small schools can meet the basic needs of newcomer students and support their academic success.

As one of many examples of innovative pedagogy in this volume, Liza Bearman and Nora Ahmed, explore the question posed by Jackie Ancess in her *Harvard Educational Review* article: "How can educators recover the purpose of small schools?" Drawing from qualitative data about a new small school in the Bronx, this chapter explores the ways in which high school students developed their voice by engaging in a year-long partnership with Teachers College, Columbia University's Student Press Initiative (SPI). As the coteachers during this endeavor, they describe the process by which they allowed students to create their own inquiry-based curriculum for an English class that centered on their experiences in the "small school experiment." The final "product" was a published book, *Small Schools, Big Questions: A Student-Led Inquiry into High School Redesign*, which included the students' written communication with various educational leaders, individual student reflections on their experience as members of a new small school's first graduating class, and recommendations to the small school community based on their own insights and experiences. By looking at current educational policy and the conditions existing in small schools today, alongside studies conducted by their students, this chapter propounds the notion that when small school students engage in "intellectually transformative experiences," these schools fulfill their original mandate and transform the academic experiences and future prospects of youth stereotyped as disadvantaged.

Martha Foote takes a more macrolevel perspective on critical small schools. In her chapter, she considers how the attributes and outcomes of the small high schools in the New York Performance Standards Consortium (Consortium) have led to low dropout rates, attendance in competitive colleges, solid GPAs and persistence into a second year at higher than national rates. In fact, many of the schools featured in this volume are currently or were members of the Consortium (Bridges, Baldwin, El Puente and Prep). Foote posits that the ties Consortium schools have to their local communities, the commitments they have to teacher and student engagement, and their promotion of active learning and alternative modes of assessment are essential features of successful new small school design. However, fundamental to the Consortium schools' success is a state variance that permits them to use their own system of performance assessments in lieu of New York's high-stakes Regents exams, thus allowing the schools to maintain their innovative approaches to teaching, learning and assessing. Through extensive data collection among all of the Consortium high schools, Foote shows how these schools not only have higher graduation rates than the New York City average, but also prepare their graduates to attend competitive colleges and achieve.

Part III: Beyond the Sphere of Schooling: Students Navigating Postsecondary Transitions

In addition to what occurs within the walls of the classroom, critical small schools are also important and innovative because of their student outcomes and how their students experience the world around them. In her research on one of the first critical small schools, Alia Tyner-Mullings' research on Central Park East Secondary School (CPESS) examines students as adults in their work or postsecondary arenas. The goals of the school—which were developed and examined through content analysis, surveys and interviews—were found to pertain to education (e.g. graduating from college), personal life (e.g., family and work), and society (e.g., becoming a public intellectual and a citizen of the world). Tyner-Mullings describes the successes and challenges the school and students faced in reaching these goals. The research found that many former students do reflect the characteristics of public intellectuals and democratic citizens. However, if there are weaknesses in the school's ability to attain its goals, they appear to be largely a result of the friction between the innovation of these schools and the traditionalism still dominant in higher education, as well as the struggles the students faced in confronting the inequalities of society. Those students who were able to break away from more traditional types of schools in their later schooling seem to have been the most successful, but others were also able to use their alternative educations to adapt to those more traditional institutions. This research can help to inform current educational structures and the ways in which they set goals and paths to achieving them.

Janice Bloom's important research describes the process that Tower High School students must face in trying to get into college. At a time when shifts in the national and global economy make higher education a prerequisite for social mobility, research points to a persistent gap in the number of young people who attend college from high and low-income backgrounds (Bloom, 2007; Carnevale & Rose, 2004; Dynarski & Scott-Clayton, 2006; Kane, 1999; King, 2004). By looking closely at the college transition process of a diverse group of seniors at Tower High School (as part of a larger study of three small schools and college access and transition), Bloom examines both the successes and failures of New York City's small schools in this critical arena. She finds that, despite explicit and extensive efforts on the part of these schools—through the use of critical small school staples like advisory and a lack of classroom tracking as a way to assist students with many of the barriers to college acceptance found in other educational sites—larger social inequalities in the distribution of social and dominant capital cultural resources too often reinforce existing class patterns in the transition to higher education. Her illustrative qualitative data from Tower

High School shows how this manifested at this site, namely through how teachers inadvertently misunderstood the importance of access to the dominant social, cultural and economic capital needed in the college application process. This resulted in perpetuating the disadvantage of many low-income students and parents in this process. She concludes by suggesting ways that these schools can work to more directly acknowledge and overcome these barriers.

Maria Hantzopoulos' chapter features Humanities Preparatory Academy (Prep), a public, college-preparatory critical small high school in Manhattan, designed for students who previously felt that schooling was unresponsive to their needs and were at-risk of dropping out. Based on ethnographic researched conducted between 2005-2008, she considers how the school engages youth academically through intentionally creating a culture of care (through strong-student teacher relationships), a culture of respect (though operationalizing the school's core values), and a culture of questioning (through a thematic, culturally-relevant and inquiry and project-based curriculum). This comprehensive approach to school culture, in turn, helped resocialize students academically and presumably gave them a platform from which to think about the world differently and imagine different alternatives for the future. However, interviews and field notes also suggest that students often encountered barriers to their sense of empowerment when negotiating external "realities" that seemingly inhibited their agency within and beyond the school. Thus, in spite of the school's attempts to create a humanizing and democratizing environment, alumni and students described brushing up against values antithetical to those that the school promoted. While students expressed feeling limited by what they were able to do in these situations, they also conveyed ways in which they negotiated these tensions to their advantage. These issues, therefore not only raise broader questions about the extent to which education can be transformative when larger structural inequalities exist, but also illuminate how young people circumvent these barriers when confronted with obstacles. This research therefore sheds light on both the internal and external successes and challenges facing a critical, small high school when its culture collides with others, and considers ways for schools to mediate these circumstances so that students are more equipped to handle them.

Together, these 10 chapters present an overview of the successes, challenges and promises of critical small schools and provide a foundation for the creation, modification, expansion and/or further research on these models and their place in New York City educational reform. It is through these pages that we hope to present the alternatives to private and charter school models, as well as the thrust to create schools that are simply small. By focusing on the lived experiences of the students, teachers, and innovators that inhabit these institutions, we hope that this volume contributes to moving the critical small schools project forward in a way that advances the original missions and visions toward equity and social justice.

NOTES

1. Other versions of parts of this section can be found in Hantzopoulos (2008, 2009) and Tyner-Mullings (2008).
2. This has now been renamed the Department of Education.
3. While the Regents Exams have existed in New York since 1865, they were not a high school graduation requirement until 1996 (Folts, 1996). The new State Commissioner, Richard Mills, caught up in the "culture wars" of the early 1990s, made standards-based reform and standardized testing top on his educational agenda. The mandate to require these tests for graduation intensified the existing debate about standards, as schools and communities were now faced with the required administration of these exams. Many politicians and even some educators welcomed the decision, insisting that prior to the existence of this policy, students were going to college without the requisite skills and knowledge (Viadero, 2001). Opponents of the tests argued that the emphasis on them watered down the curriculum, curtailed creativity, and created unnecessary anxiety (see Dillon, 2006; Winerip, 2006). In fact, a 2001 poll stated that 44% of parents nationwide thought too much emphasis was placed on high-stakes exams, while only 22% thought there was not enough (Gerwetz, 2001). In addition, while advocates like Diane Ravitch (2001) originally believed that the tests would level the playing field for children by providing an equal and adequate education for all, she has now joined opponents of testing, realizing that they have only reinforced and exacerbated the social, racial, and economic stratification that already existed (Diamond & Spillane, 2004; Kane & Steiger, 2001; Ravitch, 2010).
4. See Ancess, 2008; Annenberg Institute for School Reform, 2002, 2003; Ayers et al., 2000; Fine & Powell, 2001; Howley & Bickel, 2000; Leithwood and Jantzi, 2009; Letgers & Kerr, 2001; Powell, 2002; Ready, Lee, & Welner, 2004; Rodriguez & Conchas, 2008; Toch, 2003; Wasley et al., 2000).
5. Race to the Top, the educational inititaive sponsored by the U.S. Department of Education, also encouraged states to lift their charter caps for increased federal funding.

REFERENCES

Ancess, J. (2008). Small alone is not enough: How can educators recover the purposes of small schools? *Educational Leadership, (65)*8, 48-53.

Annenberg Institute for School Reform. (2002). *School communities that work for results and equity.* Providence, RI: AISR.

Annenberg Institute for School Reform. (2003). *Research perspectives on school reform: Lessons from the Annenberg challenge*. Providence, RI: AISR.

Antrop-Gonzalez, R., & deJesus, A. (2005). Toward a theory of critical care in urban small school reform: Examining structures and pedagogies of caring in two Latino community-based schools. *International Journal of Qualitative Studies in Education, 19*(4), 409-433.

Apple, M. W., & Beane, J. A. (2007). *Democratic schools, 2nd Edition: Lessons in powerful education*. Portsmouth, NH: Heinemann. (Original work published 1995)

Ayers, W. (2000b). The standards fraud. In J. Cohn & J. Rogers (Eds.), *Will standards save public education?* (pp. 64-70). Boston, MA: Beacon Press.

Ballantine, J. H. (2001). *The sociology of education: A systematic analysis* (5th ed.) Upper Saddle River, NJ: Prentice-Hall.

Ayers, W., Klonsky, M., & Lyon, G. (2000). *A simple justice*. New York, NY: Teacher's College.

Bajaj, M. (2009). Why context matters: The material conditions of caring in Zambia. *International Journal of Qualitative Studies in Education, 22*(4), 379-398.

Barker, R., & Gump, P. (1964). *Big school, small school*. Stanford, CA: Stanford University.

Bernard, S., & Mondale, S. (2001). The bottom line: 1980-2000. In S. Mondale & S. Patton (eds.), *School: The story of American public education* (pp. 173-213). Boston, MA: Beacon Press.

Bensman, D. (2000). *Central Park East and its graduates*. New York, NY: Teacher's College.

Bill and Melinda Gates Foundation (n.d.). Retrieved from http://www.gatesfoundation.org/Pages/home.aspx

Bloom, J. (2007). (Mis)reading social class in the journey towards college: Youth-development in urban America. *Teachers College Record, 109*(2), 343-368.

Carnevale, A., & Rose, S. (2004). Socioeconomic status, race/ethnicity, and selective college admissions. In R. Kahlenberg (Ed.), *America's untapped resource: Low-income stdents in higher education*. New York, NY: The Century Foundation.

Clinchy, E. (Ed.). (2000). *Creating new schools: How small schools are changing American education*. New York, NY: Teachers College.

Coalition of Essential Schools. (n.d.). Retrieved from http://www.essentialschools.org

Diamond, J. B., & Spillane, J. (2004). High-stakes accountability in urban elementary schools: challenging or reproducing inequity? *TC Record*. Retrieved from www.tc.edu

Dillon, S. (2006). Schools cut back subjects to push reading and math. *The New York Times*. Retrieved from www.timeoutfromtesting.org

Dynarski, S., & Scott-Clayton, J. (2006). *The cost of complexity in federal student aid: Lessons from optimal tax theory and behavioral economics* (Working Paper No.12227). Cambridge, MA: National Bureau of Economic Research.

Elmore, R. F. (1996). Getting to scale with good educational practice. *Harvard Educational Review, 66*, 1-26.

Fine, M. (2000). A small price to pay for justice. In W. Ayers (Ed.), *A simple justice* (pp. 168-180). New York, NY: Teacher's College.

Fine, M. (2005). Not in our name. *Rethinking Schools, 19*(4), 1-6.

Fine, M., & Powell, L. (2001). Small schools: An anti-racist intervention in urban America. In T. Johnson, J. Boyden, & W. Pitz (Eds.), *Racial profiling and punishment in U.S. public schools* (pp. 45-50). Oakland, CA: Applied Research Center.

Fine, M., & Somerville, J (Eds.). (1998). *Small schools, big imaginations.* Chicago, IL: Cross City Campaign for Urban Education Reform.

Fine, M., Weis, L., & Powell, L. C. (1997). Communities of difference: A critical look at desegregated spaces created for and by youth. *Harvard Educational Review, 67*(2), 247-284.

Fliegel, S. (1993). *Miracle in East Harlem: The fight for choice in public education.* New York, NY: Random House

Folts, J. (1996). History of the University of the State of New York and the State Education Department 1784-1996. Retrieved from http://www.nysl.nysed.gov/edocs/education/sedhist.htm

Gerwetz, C. (2001). Public support for local schools reaches all-time high, poll finds. *Education Week, 18.*

Gootman, E. (2006, February 2). 36 more small schools due in September, Mayor says. *The New York Times.* Retrieved January 12, 2008, from www.nytimes.org

Hantzopoulos, M. (2008). *Sizing up small: An ethnographic case study of a critical small high School* (Unpublished doctoral dissertation). Teachers College, Columbia University, New York, NY.

Hantzopoulos, M. (2009). Transformative teaching in restrictive times: Engaging teacher participation in small school reform. In F. Vavrus & L. Bartlett (Eds.) *Comparatively knowing: Vertical case study in comparative and development education* (pp. 111-126). New York, NY: Palgrave.

Howley, C., & Bickel. R. (2000). *When It comes to schooling, small works: Schoolsize, poverty, and student achievement.* Randolph, VT: Rural School and Community Trust.

Kane, T. (1999). *The price of admission: Rethinking how Americans pay for college.* Washington DC: Brookings Institution Press.

Kane, T., & Steiger, D. (2001, August 13). Right rules will damage schools. *New York Times,* A-17.

King, J. (2004). *Missed opportunities: Students who do not apply for financial aid*: Washington, DC: American Council on Education.

Klonsky, M., & Klonsky, S. (2008). *Small schools: Public school reform meets the Ownership Society.* New York, NY: Routledge.

Leithwood, K., Jantzi, D., & Steinbach, R. (2009). *Changing leadership for changing times* (2nd ed.). New York, NY: Open University Press.

Letgers, N., & Kerr, K. (2001). *Easing the transition to high school: An investigation of reform practices to promote ninth grade success.* Baltimore, MD: Center for Social Organization of schools: Johns Hopkins University.

Meier, D. (2000). Educating for a Democracy. In J. Cohn & J. Rogers (Eds.), Will-Standards Save Public Education? (pp. 3-31). Boston, MA: Beacon Press.

National Commission on Excellence in Education. (1983). A Nation at Risk: the Imperative for educational reform. *The Chronicle of Higher Education, 26,* 11-16.

O'Day, J., Bitter, C., & Talbert, L. (Eds.). (2011). *Educational reform in New York City: Ambitious change in the nation's most complex school system.* Cambridge, MA: Harvard University Press.

Performance Assessment. (n.d.). Retrieved from http://performanceassessment.org/

Powell, L. (2000, June). *Small schools and the issue of race.* New York, NY: Bank Street College of Education Occasional Paper Series.

Ravitch, D. (1974). *The Great School Wars: New York City, 1805-1973.* New York, NY: Basic Books.

Ravitch, D. (2001, June 26). Keep tough standards for high school graduates. *Daily News, 31.*

Ravitch, D. (2010). *The death and life of the great American school system: How testing and choice are undermining education.* New York, NY: Basic Books.

Ravitch, D. (2000). *Left back: A century of battles over school reform.* New York, NY: Simon & Schuster.

Ready, D., Lee. V., & Welner, K. (2004). Educational equity and school structure: school size, overcrowding, and schools-within-schools. *Teacher's College Record 106*(10), 1989-2014.

Rogers, D. (1968). *110 Livingston Street.* New York, NY: Random House

Rodriguez, L., & Conchas, G. (2008*). Small schools and urban youth: Using the power of school culture to engage students.* Thousand Oaks, CA: SAGE.

Sizer, T. (1984). *Horace's compromise: The dilemma of the American high school.* Boston, MA: Houghton Mifflin.

Sizer, T. (1992). *Horace's school: Redesigning the American high school.* Boston, MA: Houghton Mifflin.

Sizer, T. (1996). *Horace's hope: what works for the American high school.* Boston, MA: Houghton Mifflin.

Stanton-Salazar, R. (2001). *Manufacturing hope and despair: The school and Kin Support Networks of U.S.-Mexican Youth.* New York, NY: Teachers College Press.

Steiner-Khamsi, G. (2003). The politics of league tables. *SOWI, 1* (Online journal). Retrieved from http://www.jsse.org/2003/2003-1/pdf/khamsi-tables-1-2003.pdf

Toch, T. (2003). Spinning a web of relationships. In R. Rothman (Ed.), *Small schools and race* (pp. 24-31). Providence, RI: AISR.

Tyack, D., & Cuban, L. (1995). *Tinkering towards utopia: A century of public school reform.* Cambridge, MA: Harvard University Press.

Tyner-Mullings, A. (2008) Finding space: Educational reforms in practice in an urban public school (Unpublished doctoral dissertation). CUNY Graduate Center, New York, NY.

Viadero, D. (2001, October 10). Every student seen to need college prep. *Education Weekly.* Retrieved www.edweek.com

Wasley, P., Fine, M., Gladden, M., Holland, N., King, S, Mosak, E., Powell, L. (2000). *Small schools: Great strides, a study of new small schools in Chicago* (Executive Summary). New York, NY: Bank Street College of Education.

Winerip, M. (2006). Standardized tests face a crisis over standards. *The New York Times.* Retrieved from www.timeoutfrom.com

PART I

CREATING AND MAINTAINING CRITICAL SMALL SCHOOLS: CHALLENGES AND POSSIBILITIES

The process of creating new small schools can be fraught with tensions and roadblocks, especially in the formative years. While some schools have been derailed from their original intentions by these obstacles, many schools have met them in ways that have allowed them to flourish beyond the early years. The chapters in this section describe the ways that critical small schools have confronted the challenges of both launching a new school and maintaining an original vision, particularly when circumstances over time have changed. In turn, this section sheds light on the possibilities and pitfalls of realizing a vision in restrictive times.

- How have critical small schools maintained their visions when confronted with challenges to them?
- What are the relevant components of small school start-up and maintenance? Why do you believe these components are so important?
- What kinds of visions lie at the foundation of small schools?
- How can some of the lessons learned about starting new small schools be applied to public school reform in general?

CHAPTER 1

CITY PREP

A Culture of Care in an Era of
Data-Driven Reform

Jessica T. Shiller

INTRODUCTION

I had become aware of the needs of high school students. Kids were
dropping out younger and younger. I remember students who left
elementary school to go to middle school who were already showing
signs of dropping out. And to me that was frightening. That
someone at 13 is no longer going to school. And I was worried about
not only the student's future but society's future as well.

—City Prep Principal (interview, February 22, 2006)

This chapter profiles a small Bronx high school, City Prep,[1] which
opened under an initiative to create small schools in New York City
funded by the Gates Foundation. Claiming that small size would create a
personalized environment which would then lead to improved academic
achievement, The New Century Schools Initiative (NCSI) built upon an

Critical Small Schools: Beyond Privatization in
New York City Urban Educational Reform, pp. 3–20
Copyright © 2012 by Information Age Publishing
All rights of reproduction in any form reserved.

earlier wave of small schools. However, by starting hundreds of schools at once and privileging test score gains above all else, NCSI reformers overlooked the supports small schools need to build strong relationships between teachers and students. Despite this, the principal and core staff at City Prep made relationship-building a priority—strengthening its school culture and students' attachment to school. As such, they serve as an example of what is possible in a climate that prioritizes improvements in data as the main indicator of a successful school.

NCSI's founders[2] believed in the power of small schools. They thought that the potential for familiarity in small schools could provide greater opportunities for students to achieve academically (Bill & Melinda Gates Foundation, 2004; Herszenhorn, 2003). Armed with a body of research showing the success that small schools had in improving student achievement, NCSI small schools opened at "the pace of Starbucks franchises" (Freedman, 2004). In the 8 years between 2002 and 2010, almost 300 small schools were opened in the poorest communities of New York City.

NCSI founders had a tremendous amount of faith in the small schools, so much so that they left everything up to the individual schools. Although relationships were a key lever of reform, NCSI never defined what relationships between teachers and students should look like, nor did it offer support and training to teachers in relationship-building. The schools, meanwhile, were under tremendous pressure to show improved outcome data and relationship-building often was the last thing on their to-do list. A direct consequence was a frenzy at many schools to prepare students for the tests they needed to graduate, not necessarily to develop relationships between teachers and students. These new schools were test-focused, as was evident in a study conducted by Policy Studies Associates (PSA). The research firm, contracted to study 26 of New York's NCSI schools, reported that most NCSI schools "had accepted if not fully embraced the Regents exams as a way of focusing their curriculum" (PSA, 2007, p. 51).

Without any support from other NCSI schools, the City Prep staff took the relationship-building aspect of NCSI very seriously in this test-driven climate. With a principal who led the charge by training her staff on youth development principles and a partnership with a community-based organization with deep roots in the neighborhood, City Prep became a place where teachers used relationships as a vehicle to get students graduating, rather than dropping out of high school.

City Prep stood in sharp contrast to other NCSI schools that were only focused on outcome data like test scores (Shiller, 2009). In so doing, they built a community of trust between students and teachers, similarly to others schools in this volume (Valenzuela, 1999, pp. 269-271). To support this claim, this chapter presents data drawn from a qualitative study of three new small NCSI schools founded in 2002, of which City Prep was one, conducted during the 2005-2006 school year. Observations and interviews revealed how relationships were developed in classrooms and supported in professional development meetings as well as by the school's leadership.

SMALL SCHOOLS: NOTHING NEW IN NEW YORK CITY

Small schools first appeared in New York City in the late 1960s and early 1970s as alternative schools, created for dropouts of "regular" high schools by community groups (Phillips, 2000). The first city-sanctioned effort to start small schools was in East Harlem's District 4 under the leadership of Anthony Alvarado in the late 1970s (Fruchter, 2007). At this time, Debbie Meier (1995) opened and then expanded her well-known small school, Central Park East (CPE). By the 1990s, these schools achieved critical mass, with around 60 small schools in New York City (Phillips, 2000). Started by partnerships between private funders, city boards of education and educators, by the mid- to late-1990s, small schools had begun to gain some traction among researchers not only because they were innovative, but because they graduated more students, had lower dropout rates, had fewer suspensions and had improved overall performance for poor students of color (Ayers, Klonsky, & Lyon, 2000; Bryk & Driscoll, 1988; Darling-Hammond, Ancess, & Falk, 1995; Darling-Hammond, Ancess, & Ort, 2002; Fine & Somerville, 1998; Gladden, 1998; Klonsky, 1995; Lee & Smith, 1995; Wasley & Lear, 2001).

The founders of these earlier waves of small schools were not devotees to raising achievement data. Though they were concerned about achievement, they came out of a social justice tradition which had a mission for equity (Ayers et al., 2000; Fine, 2005; Klonsky & Klonsky, 2008). They wanted poor communities to receive the same kind of education that wealthy students had, one that promoted inquiry and critical thinking and that developed students' "habits of mind" (Sizer, 1985). Moreover, they valued the communities they served, and brought community members in to shape and participate in the schools. Initially, there was a great deal of enthusiasm about NCSI, and several veteran teachers and principals volunteered to help the new NCSI schools. They offered help in curriculum development, creating internal school structures and generating a professional community among teachers.

A year after NCSI schools were up and running, the city school system was reorganized into regions, and the offices established to provide direct support to the new small schools were dissolved, resulting in a void of intermediary assistance, according to staff working at NCSI schools. Some mentors from NCSI left to join the newly organized NYC Department of Education, in which they served as liaisons to a wider range of schools. Other mentors started their own small schools, and a few that originally worked with NCSI schools left the system altogether to pursue other interests. Without mentoring, NCSI schools turned to outside organizations for things like professional development, which had mixed results. As one new NCSI principal noted, "We didn't know what the heck we were talking about many times. That's the reality of it. We had this great plan and we knew we wanted it to go in a certain direction, so we learned by doing" (interview with an NCSI high school principal, January 4, 2006). As the quote suggests, schools like City Prep were left to their own devices to craft their own vision and to find ways to carry it out.

A SMALL SCHOOL SERVING A POOR COMMUNITY

City Prep can be seen from the above ground "2" train as it rolls in and out of the 149th Street station. The area, known as the Hub, is a bustling commercial district filled with shops and restaurants. Once an elementary school, the building in which City Prep is housed is flanked by empty lots on one side—a reminder of the South Bronx of the 1970s—and new housing—a sign of better times to come—on the other. Three colorful flags hang in front, representing the three small NCSI high schools in the building, one of which is City Prep.

City Prep was an outgrowth of an after-school program at a local social service organization that had served the Bronx's poor communities for decades. The organization, City Settlement (CS),[3] had scores of programs for youth—dropout prevention, tutoring, college preparation and trips, internships and leadership development. For them, having a school was a natural extension of their desire to increase the intensity of their work and actually provide more than peripheral programs for young people. A school could provide strong preparation to poor students who wanted to go to college. The principal, a Puerto Rican woman who grew up and still lives in the neighborhood in which the school is located, stepped into the position enthusiastically.

City Prep serves a mainly Latino population, over 70% of which is entitled to free lunch (see Table 1.1). Teachers at the time of the study were around 40% people of color,[4] unusually high for urban schools. City Prep, compared with two other NCSI schools in the same building (see Table 1.2)—Team Academy and Vision High School—had a lower percentage of White teachers.

City Prep did (and continues to do) well on conventional measures of achievement: an 86.7% graduation rate (see Table 1.3), far surpassing the

Table 1.1.   Demographic Data from City Prep

School	Race and Ethnicity of Students[a]		Free Priced Lunch Eligibility of Students	Total Number of students
City Prep	African American	36%	72%[b]	328
	Latino	64%		

a. Data excluded the "White" and "Asian Pacific Islander" categories since the numbers are so negligible. At City, there are no White or Asian Pacific Islanders.
b. According to the NYC Department of Education, there was also a percentage of students who were eligible for reduced-priced lunch at City Prep (approximately 12%), bringing the percentage of low-income students slightly higher than is indicated in the Table 1.1.

Table 1.2.   Race and Ethnicity of Teachers Across the NCSI Schools

School	Race/Ethnicity of Teachers[a]	
Team	African American	20%
	Latino	26.7%
	White	46.7%
Vision	African American	26.3%
	Latino	5.3%
	White	47.4%
City	African American	22.2%
	Latino	38.9%
	White	16.7%

a. Data excludes Asian and Pacific Islanders as that category included such a small percentage of the staff

Table 1.3.   Graduation and College Acceptance Rates at City Prep

School	Graduation Rate	College Acceptances
City	59 out of 68 = 86.7%	50 students accepted at 2- and 4-year colleges

(NYC Department of Education)

citywide graduation rate of 51%, and most of its seniors were accepted to college in 2006. This data remained largely unchanged in the 2008-2009 school year, when it received an "A" from the city on its annual report card.[5] What made City Prep successful was its culture of care. Staff and students developed strong relationships with one another. Motivated by these positive personal relationships, both staff and students worked hard to boost the academic achievement at the school.

A CULTURE OF CARE: BUILDING COMMUNITY FROM THE START

> We tend to forget about the experiences of teenagers. We needed to think about the professional development the staff needed in order to be able to understand the audience they are working with....We also needed to consider that in hiring, I needed to make sure that people really wanted to work with teenagers.
>
> —City Prep principal

It is difficult to start a school. Getting the school up and running is challenging enough but administrators must also make sure students know where to go, that teachers have their supplies, and that the school building is fully functional. On top of that, a school needs to develop a culture, create a curriculum that engages students and teaches them the skills they will need and provides support and training to staff members as they need it. Taken together, starting a school seems like an overwhelming task.

At City Prep, the new principal took her charge seriously and got the school up and running and flourishing by its fourth year. For her, the most important factor in creating a school was the relationships with students. Relationships were the key to academic achievement, but they did not come automatically. Therefore, the principal consistently pushed her staff to believe that the students were capable. The principal, a former elementary school teacher, said that her teachers needed to believe that "everyone is a potential genius, because I do. So, if I detect that they might believe that some people can make it but not everybody, then that's a problem." At the end of the 2005-2006 school year, she asked two teachers to leave who did not believe in the "genius potential" of their students. One was a science teacher and one was a math teacher. These are hard-to-staff areas, especially in the Bronx, but she was committed to having teachers at the school who believe in and will work with students regardless of their incoming skill level.

She set a tone for the entire school in which faculty were expected to have a high regard for their students and to build relationships with them. Her teachers took this very seriously, as one Afro Puerto Rican[6] staff member put it:

> I grew up in housing projects in the Bronx, dropped out of high school in 9th grade and got left back three times. So, finally I got my GED and went off to Binghamton and now I have my master's. I've done inspirational talks throughout New York City and plan to do that here too. Maybe they'll be able to relate and say, "Man, if you can do it, I can do it." (interview, 2005)

Several staff members thought of themselves as role models, and made building relationships with students central to their teaching practice. Although they had their struggles, City Prep's strong commitment to relationship-building was undeniable. They were not simply getting to know their students, rather the staff was engaged in practices that can be called authentic care (Valenzuela, 1999). They got to know who their students were as individuals, and as parts of families and communities. They also welcomed parents and families into the school with regular community dinners.

City Prep's strong commitment to relationship-building came across most strongly in three main areas: the advisory system, culturally-relevant instruction, and a commitment to dealing with poverty-related factors that affected student achievement. The work in these three areas provided much-needed support to students. Having a small school made this possible, but it certainly did not exist in all small schools.

Advisory

To support their teachers in becoming advisors to 15 students, the school provided weekly training through their partner organization, City Settlement. For instance, a typical Monday afternoon professional development meeting would have a facilitator showing teachers how to conduct team-building activities or would include a speaker. By devoting their professional development time to relationship-development, City Prep set itself apart from schools that were solely focused on improving their students' academic achievement (without considering the development of the whole person). For City Prep, relationships were the vehicle to improve academic achievement. The unwavering focus on relationship-building at this school helped teachers become strong advisors.

Advisory looked like an extended homeroom at many NCSI schools. All of the small schools founded with City Prep in 2002 had advisories, but many did not devote professional development time to advisory.

Team Academy and Vision High School, for example, did not provide support to teachers so that they could become better advisors. Teachers at these two schools sought out City Prep teachers on their own for assistance. They attended workshops that City Prep teachers led on advisory and borrowed their advisory curriculum. In interviews, teachers at Vision and Team said that they were not sure what to do with advisory. For them, it seemed like an additional duty on top of their teaching load with which they were already struggling. Conversely, at City Prep advisory was taken seriously. Students reported looking forward to meeting with their advisors at the end of every day, where they could talk about what was going well and what their struggles were. City Prep teachers used advisory as it was originally intended: to build reciprocal relationships with students.

Advisory was the centerpiece of City Prep, a place to celebrate achievements and to resolve problems. In comparison with other NCSI schools, City Prep advisory functioned particularly well. For example, when confronted with the problem of a group of boys who were constantly facing disciplinary action and who consistently failed classes, the City Prep principal and the staff of City Settlement responded by setting up an advisory just for these boys. Motivated by a desire to engage rather than punish students, the staff did what was common practice in programs for disengaged youth. They developed a way to motivate them. Observers saw the advisory as innovative, but this idea came directly from their years of experience with young people.

The boys' advisory was facilitated by two male teachers of color (most advisories just had one advisor) who moderated conversations with the boys about their struggles. Acting as role models for the boys, the advisors always had an agenda and wore professional clothing to class. Students were also rewarded for meeting advisory and school expectations. For instance, if the students dressed in dress code, helped others, asked for help in class, or did well on an assignment, they would be recognized for these achievements. This included getting the signature of teachers, receiving immediate feedback and recognition from the facilitators, being rewarded with things like movie tickets, or receiving certificates of recognition. Many of them were also nominated for "student of the month."

The facilitators, also men who had struggled to meet their educational goals, set the tone by creating an atmosphere of confidentiality and trust. "Nothing leaves the room," said one of the facilitators. Students' interests became the topics for conversations. One facilitator likened the conversations to a dam breaking—students gushing and sharing so much with them. This was a place for the students to share which made the students very happy. The boys also played leadership roles in the group and facilitated conversations among each other.

The principal and other teachers noticed changes in the students' behavior since the boys' advisory started. "They smile," the principal noticed, "and say hi to me." At a meeting of the facilitators and the principal, they reflected on the influence of the boys' advisory group:

> They started doing better in their classes. One student passed the science practice Regents and was invited to bring it in to show the group. They ask for help in classes. The principal noticed one student in math class asking for help with math who previously used to disrupt and do anything but math. They ask for recognition in their classes, are observed to be trying. One student, the principal noticed, broke the code of silence that students have not to snitch on one another. He came forward and admitted wrongdoing in an incident where there was a fight with a student from another school. In this investigation, the principal got a name from the dean who she was sure was innocent in the situation and rather than go on the dean's word did her own investigation and that is when this student came forward. (field notes, May 11, 2006)

In this example, teachers took a different approach to failing students—they learned from them. The goal of the advisory in this case was to find out what the boys were going through outside of school and how that impacted their lives inside of school. The boys' advisory was an example of authentic caring as teachers both taught and learned from students—finding ways to help them because they were worth helping and supporting. Their ultimate goal was to build relationships with the students, to understand their struggles and to help them improve their achievement in school.

Culturally-Relevant Instruction

Many of the teachers I talked to were unaware of the term "culturally-relevant instruction" and most teachers I observed did not use culturally responsive pedagogy (Gay, 2000; Foster, 1997, Ladson-Billings, 1994; Nieto, 1999; Irvine, 2003). However, there were a few teachers who did actively engage in culturally responsive teaching, even if they did not use the term. These were the teachers who were mentors to their colleagues and also had the strongest ties with their students.

Guided by care in what they did and prioritizing relationship-building, these teachers, frequently people of color from the same or similar neighborhoods as the students, saw their work as an opportunity to give students like themselves the help they had as young people. Several of these teachers were engaged in culturally responsive pedagogy. The following practices are common across the literature on culturally responsive teaching: making an effort to find out about students' cultures and incorporating that into the curriculum, valuing students' lives outside of school, and believing in students' abilities to be academically and socially successful by having high standards and teaching the language and content central to the dominant culture. Incorporating those practices, several staff members were able to build relationships with students as a central part of their teacher practice (see Gay, 2000; Foster, 1997; Ladson-Billings, 1994; Nieto, 1999; Irvine, 2003).

One City Prep English teacher, who described her work as "a profession, not just a job," said to her class, "I love you guys, but I need to call you on things" (field notes, November 21, 2005). In her class, students had time to do independent reading in which they were able to read books that appealed to them. The students could choose from books in the classroom library including *The Autobiography of Malcolm X, El Bronx Remembered,* and *Roll of Thunder, Hear My Cry.* This same class also read canonical literature together. The teacher provided room for students to connect their own experiences to the class, but the teacher also exposed the students to new things. She explained to her class that they cannot just read "urban fiction," as the students called it. "In college, you need to be exposed to certain books. You need to have an opinion about literature. My job as a teacher is to expose you to that literature," she explained (field notes, November 10, 2005). Allowing curriculum both to reflect the students' cultures and to teach them something from the "culture of power" (Delpit, 1995) is an essential element of culturally-relevant teaching.

In a City Prep 10th grade social studies class, the teacher regularly praised her students even if they did not see the positive qualities in themselves. In one class on the Crusades:

Teacher:	Make a prediction about what the next part of the passage will be about.
Student 1:	Invasions!
Student 2:	You are good today.
Teacher:	She is good every day.
Student 1:	Miss, I only failed English because I refuse to write essays.
Teacher:	You can write essays. You are not a failure. I see something better for you.

(field notes, December 14, 2005)

The teachers engaging in culturally-relevant practices were teachers of color, who, in most cases, reported that they had grown up in neighborhoods similar to that of the students, though there were White teachers who engaged in these practices as well. Nonetheless, since relationships between teachers were not formalized, White teachers were not formally learning from teachers of color, nor were more novice teachers formally learning from veteran teachers. Despite this lack of formalization, the school offered more culturally-relevant instruction than in the other two schools in their school building, Team Academy and Vision High School.

Another way culturally-relevant instruction was present was the school's use of funds to get Willie Perdomo, an established and renowned Puerto Rican poet, as a writer in residence and poetry mentor to the 10th grade students at the school. The entire grade was able to attend his poetry workshop as a part of their English class. Through this workshop, students were able to share their stories—stories that simultaneously communicated who they were and valued their life experience. Moreover, this workshop culminated in a special assembly devoted to students' work at which they read their poetry in front of the student body. The principal explained that she wanted Perdomo to come to the school so that the students could see that a man of color made a living from his poetry. She also acknowledged that students needed to see adults that looked like them in positions of power. As a result, the students' cultures and life experiences were validated through this artist-in-residency.

City Prep had several teachers that engaged in this form of culturally-relevant practice. Although they did not identify their practice as "culturally relevant," the practices of the teachers and the principal at City Prep incorporated students' cultures into curriculum, encouraged and acknowledged students' abilities, and taught students new content that would include them in the "culture of power" (Delpit, 1995)—all of which are elements of culturally responsive teaching.

Showing the Love: Empathy for Low Income Students

The final key area in which City Prep demonstrated their commitment to fostering strong relationships was through the acknowledgement of poverty-related obstacles to academic achievement, while holding students to high expectations. Schools that serve poor students do not often explicitly discuss and deal with poverty among their students, so this recognition made City Prep distinct. This was a direct outgrowth of the culture of CS, whose staff got to know and assisted families facing poverty in the neighborhood in which City Prep was located.

The principal had a direct role in this process since she provided financial assistance to students who could not afford school supplies, made concrete attempts to provide mentors to students, and attempted to reverse the views that school staff typically have of poor students and their families. Understanding the difficulty that students faced in their daily lives, a staff member explained how the school helped students:

> We have one young lady who has been in and out of the foster care system who just started bawling because she couldn't find the $60 for senior pictures. We are coming out of pockets paying for that. And we do it for as many students as needed. Each of us will probably take responsibility for one student. We do it every day. We give them lunch. They'll say, "What's that you're eating?" You give them money to go to the corner store and eat. (interview, 2006)

The principal and community partner, City Settlement, had a consistent view. They understood that expectations needed to be high for poor students and students of color and they saw that getting students to reach those high expectations required that the staff recognize the difficulties that poverty brings. They also agreed that the role of the school was to help students address those difficulties. One example of publicly recognizing the challenges students faced was when the school organized a poetry event with the help of Willie Perdomo. According to my fieldnotes, this event was incredibly poignant for students.

> The 10th graders read poems that told tales of drugs, violence, pregnancy, cops arresting too many people in their neighborhood and AIDS. They read to thunderous applause, many of them were too nervous to read at first, but did it anyway. At the end the principal got up and congratulated the students and talked about trying to solve some of the problems they see in their communities together. She then gave hugs to several of the students. She said that she was so proud of the students, some of whom have never read anything in front of anyone before. She said to the staff later that she hopes that they believe what they are hearing and that they recognize that the students' lives are genuinely difficult. (field notes, May, 19, 2006)

This example is in accordance with the beliefs held by the principal and the community partner; that the job of the school is not to ignore students' lives outside of school, but to understand their lives and to create an environment that addresses their needs. The principal wanted the staff "not to put barriers between themselves and the students, but to find ways to create and develop relationships with students" (interview, April 3, 2006). Additionally, the principal and community partner organized monthly town hall meetings, where there were speakers and performers that had backgrounds similar to the students'. They tried to inspire and motivate them to persist through school. For the principal, this was a priority. As she declared to her staff at a meeting, "Even though these students do not know how to express it, they are beautiful" (field notes, March 20, 2006).

The students had a deep appreciation for the teachers who believed in them and held them to high standards. One student who described a teacher who held him to high expectations: "I was not good at math, but

Ms. S just wanted me to get it. She did not give up on me and I got it."
(Student interview, April 13, 2006). Similarly, another student spoke
about a teacher who had high standards for all students. About her, this
student said,

> Ms. B did not give up on us. If there was a school spirit it would be because
> of her. There were times when she would stay working here until midnight.
> She really cared about us. She is the hardest working teacher here, making us
> do our work, right then and there. Even when she was sick, she was still send-
> ing emails and calling from the hospital. We are so very grateful to Ms. B.
> (interview, April 14, 2006)

This theme resonated repeatedly among students as many spoke
about teachers who pushed them to "shoot higher." According to students, Ms. B also shared her personal experiences with them. This
meant a lot to students and was tied into the belief that teachers held
high expectations for them. This was exemplified by one student's
description that stated, "She did not want us to sell ourselves short"
(interview, April 14, 2006).

One key attribute that distinguished City Prep from other new institutions was its leadership, and particularly, the role that the principal
played in cultivating such a nurturing and challenging environment for
students. Dedicated to developing caring relationships, she valued the
culture of students and made it clear to staff that they were expected to do
the same. It is significant that the principal was Puerto Rican and a long-
time resident of the neighborhood in which the school was located. She
was a presence in the community, and the families of her students knew
her. This contributed to the feelings of trust that students and families
had towards the staff at the school. In fact, City Prep students reported
that this was a central factor in enrolling in the school.

Although City Prep had its challenges associated with working in a low-
income community, including issues like high rates of students leaving
and entering the school and having been previously underserved, its
explicit attention to understanding the students, building relationships
with them, and valuing their cultures made an impact on the students. As
one student said, "The principal wants us to be the best" (interview, April
13, 2006). Another student echoed this sentiment:

> I never thought I would be graduating, but the teachers here care a lot....
> My parents got locked up when I was in 9th grade and I started to do bad in
> classes, I got kicked off softball team and everything. I told one of the teach-
> ers who gave me a chance. He gave me time to make up work and helped
> me. He didn't judge me. (interview, April 13, 2006)

In contrast to students at the other two schools, Team Academy and Vision High School, City Prep students communicated how they felt cared about by City Prep staff. Moreover, care was not limited to concern over whether the students attended regularly, did well in their classes or stayed out of trouble. For City Prep staff, care meant understanding students' lives outside of school, seeing their communities and families as assets to the school, and creating relationships that "removed barriers" between teacher and student. Moreover, they did not pity the students for the difficulties they faced in their daily lives, nor did they lower their expectations for them, running counter to the deficit perspective through which poor students are often viewed (Powell, 1997). This is an example of what Valenzuela calls authentic care, care which emphasizes relationship-building between teacher and student (Valenzuela, 1999).

IMPLICATIONS AND CONCLUSIONS

There is much we can learn from City Prep. The main conclusion we can draw is that relationship-building was central to the school's success. Although recent research has raised questions about relying on relationships as a single lever of change (Smylie et al., 2003, p. 101), relationship-building is an important aspect of improving academic achievement, especially among poor students and students of color (Bryk & Schneider, 2002; Darling-Hammond & Friedlander, 2007). Yet, as researchers have argued there is no guarantee that strong relationships will develop at small schools (Darling-Hammond, Ross, & Milliken, 2007). In order for relationships to develop, small schools need support. Placing people in a room together—especially people who are different from one another—does not guarantee that strong relationships will develop. Careful attention to cultivating those relationships is necessary.

City Prep paid careful attention to relationships. The principal at City Prep pushed her staff to find ways to engage each student. This stemmed from her work for an organization whose mission it was to help the most marginal students from poor communities of color. As a staff developer, she was able to train others in how to teach and work with struggling students. Understanding that this could not be left to individual teachers to figure out, she provided as much scaffolding as she could. Moreover, she was from the same kind of community that the students were from and had a strong passion for improving life for the students and families living there. This suggests that hiring school leaders who are able to connect with the communities, although they need not be from those communities, is an essential component to improving engagement in authentic care practices in schools. Those school leaders will be more likely to hire teachers and support staff who share their passion for serving the community and can teach their staff about how to connect with the community.

Another important finding with major implications for small schools starting up was that relationship-building did not simply appear at City Prep. Professional development time and energy was deliberately and consciously devoted to supporting teachers so they may engage with their students as advisors. Although not formalized, newer teachers had veteran teachers to turn to who engaged in culturally-relevant instructional practices. Neither was required for NCSI schools, but the principal thought it was necessary to support her teachers in the work of engaging and connecting with students.

One could say that what went on at City Prep was idiosyncratic and dependent on a particular school leader, but it need not be. With more attention and resources devoted to training teachers for all NCSI small schools in which teachers learned about students' cultural backgrounds and histories, seeing them as assets and resources from whom teachers could learn, teachers might see their own practice as responsive and accountable to the communities that they serve. In that context, training for advisory, and training in culturally-relevant teaching practices would make sense. Taken together, these practices would lead more schools to engage in building relationships.

What distinguished City Prep from other NCSI schools is that improving outcome data was not their ultimate goal. This strategy set this principal apart from other principals and NCSI schools where relationships were not a focus, and data was the main focus (Shiller, 2009). As such, City Prep is an example to look to for what a small school could be. It carried on the tradition of the earlier small schools devoted to social justice principles, and was a beacon of hope in a sea of new schools in a frenzy to improve test scores.

Therefore, as much attention to relationship-building is needed in small schools as is devoted to academic achievement. Building relationships is a means to academic achievement. Too much focus on achievement data can distract schools from building relationships as they put all of their energy into improving student test scores. While City Prep was pressured in the direction of the former, the leadership and staff had enough commitment to the latter to make it a priority; ultimately leading to the academic success of the students who attended the school. Thus, to make City Prep the rule rather than the exception for small schools, relationships need to be taken seriously. Support, training, and recognition for schools engaging in relationship-building with their students is essential. City Prep is a model, but it should not be unique among small schools. It should be the standard.

NOTES

1. A pseudonym.
2. Gates Foundation, Carnegie Foundation, Soros, and so on.
3. A pseudonym.
4. Defined as African American and Latino in this instance because there were no Asian, Native American, or other students of color.
5. Report card data can be found at http://schools.nyc.gov/default.htm . This data, although positive, should be read somewhat skeptically. As Jennings and Dorn (2008) point out, NYC Department of Education (DoE) data is not always reliable and valid. However, the school's strong performance data meant that it received positive attention and praise from DoE officials.
6. This staff person self-identified as Afro Puerto Rican.

REFERENCES

Ayers, W., Klonsky, M., & Lyon, G. (2000). *A simple justice: The challenge of small schools.* New York, NY: Teachers College Press.

Bill & Melinda Gates Foundation. (2004). *Making the case for small schools.* Seattle, WA: Author.

Bryk, A. S., & Driscoll, M. (1988). *The high school as community: Contextual influences and consequences for students and teachers.* Madison, WI: National Center on Effective Secondary Schools. (ED302539)

Bryk, A. S., & Schneider, B. L. (2002). *Trust in schools: A core resource for improvement.* New York, NY: Russell Sage Foundation.

Darling-Hammond, L., Ancess, J., & Falk, B. (1995). *Authentic assessment in action: Studies of schools and students at work.* New York, NY: National Center for Restructuring Education, Schools, and Teaching. Teachers College Press.

Darling-Hammond, L., Ancess, J., & Ort, S. W. (2002). Reinventing high school: Outcomes of the coalition campus schools project. *American Educational Research Journal, 39*(3), 639.

Darling-Hammond, L., & Friedlander, D. (2007). *High schools for equity: Policy supports for student learning in communities of color.* Standford, CA: School Redesign Network at Stanford University.

Darling-Hammond, L., Ross, P., & Milliken, M. (2007). High school size, organization, and content: What matters for student success? In F. Hess & T. Loveless (Eds.), *Brookings papers on education policy: 2006-2007.* Washington, DC: Brookings Institute Press.

Delpit, L. D. (1995). *Other people's children: Cultural conflict in the classroom.* New York, NY: New Press, distributed by W.W. Norton.

Fine, M., & Somerville, J. (1998). *Small schools, big imaginations: A creative look at urban public schools.* Chicago, IL: Cross City Campaign for Urban School Reform.

Fine, M. (2005). Not in our name: Reclaiming the democratic vision of small school reform. *Rethinking Schools, 19*(4), 11-14.

Foster, M. (1997). *Black teachers on teaching.* New York, NY: New Press.

Freedman, S. (2004, December 1). Nurturing small schools without hurting big ones. *New York Times,* p. B8.

Fruchter, N. (2007). *Urban schools, public will: Making education work for all our children.* New York, NY: Teachers College Press.

Gay, G. (2000). *Culturally responsive teaching: Theory, research & practice.* New York, NY: Teachers College Press.

Gladden, R. (1998). The small school movement: A review of the literature. In M. Fine & J. Somerville (Eds.), *Small schools, big imaginations: A creative look at urban public schools* (pp. 113-137). Chicago, IL: Cross City Campaign for Urban School Reform.

Herszenhorn, D. M. (2003). Gates charity gives $51 million to City to Start 67 Schools. *New York Times,* p. A1. Retrieved from Lexis-Nexis Academic database.

Irvine, J. J. (2003). *Educating teachers for diversity: Seeing with a cultural eye.* New York, NY: Teachers College Press.

Jennings, J., & Dorn, S. (2008). The proficiency trap: New York City's achievement gap revisited. *Teachers College Record.* Retrieved from http://www.tcrecord.org/content.asp?contentid=15366

Klonsky, M. (1995). Small schools: The numbers tell a story. A review of the research and current experiences. *ERIC Digest, 386*(517).

Klonsky, M., & Klonsky, S. (2008). *Small schools: Public school reform meets the ownership society.* New York, NY: Routledge.

Ladson-Billings, G. (1994). *The dreamkeepers: Successful teachers of African- American children.* San Francisco, CA: Jossey-Bass.

Lee, E, V., & Smith, B. J. (1995). Effects of high school restructuring and size on early gains in achievement and engagement. *Sociology of Education, 68*(4), 241.

Meier, D. (1995). *The power of their ideas: Lessons for America from a small school in Harlem.* Boston, MA: Beacon Press.

Nieto, S. (1999). *The light in their eyes: Creating multicultural learning communities.* New York, NY: Teachers College Press.

Phillips, S. (2000). *NYU Seminar on the future of the comprehensive high school.* New York, NY: New York University.

Policy Studies Associates. (2007 October). *Evaluation of New Century high schools: Profile of an initiative to create and sustain small, successful high schools.* Washington, DC: Policy Studies Associates. Retrieved http://www.policystudies.com

Powell, L. (1997). The achievement (k)not: Whiteness and "Black underachievement." In M. Fine (Ed.), *Off White: Readings on race, power, and society* (pp. 3-12). New York, NY: Routledge.

Shiller, J. (2009). These are our children! An examination of relationship-building in urban high schools. *The Urban Review, 41*(5), 461-485.

Sizer, T. R. (1985). *Horace's compromise—the dilemma of the American high school: The first report from a study of high schools, co-sponsored by the National Association of Secondary School Principals and the Commission on Educational Issues of the National Association of Independent Schools.* Boston, MA: Houghton Mifflin.

Smylie, M. A., Wenzel, S. A., Allensworth, E., Fendt, C., Hallman, S., & Luppescu, S., et al. (2003, August). *The Chicago Annenberg challenge: Successes, failures, and lessons for the future. Final technical report of the Chicago Annenberg research project.* Chicago, IL: Consortium on Chicago School Research.

Valenzuela, A. (1999). *Subtractive schooling: U.S.-Mexican youth and the politics of caring.* Albany, NY: State University of New York Press.

Wasley, P., & Lear, R. (2001). Small schools, real gains. *Educational Leadership, 58*(6), 22-27.

CHAPTER 2

CONSIDERING CONTEXT

Exploring a Small School's Struggle to Maintain Its Educational Vision

Rosa L. Rivera-McCutchen

INTRODUCTION

Large comprehensive high schools have been a consistent target for reform, particularly in urban areas, because the negative outcomes associated with large high school size are exacerbated where there are high concentrations of poor students and/or Blacks and Latinos (Barton, 2003; Fine, 1991, 1994, 2004; Lee & Smith, 1997; Noguera, 2002, 2003, 2006; Rothstein, 2004a, 2004b). One dominant approach to improving high schools is through the creation of small schools—both by the redesign of large comprehensive high schools into smaller units and through creating new stand-alone small schools. In New York City alone, over 200 new small high schools opened between 2002 and 2008 (Bloom, Thompson, & Unterman, 2010; see Introduction, this volume).

The rapid scale up of the small school reform movement in recent years has caused some concern, specifically regarding the conditions needed to make such reform work. A major critique of the present small school movement is that its advocates are not looking at the history of the "critical" small

Critical Small Schools: Beyond Privatization in
New York City Urban Educational Reform, pp. 21–39
Copyright © 2012 by Information Age Publishing
All rights of reproduction in any form reserved.

schools that preceded them—their successes and struggles—in order to inform and strengthen the reform (Fine, 2005; Gootman & Herszenhorn, 2005; "The Small Schools Express," 2005; see Introduction, this volume). This chapter addresses this critique by examining the evolution of Bridges Institute,[1] a small Bronx high school founded in 1994 during an earlier wave of small school reform in New York City. Specifically, the research examined the community and policy contexts within which Bridges Institute was situated, and I argue that these contexts are critical factors in understanding the successes and challenges Bridges experienced. Furthermore, the findings suggest that understanding context is crucial for creating and sustaining critical small schools that are responsive to the needs of students of color in low-income urban communities.

CONCEPTUAL FRAMEWORK

Proponents of the critical small schools approach have argued that downsizing large schools can allow for more personalization between students and their teachers (Ancess, 2003; Fine & Sommerville, 1998; Meier, 2002, 1995; Sizer, 1984/1992), as well as enhance the relationships between teachers and parents (Fine & Sommerville, 1998; Noguera, 2002). Supporters also argue that reducing the student population allows teachers to spend a greater amount of time planning engaging curricula and lessons in order to place more emphasis on meeting the academic needs of individual students (Fine & Sommerville, 1998; Meier, 2002, 1995). Studies have suggested that the greater personalization linked to small schools positively impacts student achievement (Lee & Smith, 1997) and engagement (Lee & Smith, 1995). Smaller schools are also linked to lower dropout rates and violence, and increased student attendance rates (Cotton, 1996; Darling, Ancess, & Ort, 2002; Fine, 1998; Klonsky, 1996; Oxley, 1994; Raywid, 1996).

Although the literature has indicated that smaller settings lead to more favorable outcomes, there is a consensus among researchers that small is only a *condition* through which other types of reform should be enacted (Darling-Hammond, 1995; Elmore, 1996; Fine, 1998, 2005; McLaughlin, 1994; Peterson, McCarthey, & Elmore, 1996; Smylie et al., 2003). Small size, in itself, is not enough to improve the conditions of urban high schools, or to change what Richard Elmore (1996) calls the "core of educational practice" (p. 2), which he defines as teachers' attitudes and beliefs about teaching, learning and assessment and the structural arrangements of the schools that support those attitudes and beliefs.

To change the "core," the literature on school reform suggests that schools must have strong leadership with a vision and the ability to share decision making with staff (Fullan, 1997; National Association of Secondary School Principals, 2004; Spillane, 2005), develop trusting relationships among members of the school community (Ancess, 2003; Bryk & Schnieder, 2002; Meier, 1995, 2002), and utilize reflective practice (Ancess, 2003; McDonald, 1999; Wagner, 2000). In addition to these features, small schools must also have high academic standards for their students, along with the appropriate supports for them (Ancess, 2003; Fine, 1998, 2005; McLaughlin, 1994; Wagner, 2000). Research suggests that these conditions, facilitated by small school size, are essential for successful reform. Using this framework as a basis for analysis, this chapter examines the extent to which Bridges successfully sustained small school reform over time.

METHODOLOGY

This research was primarily concerned with the ways in which one small urban high school, Bridges Institute, worked over time to create the conditions defined by the literature as important to sustaining successful small school reform, given challenging community and policy contexts. I selected this site through purposeful sampling (Merriam, 2001) because it demonstrated a commitment to small school reform over time, in spite of challenges to its vision.

I used ethnographic research methods to study the nuances of the educational processes that influenced the academic outcomes of Bridges Institute's evolution over time (Bogdan & Biklen, 1992). Data collection took place primarily during spring 2006, with additional data collected in the subsequent summer and fall. I interviewed eighteen participants, including current and former staff and administrators and alumni. I also observed numerous professional development and staff meetings as well as classes in a range of grade levels and disciplines. Data gathered during the observations and interviews were arranged and coded according to characteristics of school reform found in the research literature (Yin, 2003). Extant quantitative data, including student attendance, Regents pass rates, and graduation and dropout rates provided a base for analyses of student demographics and performance outcomes on key measures. Data on teacher experience, attendance and attrition rates were also analyzed.

SCHOOL CONTEXT

Bridges Institute opened in the Bronx in 1994 as part of a small-scale reform effort that transformed poorly performing comprehensive high schools into smaller schools. Presidential High School, the neighborhood comprehensive high school that Bridges and three other small high schools replaced, had a graduation rate of 37.3% and a dropout rate of 20.7%. The building that Bridges has occupied since 1995 (during Bridges Institute's first year, the school was housed offsite until its new building was remodeled) is located in one of the poorest sections of the Bronx, with a population that is 44% Black and 52.9% Hispanic.[2] Bordered on one side by a major expressway, the community surrounding Bridges was, for many years, mainly industrial. When the school occupied its new building in fall 1995, the surrounding blocks around the school consisted of vacant lots, auto repair shops, a Department of Sanitation facility and a cement factory.

According to census data from 2000, only 54.6% of the population 25 years or older within the school's census tract attained their high school diploma, and only 7.5% have earned their bachelor's degree. Not surprisingly, the area's median household income is quite low at $20,685. The adjacent census tracts, where Bridges students also reside, reflect similar statistics. In fact, students attending Bridges Institute reside in one of the poorest congressional districts in the nation (Serrano, 2004). By comparison, New York City's median household income is $38,393, while the more affluent Fieldston section of the Bronx has a median income of $168,061.

The prior educational experiences of students entering Bridges Institute have historically been reflective of the socioeconomic crisis of the surrounding neighborhoods. Over the course of Bridges' history, large numbers of students entered the school having been unsuccessful in their elementary or junior high schools (see Table 2.1). With the exception of its inaugural year and the 2001-2002 school year, the percentage of Bridges' entering ninth and tenth graders who were overage for grade has been significantly greater than the citywide average. In the 2003-2004 school year, nearly half of all of the students entering 9th and 10th grade in Bridges that year were overage for grade, in comparison to 27.5% citywide average. Additionally, many students come into the school with low skill levels as measured by New York State Math and English Language Arts exams (see Table 2.2). The inadequate education at the elementary and junior high school levels has had a long-lasting impact on the students who often became Bridges students. One Bridges alumnus, Julio, reflected on his experiences in the junior high in Bridges' neighborhood:

> To me it was like, for the teachers that I had before, if you really didn't try hard enough to care about what they were teaching, they were not gonna teach you. They weren't gonna waste their time. And the teacher I had for seventh and eighth grade ... she wasn't gonna pay no mind to the kids that didn't wanna learn. If you didn't wanna learn, just sit there. (interview, June 9, 2006)

**Table 2.1.   Percent Overage for
Grade Entering 9th and 10th Graders**

Year	Bridges Institute	Citywide
1994-95	13.8	43.4
1995-96	41.5	33.7
1996-97	N/A	31.1
1997-98	40.7	29.6
1998-99	48.6	28.5
1999-00	37.9	27.9
2000-01	39.2	25.7
2001-02	18.8	24.9
2002-03	37.1	25.6
2003-04	49.3	27.5
Average	36.3	28.9

Note: Data are from the NYC Department of Education Annual School Report Card.

**Table 2.2.   Percentage Entering 9th and
10th Graders Meeting Standard in Reading/ELA and Math**

	Bridges		Citywide	
Year	Reading/ELA	Math	Reading/ELA	Math
1994-95	20.0%	0.0%	50.4%	41.0%
1995-96	25.0	16.7	46.8	45.1
1996-97	–	–	41.5	52.2
1997-98	20.8	26.5	43.4	51.2
1998-99	25.5	28.8	49.5	56.7
1999-00	12.1	1.7	34.5	22.0
2000-01	6.6	3.6	33.9	23.2
2001-02	13.3	5.5	34.5	24.6
2002-03	7.3	6.0	31.0	31.0
2003-04	8.5	8.7	32.3	34.1
Average	15.5%	10.8%	39.8%	33.0%

Note: Data are from the NYC Department of Education Annual School Report Card.

Bridges' founders believed that they had to work to undo what students had previously learned about what it meant to be a learner.

In addition to negotiating a difficult community context, the school also had to navigate policy contexts that were, in the view of the staff, detrimental to the school's vision. At the same time Bridges Institute was opening its' doors, the national standards movement was gaining momentum with assessment and accountability as its core tenets. Small schools proponents, such as Deborah Meier (2002) and Theodore Sizer (1995), argued that the standards movement would lead to test-driven curriculum reform, rather than improvement in instructional practice. In their view, the standards movement was at odds with the very kind of reform taking place at Bridges Institute.

Within the first few years of its inception, another shift in the policy context came in the form of changes in personnel in the state and city bureaucracy that represented the loss of key allies of the school. In 1995, just one year after Bridges opened, NYS Department of Education Commissioner, Thomas Sobol—who had demonstrated strong support of schools like Bridges Institute—was replaced by Richard Mills. Mills embraced the standards movement and, in that same year, proposed that all NYS high school students be required to pass the Regents examinations rather than Regents Competency Tests, which tested basic skills. Although Bridges, and 27 other schools across the state in the NYS Performance Standards Consortium (referred to as "Consortium" going forward), fought against and ultimately won a variance from the Regents, the school had to quickly reorganize its instruction to comply with the mandate in the intervening years.

At the same time as those changes were taking place on the state level, New York City was experiencing high turnover in chancellors. In 1993, Joseph Fernandez, who had been supportive of what we call critical small schools and had cleared the way for the transformation of Presidential High School, was ousted from his position after only 3 years. His successor, Chancellor Ramon Cortines, spent a good deal of time in conflict with then NYC Mayor Rudy Guiliani, and resigned in 1995 after only 2 years. Rudy Crew, the next NYC school chancellor, was less supportive of small school reform, and sought more control over the schools (Hartocollis, 1997). Chancellor Crew's increasing measures curbing the autonomy of the New York City small schools led to the resignation in 1997 of Stephen Phillips, who had been the Superintendent of Alternative High Schools and Programs and Adult and Continuing Education since 1983. A long-time supporter of school autonomy and alternative assessment, Phillips had strongly advocated on behalf of the small schools movement in NYC. Furthermore, Phillips was instrumental in protecting the small size of the Bridges Institute and the other small schools that were designed to operate with no greater than 350-400 students. However, his successor, Richard Organisciak, was perceived by some as less supportive of portfolio-based assessment and did not advocate on behalf of small schools as strongly as Phillips had.

Although Chancellor Crew did support the Consortium schools in their fight against the Regents mandate, his desire to curb the autonomy of small schools made him a complicated ally. Furthermore, in 1999, after increased battles with NYC Mayor Guiliani, Crew was also removed from the chancellorship.

SUCCESSES AT BRIDGES INSTITUTE

In spite of challenging community and policy contexts, there is evidence that Bridges was successful over the years. One example was the school's 4-year graduation rate, which was consistently higher than the NYC citywide average, as well as higher than its sister schools that also emerged from the failed Presidential High School (see Table 2.3 and Table 2.4). Furthermore, the school's dropout rate was lower than the citywide rate, at 7.1% in 1998, and 11.7% in 2004. The citywide averages for high school dropouts were 15.6% and 16.3% in 1998 and 2004, respectively. Bridges Institute also consistently surpassed the 26.9% graduation rate of the final year of Presidential High School, the comprehensive high school from which it emerged (Darling-Hammond, Ancess, & Ort, 2002).[3] Further evidence that Bridges reversed the failing trends of its predecessor can be found in Table 2.5, which shows that Bridges Institute met or exceeded targets for a number of benchmarks during the 2005-06 year, as well as demonstrated improvement from the previous year in a number of areas. Note that in 2005, Bridges had a 69.6% five-year graduation rate, an impressive rate considering research suggesting that students are less likely to graduate when they fall behind in high school (Greene & Winters, 2006). Bridges' college acceptance rate, another important indicator of success, was high in 2005-2006 at 82%.

There are also qualitative indicators that Bridges achieved success with its students. Many former students returning from college for Alumni Day in 2006 indicated that college essay assignments were easy compared to what they had to do at Bridges. One student noted: "Computers, grammar, descriptive writing, how to speak in public: I learned it all here" (student personal communication, June 12, 2006). Furthermore, the visiting alumni noted that the kinds of relationships they had established with their teachers and advisors at Bridges made them recognize the importance of doing the same with their college professors, particularly in classes where the number of students was large. The importance of the relationships developed at Bridges between staff and students was

**Table 2.3.   1998 Graduation Rates for
Bridges, Sister Schools A, B and C[a], and Citywide Avg.**

	Bridges	School A	School B	School C	Citywide
1998	*n = 23*	*n = 23*	*n = 19*	*n = 19*	
Graduated	54.8%	52.1%	38.0%	39.6%	49.7%
Still Enrolled	38.1	24.4	48.0	37.5	34.7
Dropped Out	7.1	24.4	14.0	22.9	15.6

Note: Data for this table are from the NYC Department of Education.
a. As discussed previously, three other CES high schools emerged from the restructuring of Presidential HS. To protect their anonymity, they are referred to here as "Schools A, B & C." (Annual School Report Cards)

**Table 2.3.   2004 Graduation Rates for
Bridges, Sister Schools A, B and C[a,] and Citywide Avg.**

	Bridges	School A	School B	School C	Citywide
2004	*n = 77*	*n = 78*	*n = 56*	*n = 58*	
Graduated	70.1	59.0	48.2	53.4	54.4
Still Enrolled	18.2	23.1	3.7	37.9	29.3
Dropped Out	11.7	17.9	16.1	8.6	16.3

Note: Data for this table are from the NYC Department of Education.
a. As discussed previously, three other CES high schools emerged from the restructuring of Presidential HS. To protect their anonymity, they are referred to here as "Schools A, B & C." (Annual School Report Cards)

also emphasized in interviews I conducted with other Bridges alumni. Janet, former student, remarked how different relationships were at Bridges than other schools:

> The environment and the relationships were always close; it was like a big family. Since the school was so small everybody knew each other…. It was never "Ms. this or Ms. that," so you feel closer to the advisors and the teachers in general. And it has an impact on the way that you look at school. You feel like you have a closer relationship to your advisor and you feel like you can trust them more and you learn better like that, when you feel comfortable with the teacher. (interview, June 9, 2006)

These sentiments—and the use of the word "family" that was also echoed in other former students' comments—all emphasized that the relationships they established with their teachers pushed them to want to succeed academically.

**Table 2.5.   Student Achievement at Bridges—
Various Indicators and Goals by Percentage**

Indicators	2004-5	2005-6	2005-6 Target	5-Year Goal
Average Daily Attendance	83.0%	85.0%	83.7%	90%
Annual Dropout Rate	2.4	3.0	4.0	Less than 4%
HS Course Academic Pass Rate				
English	70.9	75.6	71.3	75
Math	73.5	74.0	73.7	75
Social Studies	67.3	75.9	68.1	75
Science	71.1	71.6	71.5	75
Promotion Rate				
9th to 10th Grade	70.2	72.8	72.2	90
10th to 11th Grade	65.8	69.4	–	90
Regents Cohort Pass Rate				
English	77.0	78.4	77.3	80.0
Math	81.0	80.0	80.0	80.0
Graduation Rate				
4-year (NYC Cohort)	67.2	70.7	55.0	55.0
5-year (NYC Cohort)	69.6	–	75.0	
College Acceptance Rate	68.8	82.0	70.7	90

Note: Data for this table are from the NYC Department of Education. (Autonomy Zone Performance Scorecard, 2005-6)

One factor for this success was the instructional practice at the school. The founding staff of veteran teachers instituted practices such as project- and inquiry-based learning shaped by five "Habits of Mind."[4] The school literature described these habits—which included "critically examining evidence, seeing the world through multiple viewpoints, making connections, imagining alternatives, and contemplating the significance of the material being studied" (Bridges Institute, n.d.)—as being at the center of the school's instructional work and designed to develop critical thinking skills. In the classes I observed, students and teachers often referred easily to one or more of the habits, suggesting that they had become an organic feature of the school's discourse.

Another instructional practice adopted by Bridges' founding staff was the portfolio system, which was introduced to students within their first semester. The school was designed to engage students in processes that were largely unfamiliar to them as part of creating a new range of habits and skills the staff believed were essential to academic achievement. As such, the portfolio was designed to provide a forum for the students to demonstrate their growing knowledge and mastery of a variety of subject areas. Students complete and present an interdisciplinary "Language Portfolio" prior to their admission to their junior year to a panel of teachers, parents and peers. Prior to graduating, juniors and seniors must complete and present mastery work in seven areas: math, science, social studies, literature, social issues, the arts and elective.

The Bridges philosophy of assessment was evident in one 11th grade presentation I observed, where five students sat on a panel to discuss and debate their history portfolios. The overarching question they addressed in their various papers was: *What are the forces behind change in America?* Students' portfolio papers ranged in self-selected topics and included comparing and contrasting the philosophies of Martin Luther King and the young Malcolm X, the organizational philosophies of the Ku Klux Klan versus the Black Panther Party, Nixon and Watergate, the influence of music on the antiwar movement during the 1960s, and the Chicago 8 and the 1968 Democratic National Convention. After the students summarized their papers, the two teachers they were presenting to began challenging them to address the overarching question. One of teachers, Karen, asked them to "clearly link your evidence to your viewpoint" (Field Notes, May 19, 2006). As the students answered the question, the teachers asked them questions like, "so is it media?"; "so your other topics don't really matter?" and "can one person make a change?" The teachers encouraged students to dialogue and debate one another using their historical knowledge and evidence as an anchor. The scene highlighted the value that Bridges staff members placed not only on students being able to discuss their own work, but also on their ability to respond to critique in a reflective manner.

The school's academic practices were largely maintained through the early development of a strong professional community with a shared vision. Over the years, Bridges staff frequently engaged in reflection and it was evident in my observations that their talk often centered on the various tenets of the school's philosophy. This was reflected in the teachers' articulation of the school's philosophy and mission. Esperanza, who began teaching at the school within its first few years, noted that her understanding of the mission was "to have the students be able to participate in society so they become productive in their own lives, so they can support themselves, as well as so they can support their communities" (interview, June 6, 2006). In many of the interviews I conducted, staff—both teaching and support staff—often used the term "critical thinking" in meaningful ways to describe Bridges' vision for educating their students. The school community's ability to articulate and identify the vision was an important part of their capacity to counter challenges to that vision. Laurie, a founding teacher, attributed the school's success to their commitment to the philosophy and the school's ability to "stay the course" (interview, May 5, 2006).

One important reason that the staff could so clearly articulate the school's philosophy was because for many, it closely matched their own personal educational philosophy. When I asked them why they chose to work at Bridges, many teachers answered that they were looking for a small school that valued project-based learning and, in some cases, matched the principles of the Coalition of Essential Schools.[5] The connection between personal and school philosophy can be traced back to the founding of the school and the deliberate hiring practices adopted by the school founder, Jeff Wagner. His position was that it was essential to staff the school with teachers who had experience in schools whose vision closely matched Bridges. Wagner argued:

> It was enormously important to have people who had gone through this process who had an understanding of it, who had a commitment to kids, who had a commitment to each other as well. So we had a need of people who had experienced the model, who had experienced small schools. People who were willing to give whatever was necessary in order for this to succeed. (interview, February 4, 2006)

In his estimation, he needed to hire veteran staff from small schools because they would be willing to go beyond the ordinary duties of a teacher to make Bridges a success. As a result, in its inaugural year, 77.7% of the staff at Bridges Institute had more than five years of teaching experience. This figure was the same as the citywide average for all schools. In comparison, fewer than 45% of the teaching staff at Bridges' three sister schools' had more than five years of experience.

A tradition of distributed leadership contributed not only to the staff buying into the school's vision, but also motivated them to sustain it when it was being challenged. The processes that supported this tradition were built and maintained by a core group of founding and veteran staff, including the current principal, a founding teacher herself. This core ensured that the school had the institutional memory to retain important tenets of its founding vision.

This was highlighted during an early period in the school when the school staff was largely in opposition to Mary Jones, a founding coleader of the school with Jeff Wagner, who assumed full leadership after his retirement. The staff believed that Jones was not working to support the school vision as they had come to understand and believe. As a result, they took control to effectively, as Beth—founding teacher and current school principal—put it, "run the school around her" (interview, May 1,

2006). When I asked another founding teacher, Paula, what made the staff believe they had the authority to take control of the school, she replied that Wagner had instilled in them the belief that Bridges was a staff-run school. Also, since most of the staff was veteran teachers, Paula noted that they "weren't easily intimidated" (interview, May 1, 2006). Jones subsequently left the school just 2 years after assuming sole leadership.

CHALLENGES

Although there was evidence of success at Bridges, my research revealed there were also some tensions between the school's vision and the actual practice. For example, although many alumni reported feeling cared for and adequately prepared for college, several noted that the caring sometimes interfered with the establishment and enforcement of high expectations and, for some, made the transition to college difficult. Miriam, a former student, explained:

> When you get to college it's like, "Here's your syllabus." You don't have your teacher telling you, "This is what's due today, you have extended time." Maybe they allow you, depending on your excuse, to hand it in late, but your grade still gets struck down. But it's just like it's due, it's due! (interview, June 9, 2006)

Former Bridges students found that college professors were less likely to give them the leeway their Bridges teachers had given them and, unlike many of their experiences in high school, there were consequences for not meeting deadlines. Although teachers at Bridges often tried to "go beyond" to find ways to help their students be successful, this seemed to often translate into tacit support of their students' poor habits. Mark, an alumnus, recalled that during his final year at Bridges, he found it difficult to arrive at school on time and the parent coordinator would call him to wake him up. Although he found it helpful to be awakened daily by school staff, in my estimation, he was not learning how to become responsible for getting himself to school. Not surprisingly, Mark confessed that the transition to college was difficult for him not only because he was unaccustomed to the responsibilities he had to assume, but because of the academic pressures. He noted that when he left Bridges, he thought he was smart, but upon arriving at a city university, he found himself questioning his intelligence. Mark perceived that his peers knew more than he did, and he struggled in the remedial math class he was required to take. Still, when asked what he thought of his experiences at Bridges, Mark replied:

At the end of the day, I got a little bit of everything I needed in life. I think that this was the best school for me. And maybe educational-wise, it wasn't the best, but overall, this is the best school. There's people you can talk to, Sarah, she still has my number and we still stay in contact. I don't know. You can't really describe it.... It's Bridges. It's like its own little thing. So I love it, and I wouldn't change it. (interview, June 9, 2006)

Mark acknowledged that Bridges did not provide him with the best education he could have received, but that it gave him what he needed: close relationships. This student's comment, echoed by other alumni, highlights that school staff sometimes privileged caring over high academic standards.

The "soft" caring (Antrop-Gonzalez & De Jesús, 2006; Fine, 1998; Rolon-Dow, 2005) was also evident in some of my observations of professional development meetings, where some of the teachers demonstrated having low standards for student work. In one meeting, Beth, the current principal, facilitated a group of Bridges teachers as they discussed the quality of samples of student writing. Most of the teachers had strong critiques of the student work including but not limited to: a lack of a coherent thesis, insufficient evidence to support an argument, and lack of opposing viewpoints. Still, when Beth asked the teachers to rate the papers using a common rubric used by the Consortium member schools, none of the teachers indicated that they would have asked students to revise. When I noted my surprise at the outcome after the meeting, Beth revealed that she believed teachers approached student work from a model of deficit thinking. She believed that teachers lowered their standards for their students because they perceived that since the students had so many problems in their personal lives, what they were achieving was sufficient. Though she was able to name this critical issue, it is important to note that she did not address it explicitly with her staff.

This issue of lowered expectations was one that the school struggled with since its early years. In a letter Wagner wrote to staff after his retirement in 1996, he urged them to be more demanding of the students:

Students need to get into the regular habit of dong work and being held accountable for it. We should teach up to our students. They are capable of doing more than they (or in some cases we) can imagine. We cannot afford to allow students to "get away" with not doing their work. There are effective ways to deal with this, but we have to be persistent and tough enough to carry them out, whether that means keeping students after class, bringing them in early, keeping the building open, with supervision, until 5 p.m. every day, holding regular family conferences, or whatever. (personal communication, n.d.)

While Bridges teachers and students traditionally formed close relationships—a feature that was regarded highly by alumni and noted as being a
motivator in terms of their academics—those very relationships may have
interfered with some teachers' ability to hold their students to high standards. In trying to help students be successful, some teachers may have
fallen into the habit of lowering standards to help students meet them. It
is also important to note that while the student population was over 97%
Latino and Black, with nearly 90% qualifying for free lunch, Bridges' teaching force was predominantly white and middle class. As Lipman (1998) and
Ladson-Billings (1995) have argued, the staff's lowered expectations may
have also been due in part to the lack of explicit dialogue around issues of
race and class, and how these issues can shape teachers' perceptions of what
their students are capable of doing. For students of color especially, Rolon-
Dow (2005) argues that teachers "must seek to understand the role that
race/ethnicity has played in shaping and defining the socio-cultural and
political conditions of their communities" (p. 104).

The issue of lowered expectations at Bridges Institute was compounded
by an increase in the number of inexperienced teachers over the years. As
noted earlier, Bridges inaugural teaching staff was largely comprised of vet-
erans of critical small schools. By the 1998-99 school year, the number of
teachers with over five years teaching experience had declined to 33%. As
Bridges grew in size and as the small schools movement gained momentum,
there were fewer veteran teachers of critical small schools to staff newer
small schools. Consequently, like many of the Bronx small schools to date,
in 2008-2009, 33% of Bridges Institute's 36 teachers had less than three
years of teaching experience, while only 22% of teachers had completed 30
credit hours of schooling above their master's.[6] Whereas in the first couple
of years of the school's existence, the founding staff was able to induct novice teachers into the school's culture, share curricula and build a particular
kind of professional community, in later years, the balance between the veteran and novice teaching staff shifted and this kind of induction was difficult to achieve. Part of this had to do with the fact that as the student
population increased in size during the school's first 4 years, their teaching
staff had to increase, and it was difficult to recruit experienced teachers,
much less teachers with experience in critical small schools. Furthermore,
as the school's population grew and as the staff grew larger, it became
increasingly difficult for them to have the kinds of intimate conversations
around a table that they had traditionally. In fact, at the time of my research,
the staff barely fit into some of its larger classrooms, much less its designated
conference room. If a teaching staff is too large or unstable, it is extremely
difficult to engage in ongoing dialogue around substantive issues, particularly sensitive ones like race and class. Bridges' leadership instead had to
spend time introducing novice staff to the routines and rituals of the school,

and deal with issues of classroom management that are inevitable for newer teachers. These kinds of basic survival issues took precedence over the more substantive ones, and every year, this cycle was repeated as teachers left and newer ones replaced them.

CONCLUSION

Students entering schools like Bridges have often been sorely miseducated, and teachers find themselves in the difficult position of trying to balance their efforts of supporting their students through caring, and holding students to increasingly higher standards and expectations. A difficult but necessary question must be posed: What can one school realistically accomplish in 4 years when over 60% of kids are entering at below grade level in literacy and numeracy? Unless No Child Leff Behind and local Department of Education policy mandates begin to de-emphasize traditional four-year graduation rates as a benchmark for accountability, critical small schools may be forced to make educational tradeoffs at the expense of students.

If small schools are to be successful at educating historically underserved youth, it is important to be more realistic about what it will take to achieve the goal. Small schools like Bridges need more time to remediate students and adequately prepare them for college and the workforce. With more time, teachers in these schools will have the opportunity to both nurture their students as well as transition them into more responsible and self-motivated students who are capable of meeting high standards.

Schools like Bridges also need to have a teaching force that consists of more than inexperienced teachers that leave within a few years. They need to have the resources to provide students with academic support outside of the traditional school day model. They also need the resources to provide students and their families with social and health services that their communities do not offer them.

While the policy demands on small schools need to change, so too do the conversations about what it means to have high expectations. Small school size is meant to afford teachers the opportunities to develop strong relationships with students so that they can support the students to achieve higher. With the absence of explicit conversations about race and class dynamics, teachers in schools like Bridges run the risk of falsely conflating caring with high expectations. Furthermore, given that small schools in urban communities will often inevitably face high turnover, it is crucial that they develop protocols and procedures that will institutionalize strong practice. Without a solid academic infrastructure that guides their work in the absence of a veteran staff, small schools run the risk of reproducing the failures of the large high schools they replaced.

NOTES

1.   Bridges Institute, Presidential High School and names of research participants in this chapter are pseudonyms. The names of public figures in education have not been changed.
2.   Source: Community district needs: The Bronx (2004). *Community district 3, Borough of the Bronx: Statement of district needs.* New York, NY: Author.
3.   The 1993-94 Annual School Report indicates that Presidential's class of 1994 had a 37.3% graduation rate. However, this number is inflated because it includes students who earned a GED or special education certificate.
4.   Bridges Institute's Habits of Mind were originally developed by Deborah Meier's and her staff at Central Park East Secondary School.
5.   Founded by Ted Sizer in 1984, the Coalition of Essential Schools (CES) serves as a resource to a network of schools nationwide who have committed to following its ten Common Principles that serve to guide ongoing school reform (see Feldman, Foote, Hantzopoulos, this volume).
6.   In comparison, only 18% of the 34 teachers at Eleanor Roosevelt HS—a well-regarded small school in the affluent Upper East Side of Manhattan—had fewer than 3 years of experience, while 35% of their teachers have a master's plus 30 credit hours.

REFERENCES

Ancess, J. (2003). *Beating the odds: High schools as communities of commitment.* New York, NY: Teachers College Press.
Antrop-Gonzalez, R., & DeJesus, A. (2006). Toward a theory of critical care in urban small school reform: Examining structures and pedagogies of caring in two Latino community-based schools. *International Journal of Qualitative Studies in Education, 4*(19), 409-433.
Barton, P. E. (2003). *Parsing the achievement gap: Baselines for tracking progress.* Princeton, NJ: Educational Testing Service.
Bloom, H. S., Thompson, S. L., & Unterman, R. (2010). *Transforming the high school experience: How New York City's new small schools are boosting student achievement and graduation rates.* New York, NY: MDRC.
Bogdan R. C., & Biklen, S. K. (1992). *Qualitative research for education: An introduction to theory and methods.* Boston, MA: Allyn & Bacon.
Bridges Institute. (n.d.). *Bridges Institute.* [Brochure]. Bronx, NY: Author.
Bryk, A. S., & Schneider, B. L. (2002). *Trust in schools: A core resource for improvement.* New York, NY: Russell Sage Foundation.
Cotton, K. (1996). *School size, school climate, and student performance* (Close-up #20 ed.). Portland, OR: Northwest Regional Educational Laboratory.
Darling-Hammond, L. (1995). Restructuring schools for student success. *Daedalus, 124,* 153-162.

Darling-Hammond, L., Ancess, J., & Ort, S. W. (2002). Reinventing high school: Outcomes of the coalition campus schools project. *American Educational Research Journal, 39*(3), 639-673.

Elmore, R. F. (1996). Getting to scale with good educational practice. *Harvard Educational Review, 66*, 1-26.

Fine, M. (1991). *Framing dropouts: Notes on the politics of an urban public high school.* Albany, NY: State University of New York Press.

Fine, M. (1994). *Chartering urban school reform: Reflections on public high schools in the midst of change.* New York, NY: Teachers College Press.

Fine, M. (1998). What's so good about small schools? In M. Fine,& J. I. Somerville (Eds.), *Small schools big imaginations: A creative look at urban public schools* (pp. 2-13). Chicago, IL: Cross City Campaign for Urban School Reform.

Fine, M. (2004, October). Testimony submitted at joint hearing with the New York Senate Standing Committee on Education.

Fine, M. (2005) Not in our name: Reclaiming the democratic vision of small school reform. *Rethinking Schools, 19*(4), 11-14.

Fine, M., & Somerville, J. I. (Eds.). (1998). *Small schools big imaginations: An creative look at urban public schools.* Chicago, IL: Cross City Campaign for Urban School Reform.

Fullan, M. (1997). *What's worth fighting for in the principalship?* New York, NY: Teachers College Press.

Gootman, E., & Herszenhorn, D. M. (2005, May 3). Trying to lift performance by shrinking city schools [Electronic version]. *The New York Times*, pp. 1. Retrieved from Lexis-Nexis Academic database.

Greene, J. P., & Winters, M. A. (2006). *Leaving boys behind: Public high school graduation rates.* New York, NY: Manhattan Institute for Policy Research [Online]. Retrieved from http://www.manhattan-institute.org/html/cr_48.htm

Hartocollis, A. (1997, Sep 26). Chancellor to keep teacher in her job in parents' victory. *New York Times*, pp. A.1. Retrieved from ProQuest.

Klonsky, M. (1996). *Small schools: The numbers tell a story.* Chicago, IL: University of Illinois at Chicago Small Schools Workshop.

Ladson-Billings, G. (1995, Summer). But that's just good teaching! The case for culturally relevant pedagogy. Culturally relevent teaching [Special Issue]. *Theory into Practice, 19*(3).

Lee, V. E., & Smith, J. B. (1995). Effects of high school restructuring and size on early gains in achievement and engagement. *Sociology of Education, 68*, 241-270.

Lee, V. E., & Smith, J. B. (1997). High school size: Which works best and for whom? *Educational Evaluation & Policy Analysis, 19*(3), 205-227.

Lipman, P. (1998). *Race, class, and power in school restructuring.* Albany, NY: State University of New York Press.

McDonald, J. P. (1999). Redesigning curriculum: New conceptions and tools. *Peabody Journal of Education, 74*(1), 12-28.

McLaughlin, M. W. (1994). Somebody knows my name. *Issues in Restructuring Schools (7).* Newsletter of the Center on Organization and Restructuring Schools, University of Wisconsin, Madison.

Meier, D. (1995). *The power of their ideas: Lessons for America from a small school in Harlem*. Boston, MA: Beacon Press.

Meier, D. (2002). *In schools we trust: Creating communities of learning in an era of testing and standardization*. Boston, MA: Beacon Press.

Merriam, S. B. (2001). *Case study research in education : A qualitative approach* (2nd ed.). San Francisco, CA: Jossey-Bass.

National Association of Secondary School Principals. (2004). *Breaking ranks II: Strategies for leading high school reform*. Reston, VA: National Association of Secondary School Principals.

Noguera, P. A. (2002). Beyond size: The challenge of high school reform. *Educational Leadership, 5*(59), 60-63.

Noguera, P. (2003). *City schools and the American dream: Reclaiming the promise of public education*. New York, NY: Teachers College Press.

Noguera, P. A. (2006, October 15). School reform and second generation discrimination: Toward the development of equitable schools. *In Motion Magazine*. Retrieved from http://www.inmotionmagazine.com/er/pn_second.html

Oxley, D. (1994). Organizing schools into small units: Alternatives to homogeneous grouping. *Phi Delta Kappan, 75*(7), 521-526.

Peterson, P. L., McCarthey, S. J., & Elmore, R. F. (1996). Learning from school restructuring. *American Educational Research Journal, 33*, 119-153.

Raywid, M. A. (1996). *Taking stock: The movement to create mini-schools, schools-within-schools, and separate small schools*. New York, NY: Columbia University, Teachers College, ERIC Clearinghouse on Urban Education.

Rolon-Dow, R. (2005). Critical care: A color(full) analysis of care narratives in the schooling experiences of Puerto Rican girls. *American Educational Research Journal, (42)*1, 77-111.

Rothstein, R. (2004a). The achievement gap: A broader picture. *Educational Leadership, 62*(3), 40.

Rothstein, R. (2004b). *Class and schools: Using social, economic, and educational reform to close the black-white achievement gap*. Washington, DC: Economic Policy Institute, & Teachers College

Serrano, J. E. (2004, September 20). Clearing the air. *Gotham Gazette*. Retrieved from http://www.gothamgazette.com/feds/serrano_092004.php

Sizer, T. R., (1992). *Horace's compromise: The dilemma of the American high school: The first report from A Study of High Schools, Co-sponsored by the National Association of Secondary School Principals and the Commission on Educational Issues of the National Association of Independent Schools*. Boston: Houghton Mifflin. (Original work published 1984)

Sizer, T. R. (1995). Silences. *Daedalus, 124*(4), 77.

Smylie, M. A., Wenzel, S. A., Allensworth, E., Fendt, C., Hallman, S., & Luppescu, S. et al. (2003, August). *The Chicago Annenberg challenge: Successes, failures, and lessons for the future*. Chicago, IL: Consortium on Chicago School Research. Retrieved from http://www.consortium-chicago.org/publications/p62.html

Spillane, J. P. (2005, Winter). Distributed leadership. *The Educational Forum, 69*, 143-150.

The Small Schools Express. [Editorial] (2005, Summer). *Rethinking Schools*, 2-6.

Wagner, T. (2000). *How schools change: Lessons from three communities revisited* (2nd ed.). New York, NY: RoutledgeFalmer.

Yin, R. K. (2003). *Case study research: Design and methods* (3rd ed.). Thousand Oaks, CA: SAGE.

CHAPTER 3

A CLOSE LOOK AT SMALL SCHOOL CREATION

Lessons Learned From the First Years of a Critical Small School

Jay Feldman and Anne O'Dwyer

INTRODUCTION

The current educational system in the United States faces many challenges while attempting to successfully educate a broad range of students with different needs, close the achievement gap and raise achievement for all students. The large comprehensive high school, which was conceived at the turn of the twentieth century, was designed to fit an industrial society. These schools were founded on the idea of teaching as information-delivery—a conception that has been debunked in the last generation by scholarship on human cognition (see Kohn, 1993; Rogoff, 1990; Scribner & Cole, 1973)—and were not intended to educate all students to be prepared for college. They have therefore done a grave disservice to some children and communities.

Students today must be prepared for the Information Age—a period of widespread access to information—which requires students to be critical thinkers, effective communicators, problem solvers and lifelong learners.

Critical Small Schools: Beyond Privatization in
New York City Urban Educational Reform, pp. 41–59
Copyright © 2012 by Information Age Publishing
All rights of reproduction in any form reserved.

These new expectations of schooling are in direct contrast to the structures, cultures, and instructional strategies of the comprehensive high school. Compelled to think of different alternatives for the new reality, many large urban districts, including New York, Chicago, Los Angeles, San Francisco, Boston, and Pittsburgh have opened and are continuing to create new small high schools or to convert large comprehensive high schools into small schools (Gates Foundation, 2008; Hess, 2005; Myatt, 2004; Toch, 2003). Raywid (1999) writes, "We have confirmed [the positive effects of small schools] with a clarity and at a level of confidence rare in the annals of education research" (p. 1). A large body of research has found many benefits from these new or converted schools, as small schools have been found to be safer, have greater teacher and parent satisfaction, higher achievement and graduation rates, lower dropout rates, greater student participation in extracurricular activities, reduced racial achievement gaps and a deeper sense of student affiliation (Ancess, 2003; Ancess & Ort, 1999; Bryk & Thum, 1989; Cotton, 2001, 1996; Darling-Hammond, 1997; Darling-Hammond, Ancess, & Ort, 2002; Fine, 1998; Foote, 2005; Gates Foundation, 2010; Gladden, 1998; Howley, Strange, & Bickel, 2000; Klonsky & Klonsky, 1999; Lashway, 1998-1999; Lee & Loeb, 2000; Lee & Smith, 1995; Lee, Smith, & Croninger, 1995; Raywid, 1999; 1996; Tung & Feldman, 2002; Wasley et al, 2000 and Wasley & Lear, 2001).

Many advocates of the original small school movement and current proponents of critical small schools have expressed concern that many of the small schools being created today focus solely on size and not on the democratic participation and instructional practices characteristic of previous successful small schools (Davidson, 2002; Feldman, Lopez, & Simon, 2005; Fine, 2005; French, Atkinson, & Rugen, 2007; Meier, 2004; Wallach & Lear, 2005). They have argued that size is just a mediating factor that eliminates structural barriers and allows a school community to focus on personalization, democratic participation, critical pedagogies and project based assessment as a means for ensuring high levels of student achievement, particularly for historically marginalized youth. In fact, while new smaller high schools have been found to generally increase student achievement, the outcomes, particularly in urban areas, have been more mixed than hoped or expected, as too many examples of ineffective small schools have been closed due to poor performance (American Institutes for Research & SRI International, 2004, 2006). Research has found that reducing school size does not automatically lead to positive student outcomes (Stevens, 2008).

This chapter examines the creation and first few years of a small school with an eye to understanding the best practices in critical small school development. Rather than creating small schools by simply having an idea and starting from scratch to implement it, the processes used to create the school in this study—replication, seeding and mentoring—are important practices for the critical small schools and the movement as a whole because they mirror its emphasis on democratic decision making, critical friendships and a focus on student-centered experiences. This chapter, therefore, explores this process as a successful means for creating effective small schools

SMALL SCHOOL CREATION

The process whereby a critical small high school is created, opened or sustained can be essential for its success. For instance, many of the authors in this volume explain how the importance of building and maintaining relationships (see Bartlett & Koyama; De Jesus; Hantzopoulos; Rivera-McCutchen; Shiller; Tyner) and connections to external organizations (De Jesús, this volume) can determine the effectiveness and longevity of a school. In the last decade, small high schools have been created through a variety of methods (see, e.g., Feldman, Lopez, & Simon, 2005). Some schools have been created through a conversion process, in which a large comprehensive high school is divided into multiple independent and autonomous small schools (Nehring, Lohmeier, & Colombo, 2009; Wallach & Lear, 2005). Other small schools are created as start-ups, sometimes with design teams that have been supported by a technical assistance organization (Benitez, Davidson, & Flaxman, 2009; French, Atkinson, & Rugen, 2007; Lake, Winger, & Petty, 2002). There is additional variance within these methods—some schools open with a full span of 9-12th grades while others have started with just a 9th or a 9th and 10th grade. There are pros and cons to each of these approaches, and start up teams must weigh these options in the early phases of design.

The most important part of the design process is the creation of the structures, polices, practices and curriculum that those involved in the new school will need to successfully support and prepare their students for graduation and success in college. Some schools have created their model from the ground-up, others have taken an established model for their school's structure, design, and practices, while still others have been guided by a set of common ideas.

This chapter examines the creation and first years of operation of a critical small high school created through a developmental process called **replication**, in which new schools are created based upon the model of another school. In addition, The James Baldwin High School (JBS) was created using the **seeding** of staff and students from the model school to provide a core to begin the new school. Further, staff at the model school engaged in a **mentoring** relationship with staff from the new school.

Based on student surveys, staff interviews, and student outcome data across many schools, this chapter will examine this unique mix of processes in school creation. It will focus on the school design, the first four years of school development and student experiences and academic outcomes, arguing that it was the combination of these three strategies that led to the successful start-up and early years of a new small school. In conclusion, we will consider the implications of such a process on small school creation, development and the larger question of educational reform.

METHODOLOGY

This chapter looks at the start-up process of The James Baldwin High School as well as examining data from its first few years to determine if, in fact, the school can be considered successful. This analysis draws from four sources: student surveys, school staff interviews, school documentation reports (largely from the New York City Department of Education), and student outcome data. The data was part of a larger study examining the effectiveness of the Coalition of Essential Schools Small Schools Network (CES SSN) (see Feldman & O'Dwyer, 2010) and patterns in the development of start-up and conversion small high schools (see, e.g., Feldman & O'Dwyer, 2010, Feldman, O'Dwyer, & Kleigman, 2009).

Student Surveys

During the larger CES study, we collected four years of student surveys (Academic Years 2005/06-2008/09) from more than 12,000 students at more than 40 schools, including 20 established, effective small high schools, 12 start-up new small high schools and eight new small schools created from breaking down large comprehensive high schools (which are not included in this study) (see Tables 3.1 and 3.2 for a distribution of surveys and schools). The schools were founded in different years during our research (Cohort 1 schools were founded in 2005, Cohort 4 in 2008) and the new small schools each opened with just a 9th and/or 10th grade and added a new class each year. Students at the newly created and recently converted schools completed the surveys in the fall and spring of each year; students at the established schools completed the surveys only in the spring. The fall survey each year asked participants to rate both their current and previous school. All of these schools were members of CES and were members of a nation-wide professional learning community.

Table 3.1. Number of Schools, by Type, Completing Student Surveys Across the Survey Administration Periods

			School Type			
				Startup		
	Total	*Mentor*	*Cohort 1*	*Cohort 2*	*Cohort 3*	*Cohort 4*
Fall 2005	6	2	4			
Spring 2006	21	16	5			
Fall 2006	6		5	1		
Spring 2007	26	19	5	2		
Spring 2008	23	14	5	1	3	
Spring 2009	26	16	4	1	3	2

Table 3.2. Number of Completed Student Surveys, by School Type, Across the Survey Administration Periods

			School Type			
				Startup		
	Total	*Mentor*	*Cohort 1*	*Cohort 2*	*Cohort 3*	*Cohort 4*
Fall 2005	543	232	311			
Spring 2006	2,489	2,191	298			
Fall 2006	623		541	82		
Spring 2007	3,101	2,474	502	125		
Spring 2008	2,230	1,482	393	131	224	
Spring 2009	3,029	2,039	275	140	444	131

The *student survey* consisted of 49 statements about students' perception of their school, and students used a 4-point scale: one "almost never true," two "occasionally true," three "frequently true," and four "almost always true." Students in newly created and conversion schools rated their current school and their prior school in the fall of their first 2 years, providing a baseline for comparing their experience at their current school. Afterwards, students rated only their current school.

The spring 2006 survey administration—completed by over 2,000 students at 21 schools—was submitted to a confirmatory PC factor analysis with Varimax rotation. The PC analyses revealed five conceptual categories, each consistent with CES principles. A similar pattern of factors was found for subsequent administrations of the surveys; and thus these factors were considered stable. The distribution of survey statements across the factors was used to create five subscale scores for each student at each ratings cycle. For most items/statements, a factor loading of .35 or above could be identified. Several items were "double-loaded", meaning that they correlated with more than one factor, and, in these cases, the item was typically assigned to the factor with the larger loading.

The five factors were categorized as: (1) Using One's Mind Well, (2) Classroom Practices, (3) Personalized and Equitable Practices, (4) Culture of Democracy and Trust, and (5) Family and Community Connections (see below for a representative item for each subscale). These subscales corresponded to the CES Common Principles, which describe the core beliefs and characteristics of Essential Schools[2]:

1. Using One's Mind Well:

   My teachers want me to understand my school work, not just memorize it.
   This school has helped me understand mathematics more deeply.

2. Classroom Practices:

   In my classes, we study topics deeply instead of covering a lot of topics.
   My teachers ask me to learn through projects or other "hands-on" activities.

3. Culture of Democracy and Trust:
   Teachers, staff and students treat each other with respect at this school.
   There is a real sense of community in this school.

4. Personalized and Equitable Practices:
   This school is fair—if I work hard I can get a good grade
   My teachers know my academic strengths and weaknesses.

5. Family and Community Connections:
   Through my school, I work on projects that contribute to community outside.
   My parents/guardians are very involved in the school.

Staff Interviews and Documentation

Over the course of their 5-year participation in the CES SSP, administrators and liaison staff at both Humanities Prep and The James Baldwin High School were interviewed about their experiences starting the school, their lessons learned, the impact of being part of a community of learners and their mentoring relationship. In addition, the schools submitted annual reports of progress to the CES National office describing successes and challenges, which were also analyzed by the researchers.

Student Outcome Data

Student outcome data was collected from data made publically available by the New York Department of Education (http://schools.nyc.gov). This included demographic data, graduation rates, attendance and suspension rates and performance on NY State Regents exams. We also examined the New York City Department of Education annual School Quality Review reports.

SCHOOL CREATION AND HISTORY

School Design

At the beginning of the new small schools movement in the early 2000s, staff at Humanities Preparatory Academy (Prep), the "mentor" school in this partnership, began to discuss the idea of opening a new critical small school, based upon their philosophy and practices. At the time, Prep served just under 200 high school students in Grades 9-12. A long time member of CES, Prep has a long history of providing exceptional education to newly enrolled ninth graders as well as to a significant transfer population. Prep is widely known for a number of successful practices, including the use of performance- based assessment and a well-differentiated project-based pedagogy that provides students consistent opportunities to undertake independent research, analyze current issues, collaborate and self- reflect. Prep also has a strong commitment to student voice and development, as seen in their use of advisory, town hall meetings, and the Fairness Committee (see Hantzopoulos, 2006/2011; Hantzopoulos, 2010; Hantzopoulos, forthcoming, for more information). Finally, Prep is also known for its strong professional collaboration and distributive leadership, including the use of a consensus-based organizational decision model.

Prep held conversations about beginning another school both formally and informally until the staff voted to proceed with the idea at a staff meeting. As part of their process to create a new school, Prep and the new school design team were accepted as members of the CES SSN beginning in 2003. This would allow them to take advantage of the 5 years of support provided by the CES Network for these schools to establish and sustain a mentoring partnership as well as to participate in a nation-wide professional learning community (PLC). In this PLC, schools met regularly with other small schools for intensive professional development, including quarterly meetings, Critical Friends Visits (in which a team of educators visit the school and provide constructive feedback to the host school based upon the host school's essential question for the visit), and planning time with mentor schools (see Hantzopoulos, 2009, for a more extensive discussion of the CES SSN).

Prep was very conscious of the need to have trained staff start the new school so, in preparation for Baldwin, Prep slightly increased its teaching staff. The goal was that the core of the new school would be formed with teachers experienced in Prep's practices, but also that Prep would retain enough experienced teachers to continue the quality of its educational practice. Prep set up a process for staff to apply for the new school and serve on its design team for a year. Additionally, one new teacher at Prep was hired with the explicit purpose of going to the new school (Baldwin), the following year. As a new teacher, she would learn about Prep practices before teaching at Baldwin. There was no intention that only Prep teachers would staff the new school; in fact, transfers for Prep teachers were turned down by the Prep codirectorship to ensure that some teacher positions would be open for new teachers and that Prep could maintain quality teachers. Further, Baldwin would emphasize professional development for staff by opening in the same building that housed Prep—allowing for geographical proximity to aid in the mentoring process—and encouraging the staff to participate in a leadership-training program to build principal potential from within. Prep had a codirector model, in which one director typically served mainly administrative purposes while the other focused on pedagogical professional development.

The codirectors at Prep made the hiring decisions for the design team and staff at the new school. One Prep staff member was named as interim codirector at Prep as part of his training to become the codirector/principal at the new school the following year. During the design year, most of the meetings of the new school occurred with Prep staff, though the new school team had a few meetings on its own. As they chose the name James Baldwin for the new school, the design team members read and discussed the works of James Baldwin together. This reading helped the staff to situate their work within the context of a social justice framework and also served as an inspirational tool to persevere through the challenges of the start-up process.

The James Baldwin School opened in 2005 with eight staff members— two teachers and two codirectors (one of whom also had a full-time teaching load) from Prep and three teachers (science, social studies, mathematics) and a social worker hired externally. The school began with 83 students. This included 48 ninth graders and 23 tenth graders, as well as 7 eleventh graders who had been 10th graders at Prep the prior year. These students decided to enroll at JBS because they explicitly wanted to help create the new school and all were considered reasonably serious students. However, Baldwin expected that more students would decide to enroll from Prep to help seed the school. While there had initially been more students interested in the early planning of JBS, several of them changed their minds when it came time to enroll. In its first year of operation, 45% of Baldwin students were eligible for free/reduced lunch and 6% were classified as limited English proficiency. 48% identified as Hispanic/Latino, 41% as African-American or Black, 8% as White, and 2% as Asian or Native Hawaiian/Other Pacific Islander (The New York State School Report Card Accountability and Overview Report 2006-07, NY DOE).

One explicit difference in the student bodies between the two schools was the incoming study body and the application process. As a transfer school, students apply to Prep outside the citywide process, and prep has requirements for the number of credits earned and the age of the student, and requires the student to complete a separate admissions form with short essays. Baldwin was opened as part of New York City's broader strategy to close large underperforming high schools and to create small and academically non-selective schools, and its enrollment was based upon a lottery system (see Bloom, Thompson, & Unterman, 2010). Further, there were two enrollment periods because there were so many new schools being created throughout the city. Students selected from established schools during the first enrollment period, while the second period they could select from all schools, included all the new schools opening that fall. Additionally, the James Baldwin School was required to take only students with low math and reading scores for ninth grade, whereas Prep had a bit more leeway around this clause.

When the school began, many of their practices were learned from Humanities Prep. From its inception, The James Baldwin School implemented the Fairness Committee, advisories and town hall meetings based on the Prep model. The school began with two codirectors (with one having an increased teaching load that was scheduled to be reduced by one class per year as the administrative responsibilities increased as the school grew). Much of the curriculum was also taken from Humanities Prep. In fact, the teachers who had come from Prep taught some of the same classes they had taught at the older school. Additionally, the Baldwin codirectors, unlike their Prep counterparts, were relatively new administrators and had to figure out their leadership style, their roles, and how to work together.

In Baldwin's second year of operation, 2006-2007, the enrollment increased by 41 students, to 124 students. Their demographics were very similar to those from year one, although the free/reduced lunch percent increased from 45% to 70% (The New York State School Report Card Accountability and Overview Report 2006-2007, NY DOE). Both the math and the social studies teachers—neither of whom were initially Prep teachers—had a difficult time in year one and did not return for year two, although all other staff remained.[2]

Since the staff were replicating Prep practices, and because the majority were experienced in these practices, their implementation at the new school went fairly smoothly. However, there were some challenges. For example, attempting to implement the democratic decision-making experience from Prep was not a smooth process. Although most of the staff had experience with the model as the consensus model was the foundation for Prep's culture, it took time to help students understand the process, and it was a time-intensive process for people new to it. Additionally, the first year was very busy, and many teachers had additional administrative responsibilities related to the transition and creation of a new school, and the time required to perform these tasks took time away from their ability to focus on teaching.

Further, as the new school grew, change was inevitable and with growth came growing pains. Baldwin's staff began to look in-school for decisions about its practices and policies rather than continually looking towards the Prep model. For example, because Baldwin was smaller, they were able to have town meetings with the entire community more frequently, whereas Prep did so only at the beginning and end of the school year and for special events. Because of Prep's size, the school opted to still have weekly town meetings, but these were called Quads and consisted of four advisories rather than all advisories. As Baldwin grew and became larger than Prep, Baldwin made a different decision about shrinking Town Meetings. Baldwin created two communities within the school and assigned teachers and students to those communities for classes as well as for Town Meeting. Thus, rather than have four Quads running at once, Baldwin had two town meetings and ostensibly, two separate schools, as the students in each community only took classes in their respective community. A second difference was the codirector model. Prep's codirectors were both established, experienced administrators who had been in the codirector model for years and they would, for example, have many discussions in front of staff members to set out each of their responsibilities. The Baldwin codirectors were both new administrators and had the challenge of delineating responsibilities on the fly and were more likely to discuss their responsibilities in private.

OUTCOMES

Student Surveys

As can be seen in the means of Table 3.3, Baldwin was rated as near average of all new schools (2.9 to 2.96 out of 5) by students based on our analysis of the student survey data obtained from the established successful mentor schools, other newly created small high schools, and Baldwin (the means here are the composite ratings across the five subscales, which correlated quite strongly to each other). There are two reasons why Baldwin's first year ratings are slightly lower than the average first year start-up school. First, Baldwin's first year ratings were much higher than the ratings of its students' previous schools (.40) and this difference was greater than the difference between other start-up schools and their students' ratings of their previous schools (.29). Second, what differentiated Baldwin from the other new schools in the sample was that it enrolled incoming students who were familiar with the new school. When we specifically examined the ratings of those students who were new to the practices and culture of Baldwin (that is, those students that did not come to Baldwin from Prep), we found that new students rated their new school significantly higher than they did their previous school in all five categories. Those who were more familiar with the new school rated the new school as about the same. That students who came to Baldwin from Prep, a highly regarded, established school, rated the schools similarly, indicating that Baldwin was able to quickly establish itself and its practices and that the former Prep students saw little difference. That new students rated Baldwin much higher than their previous school indicates that Baldwin was a high quality choice for new students.

Further, while Baldwin did not start out with student ratings which were comparatively high, it did not show a second-year dip as did most of the other new schools. The authors believe that three factors added to this: (1) the addition of 'experienced students'—students not only familiar with small schools but familiar with the specific practices of Baldwin—

Table 3.3.   Student Ratings of Schools by School-Type and Year of Operation

	Preconversion	Year 1	Year 2	Year 3	Year 4
Mentor Schools		2.97	3.03	3.10	3.17
Other start-up Schools	2.75	3.04	2.86	2.90	2.96
Baldwin	2.40	2.80	2.84	2.90	2.90

were a key to building and sustaining the new culture, (2) the creation of the school with a core group of staff who had worked together implementing the same practices at Baldwin as at Prep, and (3) the intensive mentoring by Prep based upon already established relationships. Since much of the staff at Baldwin and Prep had worked together in the same school, it was easier for them to work together in the new one. They already had an established mutual level of trust.

School Quality Review Data

New York City Department of Education School Quality Review is a 2- or 3-day school visit by experienced educators to each New York City school. During the review, the external evaluators visit classrooms, talk with school leaders and use a rubric to evaluate how well the school is organized to educate its students.

The Quality Review was developed to assist New York City Department of Education schools in raising student achievement. The process is designed to look behind a school's performance statistics to ensure that the school is engaged in effective methods of accelerating student learning. As a result, the Quality Review focuses on the coherence of a school's systems, measuring how well it is organized to meet the needs of its students and adults, as well as monitor and improve its instructional and assessment practices.

In the 2007-2008 and 2008-2009 school years (years 3 and 4 of the school), Baldwin was consistently rated highly during its Quality Review, both in qualitative and quantitative feedback. Within the 25 aspects of the school practices category, Baldwin did not receive one rating below proficient and most marks were at the well-developed level.[3]

According to its most recent School Quality Review (2009), conducted by an outside panel in the school's fourth year, the review team notes that Baldwin "has given careful thought to each phase of its development and is clear about its vision for the future as it undergoes transition." The school was found to have been highly successful in replicating the democratic and highly personalized approach of Prep, and students who choose Baldwin "are rewarded with highly personal experiences that recognize their talents, skills, and needs" (The New York City Department of Education Quality Review Report 2009, NYC DOE). The review team found the school's staff to be:

> intensely committed to the school's stated mission and core values, and that students and parents feel and appreciate this dedication very deeply. The school effectively analyzes data and engages the whole-school community in

ongoing adjustment of school goals, structures, and plans. Teachers receive a great deal of individualized support and frequent feedback from colleagues, and the staff is highly collegial and reflective. Staff value student voice and the school's democratic and inclusive approach supports students' in holding themselves accountable for their own learning, behavior, and for meeting their goals. (The New York City Department of Education Quality Review Report 2009, NYC DOE)

Where the panel suggested that Baldwin needs to improve practices is in providing "opportunities for differentiated instruction and monitor the curriculum to incorporate more flexible grouping, promote active learning and address the wide range of learning styles, grade levels and skill levels of the diverse classrooms." This may be something that Baldwin community members may look toward in the future.

Student Outcome Data

Finally, we found that Baldwin was successful when comparing student outcome and school practice data with other new small schools that emerged in New York City. Baldwin has performed well on the State's standardized test, the Regents exam. Baldwin's percentage of students meeting or exceeding proficiency targets on state assessments surpasses that of similar schools in the district for English and trails slightly for math. Table 3.4 compares Baldwin students with students from similar schools.[4] Note that these similar schools are not start-up schools but most have been fully established. Some research (Feldman, O'Dwyer, & Kleigman, 2009) has found that the creation of effective math programs lags behind the establishment of effective English programs at new schools. Overall, The James Baldwin School has received positive reviews, not just from the Department of Education review processes, but also from outcome data and from its students themselves. As a whole, this indicates that the school was off to a solid start and that the experiences of creating the

Table 3.4.   Comparison of Baldwin and Similar Schools on Student's Scores on Regents Exams, 2009

| | Cohort | | | |
| | 2004 | | 2005 | |
	English	Math	English	Math
Baldwin	71%	48%	59%	46%
Similar Schools	55%	57%	55%	53%

James Baldwin High School have implications for the design and implementation of other small schools.

IMPLICATIONS AND CONCLUSIONS

Creating new schools is one option for school reform that communities and school districts have increasingly turned to in order to provide students with high quality education. The creation of The James Baldwin School is an example of how a school district can use multiple supports and a preexisting school to help launch a new school fairly smoothly.

The James Baldwin School was designed and opened using three interrelated processes: (1) replication, (2) seeding, and (3) mentoring, all of which were supported effectively by a preexisting school. According to staff interviews, student surveys, and student outcome data, The James Baldwin High School has created an environment which students like and where they perform well. There are thus a number of lessons to be learned from Baldwin's creation that can support the smooth launch of new small schools.

Building From a Preexisting School

Perhaps the main ingredient for the success of Baldwin's opening was the support of a preexisting school. Humanities Preparatory Academy (Prep) served as the foundation from which Baldwin was able to launch successfully. They served as the basis for the new school's model and design, training, preparing, and providing many of the staff (teachers and administrators) that would form core faculty at the new school, providing students from their school who were experienced in the model to help create a positive peer culture, and continued mentoring of the new school in its first few years. This process began before the creation of the new school: Prep expanded its own student body and staff, as well as trained a new administrator, the year before Baldwin opened. This allowed the staff at Prep to both train Baldwin staff (teachers and administrators) as well as train its own new staff that would be replacing the faculty who would leave for Baldwin. This helped ensure that both schools would be well served by having faculty experienced in the school's model.

Replication

Creating a new school based upon practices that have been found to be effective in another school seems like a good idea. However, transferring practices from one school to another is not an easy process. Those school replications that have appeared to be the most successful are usually supported by an outside organization to ensure that the model is implemented to a high degree of fidelity (see Expeditionary Learning, Outward Bound for example). A strong replication strategy needs to ensure that staff members are trained in the model and continually supported in developing their skills in implementing its practices and articulating its ideals. In the case of the Baldwin school, what better way to replicate a model than to have staff and administration experienced in the model as core faculty?

Seeding the New School

That James Baldwin High School was "seeded" with staff and students from the model school gave Baldwin a leg up in its first years of implementation—and, in fact, both staff and students may have had higher initial expectations which both made the first year more challenging and gave the school more staying power in the long run. Staff, for instance, were not struggling to understand the practices to be replicated. However, those staff who were 'seeded' from the model school did struggle with new roles and administrative responsibilities, while new staff who came directly into Baldwin struggled to learn the new model practices. This is evident in the non-seeded new staff from the first year who struggled to be successful in the school; nonetheless, the core of the Baldwin/Prep staff has remained stable over the first four years of the school's life. Moreover, new staff who have been hired since Baldwin's second year of operation seem to have a higher retention rate, indicating that practices in the school have become more stable. Further, the use of students to seed the new school and help to develop a positive student culture was also a useful process for Baldwin. This type of student mentoring is a process that would benefit from further study.

Mentorship

In addition to seeding the new school, Prep and Baldwin were engaged in a mentoring relationship. This allowed Baldwin to continue to receive support from Prep, its model school, which itself still had faculty who remembered the school's early years and the particular challenges of a new school. The mentoring relationship was at the heart of the Coalition of Essential Schools Small Schools Network approach. Mentoring requires a degree of trust between the participants. What made this relationship different from the start was (1) the fact that much of Baldwin and Prep had worked together in the same school made it easier for them to work together in the new one and (2) the practices being implemented were so similar that there could be back and forth between the two schools.

Implications for Urban School Reform and "Critical Small Schools"

Urban school systems are still struggling with the challenge of creating a system of schools that effectively meet the needs of the youth and families in their communities. The small schools movement of the last decade has posted some promising results (Gates Foundation, 2008) but has not been without its challenges. A key challenge has been the efficient creation of multiple small schools within already existing school systems. The design, creation, and first few years of The James Baldwin School provide us with a guide for creating future schools. Through its mix of mentoring, replication, and seeding, The James Baldwin School was able to launch successfully, according to student outcome data, student and staff perceptions and Department of Education characteristics. While all small schools can learn from this model, these processes are most important for critical small schools for whom democratic decision-making, a culture of respect and critical questioning, and transformational practices are so fundamental.

NOTES

1. The Cronbach's alpha for the five scales were .90, .82, .92, .87, and .72, respectively.
2. Teacher turnover has decreased from 33% in 2005-2006 to 20% in 2006-07 and 13% in 2007-2008 (The New York State Report Card Accountability and Overview report, 2008-2009, NY DOE).
3. The scale used is: (1) underdeveloped (2) underdeveloped with proficient features (3) proficient and (4) well developed.
4. Within each N/RC category, the Department identifies Similar Schools: schools that serve similar students and have similar resources. Each school report card compares the school's performance with that of similar schools. The following factors are considered in grouping schools: a) the grade level served by the school and b) rates of student poverty and limited English proficiency. Student poverty levels are indicated by determining the percentage of children in each school who participate in the free-lunch program. By combining these factors, a measure of student need is created and used to place schools into relatively low (lowest quartile), relatively high (highest quartile), and typical (midrange) groups.

REFERENCES

American Institutes for Research and SRI International (2004). *The National school district and network grants program: Year 2 evaluation report.* Washington, DC: AIR.

American Institutes for Research and SRI International. (2006). *The National school district and network grants program: Year 4 evaluation report.* Washington, DC: AIR.

Ancess, J. (2003). *Beating the odds: High schools as communities of commitment.* New York, NY: Teachers College Press.

Ancess, J., & Ort, S. (1999). *How the Coalition Campus Schools have reimagined high school: Seven years later.* New York, NY: NCREST, Teachers College, Columbia University.

Benitez, M., Davidson, J., & Flaxman, L. (2009). *Small schools, Big ideas.* San Francisco, CA: Jossey-Bass

Bloom, H. S., Thompson, S., & Unterman, R. (2010). *Transforming the high school experience: How New York City's new small schools are boosting student achievement and graduation rates.* Seattle, WA: Gates Foundation.

Bryk, A. S., & Thum, Y. M. (1989, Fall). The effects of high school organization on dropping out: An exploratory investigation. *American Educational Research Journal, 26*(3), 353-383.

Cotton, K. (2001). *New small learning communities: Findings from recent literature.* Portland, OR: Northwest Regional Educational Laboratory.

Cotton, K. (1996). School size, school climate, and student performance. *Close-Up #20.* Portland, OR: Northwest Regional Educational Laboratory.

Darling-Hammond, L. (1997). *The right to learn: A blueprint for creating schools that work.* San Francisco, CA: Jossey-Bass.

Darling-Hammond, L., Ancess, J., & Ort, S. (2002). Reinventing high school: An analysis of the coalition campus schools project. *American Educational Research Journal, 39*(3), 639-673.

Davidson, J. (2002). Elements of smallness create conditions for success. *Horace, 19*(1).

Feldman, J., Lopez, M.L., & Simon, K. (2005). *Choosing small: The essential guide to high school conversion.* San Francisco: Jossey-Bass.

Feldman, J., & O'Dwyer, A. (2010). Patterns in student perceptions of start-up and conversion small high schools. *Peabody Journal of Education, V85*(3), 313-332.

Feldman, J., O'Dwyer, A., & Kleigman, R. (2009, April). *Authentic intellectual achievement and CES small schools.* Paper presentation at the 90th annual meeting of the American Educational Research Association.

Fine, M. (1998). Introduction: What's so good about small schools? In M Fine & J. Sommerville (Ed.), *Small schools, big imaginations: A creative look at urban public schools* (pp. 2-13). Chicago, IL: Cross City Campaign for School Reform.

Fine, M. (2005). Not in our name. *Rethinking schools, 19*(4), 11-14.

Foote, M. (2005). *The New York Performance Standards Consortium College Performance Study.* New York, NY: New York Performance Standards Consortium.

French, D., Atkinson, M., & Rugen, L. (2007). *Creating small schools: A handbook for raising equity and achievement.* Thousand Oaks, CA: Corwin Press.

Gates Foundation. (2008). *All students ready for college, career and life: Reflections on the Foundation's Education Investments 2000-2008*. Seattle, WA: Authors.

Gladden, R. (1998). The small school movement: A review of the literature. In M. Fine & J. Somerville (Eds.), *Small schools big imaginations: A creative look at urban public schools*. Chicago, IL: Cross City Campaign for Urban School Reform.

Hantzopoulos, M. (2009). Transformative schooling in restrictive times: Engaging teacher participation in small school reform during an era of standardization. In F. Vavrus & L. Bartlett (Eds). *Comparatively knowing: Vertical case study research in comparative and development education*. (pp. 111-126). New York, NY: Palgrave.

Hantzopoulos, M. (2011). Deepening democracy: Rethinking discipline in schools. (Reprint with permission from *Rethinking Schools* in *Schools: Studies in Education*. University of Chicago Press. Spring 2011, Vol. 8(1), 112-116).

Hantzopoulos, M. (2011). Institutionalizing critical peace education in public schools: A case for comprehensive implementation. *Journal of Peace Education, 8*(3), 225-242

Hess, F.M., (2005). *Educational "innovation" v. educational innovation*. Policy Paper for the American Enterprise Institute for Public Policy Research. Retrieved from http://www.aei.org/paper/24250

Howley, C., Strange, M., & Bickel, R. (2000). *Research about school size and school performance in impoverished communities*. ERIC Digest. Charleston, WV: ERIC Clearinghouse on Rural Education and Small Schools (ED 448 968).

Klonsky, S., & Klonsky, M. (September, 1999). Countering anonymity through small schools. *Educational Leadership 57*(1), 38-41.

Kohn, A. (1993). *Punished by rewards*. Boston, MA: Houghton Mifflin Press.

Lake, R., Winger, A., & Petty, J. (2002). The New Schools Handbook. Center on Reinventing Public Education, Seattle WA.

Lashway, L. (1998-1999). School size: Is small better? *Research Roundup 15*(2), 2-5.

Lee, V. E., & Loeb, S. (2000, Spring). School size in Chicago elementary schools: Effects on teachers' attitudes and students' achievement. *American Educational Research Journal, 37*(1), 3-32.

Lee, V. E., & Smith, J. B. (1995). Effects of high school restructuring and size on early gains in achievement and engagement. *Sociology of Education, 68*(4), 241-270.

Lee, V. E., Smith, J., & Croninger, R. G. (1995, Fall). Another look at high school restructuring: More evidence that it improves student achievement, and more insight into why. *Issues in Restructuring Schools, 7*, 1-10.

Meier, D. (2004). *Many children left behind: How the No Child Left Behind Act is damaging our children and our schools* (Edited, with George Woods). Boston, MA: Beacon Press.

Myatt, L. (2004). Fulfilling the promise of small high schools. *Phi Delta Kappan, 85*, 770-772.

Nehring, J. Lohmeier, J. H., & Colombo, M. (2009). Conversion of a Large, Urban High School to Small Schools: Leadership Challenges and Opportunities NASSP Bulletin 93: 5.

The New York State School Report Card Accountability and Overview Report 2006 – 07, NY DOE. (http://schools.nyc.gov/SchoolPortals/02/M313/AboutUs/Statistics/default.htm).

The New York City Department of Education Quality Review Report 2009, NYC DOE. (http://schools.nyc.gov/SchoolPortals/02/M313/AboutUs/Statistics/default.htm).

Raywid, M. A. (1999). *Current literature on small schools.* Eric Digest. Charleston, WV: ERIC Clearinghouse on Rural Education and Small Schools (ED425 049).

Rogoff, B. (1990). *Apprenticeship in thinking.* New York, NY: Oxford University Press.

Scribner, S., & Cole, M. (1973). Cognitive consequences of formal and informal education. *Science, 182,* 553-559.

Stevens, W. D. (2008). *If small is not enough … ?: The characteristics of successful small high schools in Chicago.* Consortium on Chicago School Research at the University of Chicago.

Toch, T. (2003). Small schools, big ideas. *EdWeek.* Retrieved from http://www.edweek.org/ew/articles/2003/12/03/14toch.h23.html

Tung, R., & Feldman, J (2002). *How Boston Pilot Schools use freedom over budget, staffing, and scheduling to meet student needs.* Boston, MA: Center for Collaborative Education.

Wallach, C. A., & Lear, R. (2005). *A foot in two worlds: The second report on comprehensive high school conversions.* Seattle, WA: Small School Project.

Wasley, P. A., Fine, M., Gladden, M., Holland, N.E., King, S. P., Mosak, E., & Powell, L. C. (2000). *Small schools: Great strides—A study of new small schools in Chicago.* New York, NY: Bank Street College of Education.

Wasley, P. A., & Lear, R. (2001). Small school: Real gains. *Educational Leadership, 58*(6), 22-27.

PART II

INSIDE THE LEARNING COMMUNITIES: THE CULTURE, PRACTICES AND FORM OF CRITICAL SMALL SCHOOLS

The following section examines the various practices, pedagogies, and school structures that contribute to student engagement in critical small schools, particularly for students that have been historically underserved in their schooling experiences. While the models vary from site to site, these chapters explore how some schools have found ways to keep their students from disengaging from their education, which offers suggestions for schooling even beyond the critical small schools arena. Throughout this section, we see evidence of student-teacher relationship building, culturally-relevant pedagogy, strong school culture, community connections, and a commitment to inquiry-based learning. Here, we demonstrate that the ingredients of critical small schools include more than just their size.

- What seem to be the most effective ways in which critical small schools have successfully (re)engaged students in their learning? Why are these pedagogies and structures effective?
- How do the various pedagogies and structures described in the chapters vary and in what ways do they overlap?
- How does context influence the ways in which critical small schools enact their pedagogies and structures? How might this inform broader educational reform.

CHAPTER 4

AUTHENTIC CARING AND COMMUNITY DRIVEN SCHOOL REFORM

The Case of El Puente Academy for Peace and Justice

Anthony De Jesús

INTRODUCTION

During the past decade, school reform in New York City has accelerated at a pace rarely seen in the history of the city's schools (Ravitch, 2010). Facilitated by a neoliberal school reform agenda at the federal, state and philanthropic levels, New York City's Department of Education has closed more than 20 under-performing high schools in recent years and established more than 200 new schools in their place including 123 small *schools of choice* intended to be viable alternatives to the closing schools (Bloom, Thompson, & Unterman, 2010).

Bolstered by a new mayoral controlled governance structure and led by Chancellor Joel Klein (a former U.S. Attorney who prosecuted the Microsoft Anti-Trust case), the city was able to attract the resources of private

Critical Small Schools: Beyond Privatization in
New York City Urban Educational Reform, pp. 63–78

philanthropy (e.g., the Bill and Melinda Gates Foundation) in order to restructure large failing high schools into smaller learning communities through the New Century High Schools initiative (Bloom, Thompson, & Unterman, 2010). This era of new small school creation built upon the success of prior small school reform efforts but differs considerably in scale and scope of vision from the progressive educators and community leaders who established an earlier generation of model small schools (Bensman, 2000; Meier, 1995; Rivera & Pedraza, 2000). While the new small schools create the potential for more favorable learning environments and show initially promising outcomes, the broader set of district driven reforms they are part of gives short shrift to the community informed approach of earlier small schools. This chapter explores the experiences of students at one small school in Williamsburg, Brooklyn— El Puente Academy for Peace and Justice which was established a decade before the city's current small school initiative, and draws upon student voices to show the generative potential of community driven reform.

METHODOLOGY

Based on interviews with students, participant observation and a review of the literature written on El Puente Academy for Peace and Justice, this chapter analyzes the voices of students as they discussed their educational experiences at the school. Using purposeful sampling (Maxwell, 1996; Patton, 1990), a cohort of eight students was assembled which reflected a cross section of the school's student body ($n = 150$) at the time.[1] The students were from working class and poor backgrounds; were male and female; U.S. born and immigrant—Latino/a and African American and reflected a range (low-high) of involvement in community activities and academic performance and overall engagement in school (see Table 4.1). The latter of which was an important consideration in assembling the cohort.

The perspectives of these students offer compelling insight into what is unique about El Puente's structure and curriculum which emphasizes the history of students' communities and the importance of reciprocal relationships in engaging young people who have been traditionally marginalized in public schools. Using the language of caring, students revealed that the school emphasizes high academic expectations and supports the development of high quality interpersonal relationships between adults and students who provide them with academic and interpersonal support. Students also reported that the reciprocal nature of their relationships with adult facilitators at El Puente engaged them academically and pointed them toward postsecondary success. The theoretical literature on

Table 4.1. Student Characteristics

	Pseudonym	*Age*	*Grade*	*Birthplace*	*Leadership*	*Academic %*
1.	Ricardo	15	10	Dominican Republic	no	low
2.	Diego	15	10	Mexico	yes	high
3.	Carmen	14	9	U.S. (Puerto Rican)	no	moderate
4.	Ramon	16	11	U.S. (Puerto Rican)	no	moderate
5.	Trina	14	9	U.S. (African American)	yes	high
6.	Teresa	18	12	U.S. (African American)	yes	high
7.	Orlando	17	11	U.S. (Salvadoran/Ecuadorian)	yes	high
8.	Reggie	17	11	U.S. (African American)	no	low

caring in education (Noddings, 1984, 1992; Valenzuela, 1999) provides a useful framework for analyzing the experiences of El Puente Academy's students.

BACKGROUND

El Puente Academy for Peace and Justice is a small, innovative community high school in New York City that emerged from and is part of El Puente, a Latino community-based organization in Brooklyn, NY. Founded in 1982 by community activists who sought to stem the tide of violence among young people in this predominately poor and working class Latino community, El Puente today is a vibrant community institution that comprises the Academy, four youth leadership centers (after-school programs) and various other community development initiatives. El Puente's founders started the organization in response to a protracted period of youth violence during the late 1970s and early 1980s and the lack of social service agencies and schools capable of addressing these problems. From its inception, El Puente's founders were deeply engaged in advocacy efforts to improve public schools—particularly Eastern District High School, the large traditional zone school for the neighborhood which was plagued by an 80% dropout rate (Nix, 1987) and symbolized for El Puente's founders what was wrong with the Board of Education. Lack of Latino representation at the school board, school administration and classroom levels strained relations between teachers and Latino students leading to acrimonious relations. Of this situation, one of El Puente's founders interviewed by the New York Times observed: "Young people are being given a message: Your culture is not good enough; your language stinks; you have to adjust to our culture, it's an insensitive cultural response

by the Board of Education and the educational system in general"
(Carmody, 1988). The conditions to which Latino students were subjected
in Eastern District resonate with Valenzuela's (1999) articulation of
subtractive schooling, which suggests that such schools:

> Are organized formally and informally in ways that fracture students cul-
> tural and ethnic identities, creating linguistic and cultural divisions among
> the students and the staff.... Teachers fail to forge meaningful connections
> with their students; students are alienated from their teachers and are often
> (especially between groups of first generation immigrants and U.S.-born)
> hostile toward one another as well; and administrators routinely disregard
> even the most basic needs of both students and staff. The feeling that "no
> one cares" is pervasive-and-corrosive. (p. 5)

In their efforts to develop effective youth development and after school
programming, El Puente's founders identified the need to address the
schooling of the young people in their community, known as Los
Sures—the south side of Williamsburg. When invited by New Visions for
Public Schools to start their own public high school, the founders of El
Puente Academy sought to create a holistic after school learning community that would affirm the language, culture and identities of Latino students and link the individual development of students to a broader vision
of community development. According to Rivera and Pedraza (2000) the
founders of El Puente:

> Rejected a service-provider ideology and instead sought to provide Wil-
> liamsburg residents (who are mostly Latino/a) with opportunities, spaces
> and experiences so that they can determine what is best for them to live
> holistic, healthy and productive lives. In essence, El Puente's founders
> embraced a belief in and practice of self-determination and community
> development. (p. 232)

In 1993, El Puente Academy for Peace and Justice opened as a New York
City public high school under the auspices of New Visions for Public
Schools, a non-profit initiative founded "to create a critical mass of small,
effective schools that equitably serve the full range of children in New
York City" (Rivera & Pedraza, 2000, p. 227).

Now in its seventeenth year, El Puente Academy serves 200 students in
grades nine through 12, 83% of which are Latino/a (15% are African
American). The majority of students are residents of North Brooklyn.
While a New York City Public School, the fact that El Puente was founded
by Latino community activists who explicitly sought to create a school
whose purpose is linked to explicit values of community development and
human rights speaks to an interest in the educational success of students

being linked to the well being and interests of local Latino residents (community driven reform) rather than those of school district administrators or city planners (district driven reform). These community interests were underscored by students who described their appreciation for culturally-relevant pedagogy and curriculum at the school as well as the close inter-personal relationships they forged with adults at the school. Students con-sistently used the language of caring to describe their educational experiences at El Puente.

A CULTURALLY-RELEVANT PEDAGOGY AND CURRICULUM

El Puente Academy organizes annual integrated curricular projects across disciplines and seeks to link them to students' cultural and historical journeys as well as the history and geopolitics of the local Williamsburg community. This approach is consistent with Ladson-Billings (1995) classic articulation of *culturally-relevant pedagogy* that "addresses student achievement but also helps students to accept and affirm their cultural identity while developing critical perspectives that challenge inequities that schools (and other institutions) perpetuate" (p. 469). El Puente's The Sugar Project, for example, was inspired by a local Williamsburg landmark—the Domino Sugar factory—and linked English, global studies, biology, dance and visual arts.

Young people studied the history of sugar and its effects (i.e., slavery dependent cultivation in the Caribbean and Latin America) as well as the patterns of consumption in the United States. Students in biology conducted a school-wide survey of the amount of sugar and sugar-based products consumed daily by young people in Williamsburg. The English and global studies classes investigated the histories of people who worked on sugar plantations and studied the cultures of resistance which grew out of their struggles. Video, dance and visual arts classes studied the cultural and spiritual expressions that emerged from struggles and oppression related to sugar in Africa, Latin America and the Caribbean.

As this description reveals, curriculum at El Puente is neither static nor prescribed, rather it is a constructivist process which is understood by staff and students as a form of practice— "a state of mind, and a way of life" as one facilitator put it. Another example—the *Sankofa* curriculum (based on the Swahili term that means "going back to the roots") is a ninth and tenth grade English, global studies and fine arts curriculum and is organized around the essential questions, "Who am I?" and "Who are we?" Students explore poetry, art and cultural histories, which address issues about personal identity, and present individual portfolios of art projects, writings and research about themselves and their families. Orlando, a U.S. born sophomore of Salvadoran and Ecuadorian parents described how the curriculum helped him clarify confusion about his Latino identity:

> This year, one important thing that I really learned was what the difference was between Latino and Hispano. I used to be confused before, I didn't know the difference. Like when you say that you're Spanish or something like that—it's like you're saying you belong to Spain but they're the ones that conquered us and gave us our language. But (saying) Latino, is recognizing your whole group and you're background—like we're part African and Indian, and there are other parts too, it's not just one thing. Now I say that I'm Latino, cause I know where I come from. —Orlando (interview, October 4, 2000)

By basing its curriculum and pedagogy on students' community and cultural resources, El Puente Academy seeks to remedy culturally subtractive and marginalizing schooling experiences for Latino/a students and provide them with an academic and cultural foundation for acquiring the academic and social knowledge and skills for success in the United States (e.g., New York State learning standards).

Through the appropriation of both student funds of knowledge and the codes of power (Delpit, 1995) of the dominant society, El Puente makes great strides toward providing Latino/a students with the kinds of educational experiences necessary, not only for their educational/occupational success in the U.S. but also with the orientation to apply these skills toward the development of their community.

Creating a Culture of Engagement Through Principles of Peace and Justice

El Puente Academy's strong emphasis on relationships stems from its history and institutional identity and is organized symbolically around the organizations' mission: *To Inspire and Nurture leadership for Peace and Justice* and its 12 principles for peace and justice.[2] El Puente's principles, embedded in their organizational culture, are prominently displayed throughout the school and in publications and are evoked on nearly a day-to-day basis by students and staff. Students discussed at length how the principles were central in their experiences as members of the El Puente learning community. Carmen, a Puerto Rican freshman student, reflected on how the visual representation and community practice of the 12 principles (particularly the principle of "love and caring") impacted her during her first day as a student at El Puente:

When you first go into the school you see a big round circle and it says all the stuff the school is about (the 12 principles). When I first saw it, I thought it was like a (night) club or something. I saw loving and caring and didn't really understand at first. Then, I saw people giving each other hugs, just saying welcome. (interview, January, 2001)

When I asked Carmen what school and principles meant to her she replied:

It's about loving and caring, support, community, like we're all one—united. The way people interact with each other, you know? They give you support when you need it. The facilitators are good. They care about the students. Basically, they treat you like friends. You can call them by their first name, just like they call you by your first name. It mainly has to do with respect. They're caring. (interview, January, 2001)

She connects her understanding of the 12 principles to the respect and support she received from facilitators and students. In our discussion, using the language of caring Carmen described how she felt about her facilitators at El Puente in contrast to her prior experience with teachers in middle school.

Carmen:	In other schools, the teachers don't care if they even teach, as long as they're getting paid. They gotta give enough credit to the teachers in this school. If you compare these ones to in other schools ... I don't know, they really don't care—as long as I'm getting paid, "go ahead, talk." That's how it was at my old school.
A. De Jesús:	So these facilitators care more about teaching?
Carmen:	Yeah and they care about their students.
A. De Jesús:	Would you say that's a big difference?
Carmen:	Yeah, to come from another school to this.

Carmen's observation relates well to Valenzuela's (1999) educational caring framework. Building on a framework developed by Noddings (1984, 1992), she analyzed competing notions of caring among predominately Anglo teachers and Latino students that are rooted in fundamentally different cultural and class-based expectations about the nature of schooling. In the traditional high school which Valenzuela studied, these expectations inevitably clash and when they do, they fuel conflict and power struggles between teachers and students who see each other as *not caring:*

The predominately non-Latino teaching staff sees students as not sufficiently *caring about* school, while students see teachers as not sufficiently *caring for* them. Teachers expect students to demonstrate caring about schooling with an abstract, or *aesthetic* commitment to ideas or practices that purportedly lead to achievement. Immigrant and U.S.-born youth, on the other hand, are committed to an *authentic* form of caring that emphasizes relations of reciprocity between teachers and students. (p. 61)

While the teaching staff at El Puente at the time of my study were approximately half Latino and half White (with a small percentage of African Americans), it is clear from student responses that the practice of authentic caring is rooted in El Puente's mission and principles and in the opportunity for El Puente's students to engage in authentically caring relationships with a diverse group of facilitators.[3]

Teresa, an African American senior, spoke to the importance of the 12 principles in operationalizing the school's mission and practice. As a student who transferred to El Puente after a difficult first year at a large traditional school, she illustrates the significance of the 12 principles in contrast to her experience in her previous school.

This whole thing of basically having 12 principles is different right there— you can't ask no other school like "what's your mission?" 'cause I don't really think they have none (laughs). I think it's just to get those students out— cause they also push a lot of students ahead without them making their grades. *And I haven't seen that done in this school.* (interview, March 2001)[4]

Teresa's critique of the lack of a mission of her former school and the practice of "pushing out"[5] students suggests that educational engagement at El Puente is related to both high expectations and a high level of support placed on her by facilitators and is operationalized by an espoused commitment to the 12 principles. Teresa went on to discuss her experiences with facilitators:

They're caring; they take their time out with the students. Make sure they're passing their classes. If you're not passing, they stay after school knowing they could be doing other things. 'Cause most of the teachers take out their time and stay here with you and make sure you got the work down. (interview, March 2001)

Some critics might express concern that the highly personalized and informal relationships valued at El Puente diminish boundaries and authority relationships between youth and adults. Teresa, however, believes that facilitators at El Puente negotiate relationships that are indeed bounded, respectful and conducive to student development.

I think they come down to our level in a mature way. Like they can hang out with us and talk to us on our same level—but it's like they're not really with us. They know how to have a good time with us—how to talk to us—how to find out what we're thinking but at the same time not really act childish.

They still know their place—have a good time and let the student know that they are older and they do have a certain respect—so if you're sitting down with a facilitator you don't cuss or anything. (interview, March 2001)

While new students to El Puente often experience "culture shock" when El Puente's expectations and pedagogy are explained, El Puente's 12 principles emphasize the nurturing of reciprocal relationships and relate to Valenzuela's (1999) articulation of *educación*, a term that within Latino culture is strongly related to social ties and reciprocal relationships (p. 61). Teresa further suggested that students also play an important role in facilitating the school's culture of engagement by helping socialize newer students to the "ways of the school."

My grades improved, my personality—I get along with a lot of people better 'cause they're like—friendly. When I first came here—a lot of students were trying to get to know me and I was like- "why are you asking me all these questions?" and they were like "I'm just tryin' to get to know you." and I was—like "all right!" Cause, I didn't like that at first—but now I understand why they do it. (interview, March 2001)

As did Teresa, most students over time come to embrace a community-based approach to learning based on *confianza* or what Rauner (2000) calls an *ethic of care*:

Organizations can be caring by consciously arranging their practices, programs and policies along an ethic of care. Individuals in their professional capacity perform caring actions, but the organization, by virtue of its structure and functioning, also can facilitate and promote effective caring behavior. (p. 3)

El Puente's ethic of care is organized around the 12 principles, curriculum and support mechanisms that facilitate the transformative experiences of caring described by students. These include the Holistic Individualized Process (HIP).

"It would mean a lot to see your eyes when you speak to me:" The Holistic Individualized Process

With the preponderance of violence experienced in schools throughout the United States in recent years, and El Puente's institutional origins in response to a wave of youth violence, the physical safety of students is clearly a high priority. However, metal detectors, increased security, elaborate forms of surveillance and coercive control apparatus are not hallmarks of El Puente's commitment to the principle of safety. While El Puente seeks to provide a form of cultural protection by fostering a small tightly knit learning community, the *Holistic Individualized Process*, as it is known, avoids a reliance on unilateral discipline policies and seeks to understand more broadly the needs of individual students and the origins of conflicts among members of the learning community to the extent it is possible. Through strengths based assessment (Blundo, 2010) and reflection, young people develop goals with adult mentors and create individualized action plans. Consistent with the school's commitment to holism, students focus their goals and action plans through a weekly HIP seminar. The seminar emphasizes well-being in the areas of body, mind, spirit and community within the following four major components: individual and collective self-help, group development, wellness and community action and development. The HIP process is tied to the schools' 12 principles and is characterized by resisting the deficit orientations that proliferate within and outside of schools. Rather than seeing young people as problems (or solely as diagnoses), HIP is a manifestation of El Puente's attempt to create its own language for what traditionally is known as student support services or simply, counseling. Julie, one of El Puente Academy's HIP coordinators described the HIP to me:

> Instead of like looking at all young people as what their deficiencies are or that they have these problems and we have to fix them, we look at them as a whole person and see what (experiences) they bring to the table. And a lot of it is positive and a lot of it has to do with environmental factors and a lot of it has to do with some strengths that they have but they have put in other areas in their life that need to be refocused. If we look at them as an individual instead of looking at their deficit we can see what's really going on and we can work from there. It's a much more empowering model, it's much more youth-focused, it's positive and it allows you to go more places than if you look at them through all of the things that they have wrong. (interview, April, 2001)

Julie's description and my observations of HIP's implementation are consistent with the strengths based framework within social work practice. According to Blundo (2010) the

> strengths perspective focuses not on the defectiveness of the client system in an attempt to undo these problems but on the inherent competencies, and resiliency that are the building blocks of a better future.... It assumes the expertise of the client and privileges client knowledge and capabilities.

Importantly, HIP is not the exclusive domain of the "counseling" staff and while trained counselors and health professionals are key HIP resources and coordinators, all staff (and some trained students) participate in HIP. A compelling example of HIP in action is found in the following excerpt of dialogue I observed during an intervention between two students (one male and one female) who were threatening to assault each other during class. Julie was asked to mediate:

Julie:	What happened?
Sergio:	Just suspend me! I don't want to fuckin' talk about it! Just suspend me!
Julie:	You are really angry and hurting inside, tell me what happened.
Sergio:	I don't want to talk about it—just suspend me! I want to go home! That's what they would do at my old school—why don't you just send me home?
Julie:	I know you haven't been here (at El Puente) long but we don't do that at this school. You're very angry, why don't you take a deep breath and relax.
	(Sergio sarcastically takes a deep breath)
Julie:	Can you look at me and tell me what happened?
Sergio:	*(With head tilted and eyes looking down, avoids eye contact)*: She was yelling at me loud and pissed me off – so I threatened to hit her.
Julie:	Can you look at me when you speak? *It would mean a lot to see your eyes when you speak to me. They're the window to the soul.*
	(Sergio repeats himself while nervously attempting eye contact.)
Julie:	Thank you Sergio. Lissette, can you tell me your side?
Lissette:	Yeah, like he said—he was talking bad about my mother and I have a very close relationship with my mother who is sick with cancer, so it really hurt me to hear that so I yelled at him and he told me to shut up.
Sergio:	Yeah, but I was joking, I didn't know that your mother was sick. I don't have a good relationship with my mother—so it's easy for me to talk about mothers. That's my bad. I didn't mean nothing bad.
Julie:	Do you think transferring your negative feelings toward your mother to other people is going to make your situation better?
Sergio:	No, but sometimes I don't think about how other people feel about it 'cause I don't know what its like to have a mother who's there for you.
Julie:	That's a really sad situation Sergio and I don't think that there is much that I can do to make it better but I do know that expressing that anger toward other people like you did is not going to help your situation. Do you agree?
Sergio:	Yeah—you have a point.
Lissette:	I can't imagine what it would be like to have a bad relationship with my mother. I kinda over reacted too—sometimes I'm like that—you know. It gets me into trouble. I'm sorry.
Sergio:	I'm sorry for talking bad about your mother.

(field notes)

While Sergio's conditioning in his previous school was to anticipate (if not expect) a suspension and avoid addressing the underlying causes of the conflict, this vignette illustrates a powerful alternative to the punitive disciplining event in schools.

Mediations such as this are commonplace at El Puente where diligent efforts are made to address the underlying emotional needs of students that may lead to conflict. HIP constitutes a strong example of El Puente toward avoiding unilaterally punitive or "zero tolerance" approaches in addressing school conflict and is a compelling practice that is highly successful. To be sure, there are situations that may require more serious disciplinary action and sustained intervention, but El Puente's commitment to the principle of safety facilitates greater trust among students and adults at the school and creates the conditions where students can reflect on their behavior and receive support from staff rather than constantly expect punitive and coercive adult power. HIP coordinators and staff strive to support students in confronting feelings that are uncomfortable, and often left unaddressed in other schools, in a way that communicates that they are valued as individuals and members of the community. Because so many students (and adults at times) are conditioned to unilateral discipline policies and models of punishment (as was Sergio in the above example), the HIP process attempts to prevent conflict by strengthening students' interpersonal capacity to function as contributing and healthy members of a community. Julie observed:

> When somebody gets in trouble at El Puente, they never want to get in trouble again because it's painstaking, it's like every level they go through is a whole process unto itself. If it's two people that are fighting, the process goes like this. Two people are fighting they are brought up, the crisis intervention team comes together and they focus on okay, who is available, who's close to these people and we set up a plan of action. —Julie (interview, April, 2001)

As challenging as this process is for many students (and adults), HIP provides insights into how El Puente confronts the global concern of violence and manifests a commitment to proactive conflict resolution, a strengths based approach and the principle of safety. El Puente students recognize and appreciate this commitment in contrast to their knowledge of other schools.

Reggie, a student who struggled academically and behaviorally earlier in his high school career, now clearly articulates his goal of attending a state university in the south. An African American junior who, through his friends is aware of the practices utilized in other schools to curtail violence and conflict, explained to me why El Puente is a safer place for him:

> It's not worth it to fight or to get in conflicts you know, 'cause this school right here, there's something special about it, you know. They treat you with a lot of respect. They give you a lot of freedom here. They don't hassle you. They don't check you when you come to school. They don't have metal

detectors. They trust you. You know? This is a good school. Most schools now—they got metal detectors—they pat you down. I don't be wantin' that! My friends tell me: "Yo! I don't want to go to school. They're not teaching me nothing. They (the teachers in their schools) don't care! This school (El Puente), if you cut school or don't come to school—they call your house and ask why. Other schools—they don't care—they just mark you absent. If you don't come—absent, late, cut. They don't care! (interview, February 2001)

Reggie's statement suggests that his sense of feeling respected and trusted by facilitators solidifies confianza and informs a school cultural norm of safety rather than the preoccupation with control and punishment that is so prevalent in urban schools (Noguera, 1995). Reggie's experience at El Puente has been so positive that he credits the school with the fact that he is currently in school:

Yeah, if I was at another school, I think I would be out playing basketball right now or sitting at home asleep—while my mom's at work. Only once I cut school—and they called my house. I don't cut school no more. (interview, March 2001)

While no single strategy can inoculate schools from the barrage of violence and conflict so present in the lives of young people, the HIP process additionally attempts to protect students from punitive discipline policies which reinforce violence (in the form of coercive and rigidly applied codes of conduct) rather than prevent it (Noguera, 1995).

CONCLUSION

The voices of El Puente students presented in this chapter reveal that authentic forms of caring based on Latina/o values and struggles for educational rights are embedded in the formal and informal structures and curricula of El Puente Academy. Students consistently reported that they were significantly engaged in the learning process through high quality interpersonal relationships with adult facilitators and that these relationships were characterized by high academic expectations of the students by staff. Additionally, participant observation provided evidence that the risk of conflict and violence was diminished as a result of the reciprocal relationships fostered between adults and students and El Puente's strengths based approach to discipline.

El Puente espouses an explicit commitment to creating curriculum that affirms student identities as well as employs culturally-relevant pedagogy (Ladson-Billings, 1995) rather than a politically "neutral" curriculum that tacitly supports the status quo. Valenzuela (1999) argues that these are essential weapons in combating the detriments of subtractive schooling. She notes:

> students' cultural world and their structural position must be fully apprehended, with school based adults deliberately bringing issues of race, difference and power into central focus. This approach necessitates the abandonment of a color-blind curriculum and a neutral assimilation process. (p. 109)

Because El Puente was organically created and sustained by and for community members, as opposed to large, impersonal and bureaucratic school districts; teachers were able to authentically privilege and honor their respective funds of knowledge and dismantle the subtractive schooling (Valenzuela, 1999) practices that were so commonplace in students' previous schooling experiences. In this regard, El Puente represents the notion of community driven reform and was part of the first generation of schools that have informed today's district-driven small school reform. These findings are important because they support the argument that while schooling on a smaller scale is an important condition for engaging Latina/o youth in learning, what goes on within those small structures is infinitely more important. This research points to the importance of opportunities for communities of color to play a primary role in the creation of small high schools that reflect their social, cultural and political interests. Finally, this research suggests that policymakers and school reformers must consider the ways in which they structure opportunities at every level for communities to be involved in the schooling of their own. That is, of course, if they care to do so.

NOTES

1.   This research emerged from a case study project conducted in collaboration with the Center for Puerto Rican Studies at Hunter College (CUNY) and El Puente Academy staff. Data collection began during the 1999/2000 school year and was completed at the end of the 2000/2001 school year. The project featured a participatory design where a group of El Puente Academy staff with a University based researcher (myself) developed research questions and protocols and interviewed students and parents. While the research design process was a collaborative one, the bulk of data collection and all of the analysis herein is provided by this author.

2.   El Puente's 12 principles developed by its founders, Luis Garden Acosta and Frances Lucerna, also the academy's founding principal, are Love and Caring, Collective Self-Help, Peace and Justice, Mastery, Holism, Development, Mentoring, Creating Community, Unity through Diversity, Respect,

Creativity and Safety. El Puente lists its four cornerstone principles as love and caring, collective self help, peace and justice, and mastery.

3. This was the demographic composition of El Puente's faculty at the time of my study.

4. Italics mine

5. As Katz (1999) argues the term dropout implies a conscious choice on the part of the student to leave school "as if all options were open to them. However students of color leave school largely because they feel discriminated against, stereotyped, or excluded (Fine, 1991; Oakes, 1985; Rumberger, 1987, 1995). The terms "push out" puts the responsibility on where it should accurately fall: schools and schooling in the United States" (p. 812) .

REFERENCES

Bensman, D. (2000). *Central Park East and its graduates: "learning by heart."* New York, NY: Teachers College Press.

Bloom, H. S., Thompson, S. L., & Unterman, R. (2010). *Transforming the high school experience: How New York City's new small schools are boosting Student Achievement and Graduation Rates.* New York, NY: MDRC.

Blundo, R. (2010). "Strengths-based framework" *The encyclopedia of social work.* Ed. Terry Mizrahi and Larry E. Davis. 2008 National Association of Social Workers and Oxford University Press, Inc. CUNY Hunter College. 26 September 2010. Retrieved from http://www.oxfordreference.com/views/ ENTRY.html?subview=Main&entry=t203.e381

Carmody, D. (1988). Education: Hispanic dropout rates puzzling. *The New York Times*, p. 8.

Delpit, L. (1995). *Other people's children: Cultural conflict in the classroom.* New York, NY: New Press.

Fine, M. (1991). *Framing dropouts.* Albany, NY: SUNY Press.

Katz, S. (1999). Teaching in tensions: Latino immigrant youth, their teachers, and the structures of schooling. *Teachers College Record, 100*(4), 809–840.

Ladson-Billings, G. (1995). Toward a theory of culturally relevant pedagogy. *American Educational Research Journal, 32*, 465–491.

Maxwell, J. A. (1996). *Qualitative research design: an interactive approach.* Thousand Oaks, CA: SAGE.

Meier, D. (1995) *The power of their ideas: Lessons for America from a small school in Harlem*, Boston, MA: Beacon Press.

Nix, C. (1987, June 27). Eastern high's daily assault on failure. *The New York Times*, p. A1.

Noddings, N. (1984). *Caring: A feminine approach to ethics and moral education.* Berkeley, CA: University of California Press.

Noddings, N. (1992). *The challenge to care in schools: An alternative approach to education.* New York, NY: Teachers College Press.

Noguera, P. (1995). Preventing and producing violence: A critical analysis of responses to school violence. *Harvard Education Review, 65*, 189–212.

Oakes, J. (1985). *Keeping track: How schools structure inequality.* New Haven, CT: Yale University Press.

Patton, M. Q. (1990). *Qualitative evaluation and research methods* (2nd ed.). Newbury Park, CA: SAGE.

Ravitch, D. (2010). *The death and life of the great American school system: How testing and choice are undermining American education.* New York, NY: Basic Books.

Rauner, D. M. (2000). *They still pick me up when I fall: The role of caring in youth development and community life.* New York, NY: Columbia University Press

Rivera, M., & Pedraza, P. (2000). The spirit of transformation: An education reform movement in a New York City Latino/a community. In S. Nieto (Ed.), *Puerto Rican students in U.S. schools* (pp. 223–246). Mahwah, NJ: Lawrence Erlbaum.

Rumberger, R. (1987). The impact of surplus schooling on productivity and earnings. *Journal of Human Resources, 22,* 24–50.

Rumberger, R. (1995). Dropping out of middle school: A multilevel analysis of students and schools. *American Educational Research Journal, 32,* 583-625.

Valenzuela, A. (1999). *Subtractive schooling: U.S.-Mexican youth and the politics of caring.* Albany, NY: State University of New York Press.

CHAPTER 5

ADDITIVE SCHOOLING

A Critical Small School for
Latino Immigrant Youth

Lesley Bartlett and Jill P. Koyama

INTRODUCTION

The population of Latino immigrants living in the United States grew from 22.4 million to 35.3 million between 1990 and 2000 (Logan, 2001); in fact, 54% of the most recent and unprecedented wave of immigrants is from Latin America (McCabe & Meissner, 2010). Additionally, according to official statistics, the number of immigrant children and children of immigrants in U.S. schools—the majority of which are designated as "English Language Learners" (ELLs)—escalated from 6% in 1970 to 20% in 2000 (Jaffe-Walter, 2008) and were a population that immigrant scholars called "overlooked and underserved" (Capps et al., 2005, p. 5; Ruiz de Velasco & Fix, 2000). An estimated 35% of Latino youth living in the U.S. are foreign-born (López, 2009, p. 2).

Schools in the United States are increasingly responsible for educating these immigrant children, and yet, too often, they are not prepared or structured in a manner to do so successfully. A new type of school has emerged to meet their needs: the newcomer school. A survey of 115 new-

Critical Small Schools: Beyond Privatization in
New York City Urban Educational Reform, pp. 79–102
Copyright © 2012 by Information Age Publishing
All rights of reproduction in any form reserved.

comer programs in 29 states, plus Washington, DC, provides the best available overall description of these efforts (Boyson & Short, 2003; Short & Boyson, 2000). These programs generally defined and admitted students on the basis of English proficiency, time in the United States and native language literacy skills. Almost two-thirds of all programs served fewer than 100 students, demonstrating that newcomer schools tend to be particular kinds of small schools. In 85% of the programs, between 80 and 100% of students were eligible for free or reduced lunch, indicating the low socioeconomic status of newcomer students. Most of these newcomer programs (76%) were in urban settings, and the majority (54%) served high school populations. Newcomer programs generally share the similar goals of helping students acquire English skills while providing some instruction in core content areas. Sheltered instruction was found to be the most common means of teaching content (applied in 89% of programs), employing English as the main language of instruction, but using specialized strategies to assist with understanding. Only 11% of programs gave content instruction primarily in the home language, as is the case in the school we examine here.

In this chapter, we present a small newcomer school that has done a remarkable job of meeting the educational and social needs of Latino immigrant students in New York City. The research presented in this chapter draws from a qualitative case study of a bilingual high school for Latino newcomer immigrant youth in the Washington Heights neighborhood in New York City. The school, Gregorio Luperón High School, represents a unique effort to serve the educational needs of immigrant newcomer youth. For a period of four years, we worked with a team of researchers to conduct school-based observations, to interview administrators, faculty, students, and parents, and to trace the impact of public policies on the school. In what follows, after discussing the "subtractive" economic, social and educational circumstances that influence the education of Latino immigrant youth in New York City, we examine how Gregorio Luperón High School, like other critical small schools across the nation, created and supported a thriving learning community despite these challenges. In particular, we demonstrate how the school fostered instructional and assessment policies that built additive linguistic and cultural practices that resulted in a "successful" bilingual school for Latino newcomers. In this sense, Luperón was not a typical small high school for newcomer youth, but rather one that exemplified the characteristics of a critical small school: a school organized by strong, supportive relationships between the community and the school and between teachers and students, as well as among students, and a community of commitment to equity united by a sense of struggle for justice.

SUBTRACTIVE CIRCUMSTANCES

Schooling for Latino immigrant youth takes place in the midst of various subtractive circumstances that create significant vulnerabilities including poverty, unemployment, racism and language discrimination, decimation of bilingual education, high-stakes testing, and the significant challenges facing all of urban education. It is important to understand these conditions in order to address them.

Economic Circumstances

Latino immigrant students are vulnerable in many ways. First, poverty exposes many Latino students, and especially those who are immigrants, to risk—while 27% of the former live in poverty, 35% of the latter do (Fry & González, 2008, pp. ii-iv). The per capita mean annual household income in 2005 for Latinos in the United States was $15,341 which is significantly lower than the national average of $25,817 (2006 American Community Survey, as cited in Rivera-Batiz, 2008). This number also contrasts sharply with the non-Latino White population's per capita mean annual household income at $29,595. Latinos are also behind non-Hispanic Black households whose per capita mean annual income is at $17,180 (American Community Survey, as cited in Rivera-Batiz, 2008). As a result of the high levels of unemployment and low levels of income, 24.5% of Latinos lived in poverty in 2007, compared to 15.6% of the total population (United States Census Bureau, 2007). The highest rates of poverty for Latinos occur in families with children under 18 years old and nearly 32.4% of this population were estimated to be living in poverty in 2007 (U.S. Census Bureau, 2007).

In New York, where Latinos constituted 32% of the immigrant population in 2002, they have had disproportionately low levels of socioeconomic attainment as compared to other ethnic and racial groups (New York City Department of City Planning, 2000). The average unemployment rate for Latinos in New York City in 2007 was estimated to be 5.6%, as compared to the 4.4% unemployment rate for the total population (American Community Survey, 2007). These numbers in the city, as well as across the country, were undoubtedly exacerbated by the economic crisis late in the decade, likely further narrowing academic opportunities for Latino children who often attend underfunded public schools.

Educational Circumstances

While economic circumstances hamper the opportunities available to immigrant Latino families, prevailing educational policies and practices have a similar effect on Latino students. First, the contemporary period is marked by opposition to bilingual education. Access to bilingual education was established by the Bilingual Education Act of 1968 and the Lau v. Nichols judicial decision of 1974 but has been significantly eroded by the English-only movement, successive state-wide legislation that drastically restricted bilingual education and the efforts of various legislators and anti-bilingual political hopefuls such as Ron Unz (a leader of antibilingual initiatives in California and Arizona) (Crawford, 2004; García, 2009a; García & Kleifgen, 2010; García, Kleifgen, & Falchi, 2008). During the past five decades, bilingual education programs have given way to English as a Second Language (ESL) programs, and the term "bilingual education" has been associated only with transitional bilingual programs, where the goal is to mainstream students (and cease support for the development of academic literacy in the first language) as soon as possible.

Second, Latino immigrant students in the nation tend to live in highly segregated areas where the schools lack resources and well-trained teachers (Orfield & Eaton, 1996; Orfield & Lee, 2005). Many schools with large English-learner populations also have large low-income populations. In urban centers such as New York, Los Angeles, and Chicago, where Latino youth comprise the majority of the school age population, Latinos are disproportionately consigned to overcrowded and underfunded schools of low quality (Oakes, 2002; Noguera, 2003, 2004; Conger, Schwartz, & Stiefel, 2007). In New York City public schools, where roughly 40% of the students were Latino in 2008, Latinos had the highest dropout rate of all ethnic groups, with the exception of the few American Indian students in the system (De Jesús & Vásquez, 2005). In 2007, the New York City Department of Education (2008) found that Latinos had a graduation rate of 53.4% as compared to a 79% graduation rate for white students.[1] According to the Commission on Independent Colleges and Universities (year unknown), only one-third of Latino New Yorkers graduate high school in 4 years—a rate which is lower than those of all other ethnic groups.

Third, immigrant students' previous educational experiences may negatively impact their retention and attainment. Some students attend school regularly but experienced low quality education in their native countries. Some first-generation students have not experienced continuous education prior to their arrival in the United States. In 2000, an estimated 6% of first-generation immigrant students reported interrupted formal education in their home country; notably, the school dropout rate for that group in the United States was 70% (Fry, 2005, p. 3). Immigrant students with interrupted formal education constituted 38% of all foreign-born school dropouts (Fry, 2005, p. 8).[3]

Latino students who have immigrated to the United States and have received some schooling abroad are also significantly more likely to dropout of school than Latino youth who have received all of their education in U.S. schools (Van Hook & Fix, 2000; Vernez & Abrahamse, 1996). According to the National Center for Education Statistics, "The status dropout rate[3] of 44.2% for Hispanic 16- through 24-year-olds born outside the 50 states and/or the District of Columbia was more than double the rate of 16.1% for Hispanic youths born in the United States with at least one parent born outside the United States, and the rate of 16% for Hispanic youths with both parents born in the United States" (Van Hook & Fix, 2000, p. 14; see also Fry & Lowell, 2002). This is startling, given that even Latinos schooled exclusively in the United States have comparably high dropout rates: 15%, as compared to 12% for Black youth (Fry, 2003). Foreign-born students who arrive as teens are particularly vulnerable to dropping out. According to Fry (2007), "in 2000, more than 80% of foreign-born school dropouts were recently arrived youth" (p. 597).

A fourth educational factor contributes massively to the subtractive circumstances facing newcomer students. Immigrant students in general and English learners in particular have specific linguistic needs. Forty-four percent of first-generation students speak English with difficulty (Fry & González, 2008, p. ii-iv) and 7 million schoolchildren in the United States speak Spanish as their primary language (Capps et al., 2005). Their language instructional needs and the practices that best attend to them have been widely documented elsewhere (Crawford 2004; Cummins, 2000; García, 2009a). The many English learners who, more often than not, attend schools that subtract their "cultural and linguistic knowledge and heritage" (Valenzuela, 1997, p. 326) experience linguistic and cultural segregation from those for whom English is their primary language. Fifty-three percent of emergent bilinguals attend elementary and secondary schools where over 30% of their classmates are also language minorities; conversely, 57% of English-proficient students attend schools where less than 1% of all students are English language learners (Van Hook & Fix, 2000, p. 10).

Schools with large Latino immigrant populations too often fail to meet the unique needs of these students. Their culture and language is not reflected in the school curriculum (Gándara & Contreras, 2009) and teachers who lack an awareness of the realities of this population have difficulty relating to them and may develop negative perceptions of them (Valdes, 1996; Valenzuela, 1999). As Valenzuela notes, Latino youth often experience *subtractive schooling*, in which their cultural and linguistic knowledge and heritage, which could promote bicultural and bilingual competence, are subtracted from their formal learning environments. Further, these youth often feel stigmatized by other students when they are removed from the regular classroom for language classes, such as English as a Second Language (ESL) classes. Further, many of the language education models for English learners were developed for students born in the United States, rather than for recently-arrived immigrants. Such "subtractive schooling" (Valenzuela, 1999) positions Latino immigrant students at the lowest rung of the school's linguistic and cultural ladder.

Fifth, educational opportunities for Latino immigrant students have been negatively shaped by federal, state and local policies. The federal No Child Left Behind (NCLB) Act (U.S. Department of Education, 2001), with its aim to increase achievement for all students through school accountability, led to expanded, standardized, statewide assessments as measures for learning. However, the legislation has done little to address resource inequities, shortages of teachers trained to serve emergent bilinguals, inadequate ELL curricula and ineffective programs for Latino newcomers (Crawford, 2004). The testing demands of NCLB have narrowed curriculum, promoted excessive test preparation, and forced educators to abandon programs that have, over the long-term, proved successful for this substantial and growing sector of the public school population (Abedi, 2004; Menken, 2008). English language learners are often juggled between ESL classes and mainstream content instruction throughout the school day.

NCLB's exaggerated focus on testing risks further exclusion of historically underserved racially and linguistically diverse immigrant populations. As Kim and Sunderman (2005) show, group accountability targets place racially diverse schools and/or schools with large emergent bilingual populations at greater risk of failing "Adequate Yearly Progress" (AYP). In fact, the academic progress and measured performance of emergent bilinguals, as a group, becomes critical to the school's overall performance.[4] Some schools therefore avoid serving students categorized as "LEP." For example, many charter schools and small high schools elect not to accept English language learners in an effort to maintain higher standardized test scores (Ravitch, 2010).[5] Further, as noted by Crawford (2008), NCLB

does little to address the most formidable obstacles to [the] achievement [of English language learners]: resource inequities, critical shortages of teachers trained to serve ELLs, inadequate instructional materials, substandard school facilities, and poorly designed instructional programs. Meanwhile, its emphasis on short-term test results—backed up by punitive sanctions for schools—is narrowing the curriculum, encouraging excessive amounts of test preparation, undercutting best practices based on scientific research,

demoralizing dedicated educators, and pressuring schools to abandon programs that have proven successful for ELLs over the long term. (p. 2)

Some argue that, for emergent bilingual students, broad sweeping one-
size-fits-all federal policies like NCLB use language to categorize, test and
discriminate against students in much the same way that policies used to
employ race: such policies ignore income, culture and other factors that
impact English Language Learner's (ELL) academic engagement and
achievement (Gutiérrez & Jaramillo, 2006; Monzó & Rueda, 2009).

State and city policies, likewise, greatly affect immigrant youth. States
implement NCLB through their determination of AYP requirements. Different states, and even different school districts within a state, employ var-
ied criteria to classify, educate and assess ELLs. New York State has
influenced the education of English language learners in large part
through its increasingly higher standards on Regents examinations, which
are now required to graduate high school and therefore can compel those
who cannot pass the requisite number of standardized tests to "dropout."
Further, the centralization of mayoral control over schools in New York
City, and the subsequent large-scale and sometimes confusing reorganiza-
tions, have led to increased prominence for standardized test scores and
only a slight (and debatable) decrease in the dropout rate (Ravitch,
2010,p. 89).

However, New York City has demonstrated a somewhat unusual
(though not nearly strong enough) commitment to improve the schooling
of emergent bilinguals in the face of national trends. Since 2003, the
Department of Education has provided professional development for
more than 20,000 teachers, administrators, school staff and parents. In
addition, it has provided grants to support students with limited literacy
in their home language and interrupted formal schooling (known in NYC
as Students with Interrupted Formal Education—SIFE), and to develop
"dual language" bilingual programs. It has also generated major initiatives to create support networks and model solutions for schools striving
to improve the academic achievement of emergent bilinguals. One
important initiative concerns the emergence of nine international schools
serving immigrant youth from more than 90 countries. These schools,
which are located at the intersection of federal, state, and some policy
contexts that are "hostile to immigrants who are ELLs, to teachers' professional communities, and to inquiry-based learning and performance-
based assessments;" nonetheless, they "continue to work against the tide
of detrimental policies while sustaining school communities dedicated to
the needs of immigrant youth" (Jaffe-Walter, 2008, p. 2042). The small
size of these schools, their instructional aims and their pedagogical
approaches foster a supportive institutional culture that resists narrowing

educational policies and focuses on inquiry-based learning and multifac-eted performance-based assessments (Jaffe-Walter, 2008; Fine, Jaffe-Walker, Pedraza, Futch, & Stoudt, 2007).

To address these seriously subtractive conditions, a group of Latino activist educators, with community support, gathered to form a small, critical, bilingual high school. In the following sections, we first detail the research methods used in this study and offer a brief description of the site before explaining the linguistic and cultural support provided to immigrant students.

DOING THE STUDY: RESEARCH METHODS AND THE SITE

This chapter draws from a 4-year, longitudinal, multimethodological study that involved a team of researchers.[6] Using purposeful sampling, the school was selected as a site of study because it was experiencing unusual levels of success with Latino immigrant youth. Research strategies included an initial survey of newly arrived students in 2003; classroom observations focused on English as a Second Language and Native Language (Spanish) classes in the first year and other content areas in subsequent years; focus groups with teachers and students; interviews with teachers, administrators, and parents; observations at PTA meetings; and a longitudinal study of 20 newcomer youth, which involved observing them in classes over a period of four years and conducting an annual interview with them.[7] This chapter draws primarily upon the data collected from interviews with students, teachers, and administrators.

Gregorio Luperón High School

In 1993, a group of Latino educators began working together to respond to the immense educational needs of immigrant youth in New York City and to develop a new small school for Spanish-speaking, newcomer youth who had been in the country for fewer than six months. Gregorio Luperón High School for Science and Mathematics opened in 1994 in Washington Heights—the neighborhood with the United States' highest concentration of Dominicans—as a 2-year orientation program to transition Latino immigrant students into area high schools. The program converted to a 4-year secondary school in 2001. Ninety-seven percent of the students currently attending Gregorio Luperón are deemed English language learners (what we, following García, 2009, are calling "emergent bilinguals"), the highest percentage of all of the city's high schools.

Luperón's mission statement reflects its commitment to bilingualism; the school "aims to nurture, challenge and prepare students ... to achieve high standards of scholarship and leadership in both Spanish and English speaking society." To achieve this goal, Luperón employs what García and Bartlett (2007) call a speech community model of education, in which educators focus on language acquisition as a social process that involves an entire speech community while attending to sociocultural and sociopolitical contexts, including the ways in which practices, identity and power interact to provide a context for learning English. This speech community model has a focus on *macroacquisition,* defined by Brutt-Griffler (2004) as "a process of social second language acquisition" (for more on this process, see Bartlett & García, 2011).

At Luperón, the faculty members have developed a dynamic bilingual model, in which they teach English for three intensive periods per day while simultaneously teaching content courses primarily in Spanish for the first two years. Content courses also employ strategies to support English acquisition across the curriculum through "translanguaging" (Bartlett & Garcia, 2011), an approach that includes pedagogical strategies such as constantly translating key vocabulary terms into both languages, working across both languages when speaking, listening, reading and writing over the course of a lesson, and comparing content-specific genre structures in the two languages. Native language literacy instruction of this type, used in approximately 40% of newcomer schools (Short & Boyson, 2003), merits careful scrutiny. The approach, only possible in schools that have a concentration of large numbers of students from the same linguistic background, valorizes students' linguistic and cultural assets and supports students' development of second language literacy (see also Bernhardt & Kamil, 1995; Bialystok & Cummins, 1991; Carson, Carrell, Silberstein, Kroll, & Fruehn, 1990; Cummins, 1991; Gabriele, Troseth, Matohardjono, & Otheguy, 2009; Walsh, 1991).

Compared to national and city-wide averages, Luperón has had remarkable success shepherding newcomer immigrant youth through graduation. The official rates in 2008 showed that Luperón enjoyed an 83.8% four-year graduation rate. It far outperformed peer schools with similar populations, resulting in the New York City Department of Education declaring the school as performing at 119.8% of its "peer horizon" in graduation rates.[8]

Overall, the school meets or exceeds New York City's evaluation criteria, which include instruction, assessment, evaluation and capacity building goals (New York City Department of Education, 2008). It also received an A grade (100.4%) on the 2007-2008 Progress Report issued by New York City's Department of Education. According to the report, which measures school environment (15% of total grade), student performance (25%), and student progress (60%), Gregorio Luperón was in the 99th percentile of all high schools citywide and met 100% of its improvement target from the previous year.

ADDITIVE SCHOOLING

In the midst of subtractive circumstances, some small, critical high schools are developing what some authors have termed "additive schooling." In their study of two such high schools, Antrop-Gonzalez and de Jesús (2006) discuss several key factors of additive schooling, including a culture of high expectations, respect for the lived experience and cultural knowledge of students and their families, and an emphasis on supportive personal relationships between teachers and students and among students (see also de Jesús & Vásquez, 2005; and de Jesús, this volume).

This section demonstrates how an additive approach to schooling is developed at Luperón through the ongoing relationships between students, their peers, teachers and administrators—each contributing in significant ways to a safe school environment that values Latino language, identities and experiences and supports students in adapting to the challenges they face as immigrants. Developing and strengthening an additive school culture is a dynamic and interactive process, depending on mutually reinforcing actions and relationships between students as well as between students and the adults who support them.

Students' sense of belonging in school has been shown to have a strong relationship with their academic achievement (Koyama & Gibson, 2007; Louie & Holdaway, 2009). The social relationships that students developed with teachers and administrators at Luperón fostered their sense of belonging. Faculty worked hard to support low-performing students and hold high expectations for all. Further, Luperón specifically worked with students to imbue them with a strong linguistic and cultural affiliation, in the hopes that the identification would help them feel rooted during the alienating, lifelong process of adapting to life in the United States. Adults at Luperón helped to ease students through the transition to new cultural rules and expectations of schooling in New York. As shown throughout this section, the school felt familiar and familial to the newcomer students, and the shared sense of culture and language, and more importantly the academic and emotional investment on the part of teachers and administrators, buffered their experiences and status as immigrants.

Relationships With Teachers, Administrators, and Staff: Familia

Over the course of our study, we found that students at Luperón expressed great satisfaction from the relationships they enjoyed with their teachers, with administrators and with the staff at their school. Five themes emerged from interviews with students regarding the ways in which teachers supported them: teachers worked hard to ensure that students understood content; teachers valorized Spanish and English equally; many teachers shared common cultural and even immigration experiences; teachers held high expectations; and teachers were open to discussing with students relevant issues beyond academic topics. In this section, we explore those five themes. We then discuss the frequently evoked metaphor of *familia* for discussing the culture of Luperón.

Many students expressed their appreciation of how hard teachers worked to ensure that students understood the content in their class-rooms. Delia's[9] comments were typical in this regard:

Interviewer:	What would you say to a new student about the teachers?
Delia:	I would say they are excellent. The teachers want what is best for you, when they see that you are having trouble, for example on a test, they try to talk to you, explain what you didn't understand, so that you understand the class better. They always want to help you.

(interview, 2006)

Several students commented that, unlike their teachers back home, Luperón teachers were concerned with making sure students understood the academic content:

Interviewer:	What do you think of your teachers?
Fausto:	There are people that say that here in New York teachers are bad, but what happens is that over there in Santo Domingo what one is used to is to going to school and having teachers tell you 'copy what it says on this book' and that's it! What you learn is what you understood. But not here, here one has to... they [teachers] explain to you, if you don't know something you tell them to explain it to you; and after school most of the teachers have a particular day in which they give tutorships and classes after the regular school period, and if you need help with anything they help you.

(interview, 2006)

Another student concurred with this opinion:

Interviewer: How would you compare your teachers at Luperón to your teachers in Santo Domingo?

Francisco: The teachers here show more interest in the class and they care more about the students, and if there is something wrong they call their parents... and they give classes that you can understand it. If you don't understand they repeat it again for you. Not in Santo Domingo, if you don't understand you're screwed.

(interview, 2006)

On a similar note, several students also stated that their teachers in the U.S. were better prepared for daily classroom activities.

Second, students appreciated the high value teachers placed on both Spanish and English. Many of the teachers were themselves Dominican immigrants who spoke Spanish fluently and had learned to speak English fluently. At the beginning of our study, two of the ESL teachers spoke Spanish fluently, and two others, who were not native Spanish speakers, had studied it and were able to communicate well in it. Given the structure of the curriculum, in which students spent approximately two years learning content in Spanish while acquiring sufficient academic English skills, Spanish was positioned as an asset, not a deficit. This equalization of status between the languages led to very positive attitudes toward both English and Spanish. For example, a student told us:

Spanish is the language in which you communicate with your culture. English is like improving oneself. If you don't know English, you're not going to get anywhere. It is the most important thing after Spanish. (per. 2, focus group, March 22, 2004)

Because English monolingualism is not marked as the norm, there is no threat to students' Spanish language identity. As a result, English and Spanish were both valued by students as well. For example, in one of the focus groups, a female student commented:

Spanish is my native language. I love English. That language is spoken in all countries, it is very important, for everything, more than anything here. It is the official language here and it has to be. (focus group 2, March 22, 2004)

At Luperón, the bilingualism of many teachers and the high regard all teachers demonstrated for Spanish meant that Spanish maintained a high status, and students continued to improve their academic Spanish while developing academic English. Because their investment in their identities as Spanish-speakers was not threatened, students were free to develop and maintain a positive attitude toward English.

Further, several Dominican students expressed a strong, mutual sense of identification between themselves and the teachers:

Interviewer:	When you say they bother you, what do you mean?
Tony:	Well, from the time one arrives, the teachers here give a hand, they want to help you, as if they aren't here just for the salary but because students really matter to them, helping students progress matters. Many of them came at the same age, young. They had to learn English and there was no bilingual education. So they understand our situation

(interview, 2007)

During several observations, we heard immigrant teachers narrate their own immigrant and educational experiences to their students, using their biographies to encourage the youth to study hard and excel. These stories offered models for how to use schooling as a path to social and economic mobility. Four of the students we interviewed during the research project chose their colleges specifically because a teacher-mentor had previously attended those institutions.

Though occasionally students complained about teachers, for the most part, students' comments about their teachers at Luperón were exceedingly positive. In fact, one of the few complaints we heard regularly about teachers related to their high expectations for students—and even those complaints were, in some ways, hidden praise. So, for example, when asked what she liked most about her teachers at Luperón, Isabel said:

Isabel:	They bother you a lot, so you do things you have to do, but they do it because they know you can do it.
Interviewer:	When you say they bother you, what do you mean?
Isabel:	That they practically force you to do things, because they know you have sufficient ability to do things.
Interviewer:	And how do you feel about that?
Isabel:	Under a lot of pressure, but you know they have to do it... At least here you have the option of taking individual classes and tutorships. In Santo Domingo this doesn't exist, you would need to pay for a tutor.

(interview, 2006)

Francisco offered similar comments. When we asked what he would miss if he left New York, he first said his mom, the transportation system and the friends he has made here. Then he added the school, explaining that he would miss "the teachers nagging you, you know, every day they are on top of you, saying, do this and do that" (interview, 2007).

The teachers at Luperón were also attentive to more than the students' academic selves; teachers offered important forms of emotional support as well. For example, when we asked Laura what she considered to be most difficult about Luperón, she said "Nothing, because there are always people to help at Luperón. If there is something you don't understand, they help you. And it's a way of unburdening oneself" (interview, 2005).

This sense of openness between teachers and students generated trust, a crucial element of the Luperón school culture. When asked in 2008 what he liked most about the teachers at Luperón, Eduardo said, *"confianza, siempre ha habido confianza"* [the trust, there has always been trust]. He elaborated, explaining that his brothers attended other schools, where they were treated as numbers and people related to one another through laws and guidelines. By contrast, he said, "at Luperón there is enough trust to be able to share with each other." Such comments were common among the students we interviewed. Generally speaking, the students felt that their teachers were invested in their success and well-being; they enjoyed the *confianza* they shared at school. The school's evident community of commitment (Ancess, 2003) served as a protective factor for these newcomer youth, for whom the process of migration had provoked feelings of vulnerability and a lack of trust.

Several students spoke about their relationships with specific teachers—not only the Dominican ones. For example, several students mentioned their close relationships with their ESL teachers. One referred to a teacher as her "mamá," and that teacher called the student "her baby;" another said of his English teacher, "She's like my second mom. She taught me to speak all over again" (field notes, 2005). At the end of our 2005 interview with Tony, we asked if there were any other topics he'd like to talk about. Tony said, "Maybe that I speak a lot with [my English teacher]." He said that when school ends, in the ten minute period before tutoring begins, he often goes up to speak to the teacher. "I feel an admiration for [him]," he said, "I like his ideas about things." They originally met through newspaper and chess club. They talked in English (the teacher did not speak Spanish) about college, life and political points of view. Tony said he felt the teacher had become a mentor to him, in the absence of his brother who had left home. "He has shown me how to think about myself," said Tony.

As suggested by these quotes, students frequently employed the metaphor of "family" to describe the unique environment at Luperón. One student was so inspired by the metaphor that she dubbed adults at the school as fictive kin:

Interviewer: What would you tell a new student about Luperón?

Delia: That it's the best school that I could have hoped for. I love this school. I stay here sometimes until 7 PM, because here you feel like a family, like you are at home, like you are in the Dominican Republic. The people here feel like family. I call [the principal] my uncle, I call [one of the secretaries] my grandmother, I give everyone a name, and I feel like I'm with my family…. It's a school where you learn English quickly, and learn well, and they help you when you need it. If they see that something is not going well in your class, they seek the best way to get close and explain things as they are; and the teachers act like you are their child, and think about your future; they get in your personal life, but not in a bad way, just to help you.

(interview, 2006)

These supportive, familial relationships were common not only with teachers but also with the principal, Juan Villar. He often referred to students as "our kids." But it was more than mere rhetoric, as observations bore out. For example, in the middle of one interview we conducted with him, three excited young women came in to tell him that they were departing for a tour of a college upstate. Villar quizzed them about their preparations before asking if they had sufficient pocket money and making sure they had his cell phone number with them (observation, 2006).

Further, close relationships were enjoyed by all, not only the most high-achieving students. When Lesley once stopped by Villar's office to ask about a student she had not seen in a while, Villar reported "he's doing okay, because he's not on my list." Upon asking about that list, Lesley learned that Villar keeps a list of the students who aren't doing well in classes, so he can coordinate more support for them and keep in touch with their parents. He said,

I enjoy working with these students; their progress makes me happier than to see students who always get 95 or more in all their classes. I would throw a party if Laura [a struggling student] got a 65 in her English class, but it wouldn't be the same for someone who always gets A's. (interview, 2006)

This sense of family was also adopted by several long-term staff members. During one observation, we saw the school janitor showing several students pictures of his family and their recently adopted child. Further, we noticed that several of the young women, in particular, would seek personal advice from Jessica, the secretary (observations, 2007). These small glimpses of interactions between faculty, staff and students exemplify the ways in which a family environment was cultivated at Luperón.

The metaphor of *familia* proved a crucial feature of school culture at Luperón. Antrop-Gonzalez and De Jesús (2006) suggest that additive schooling for Latino students relies upon the careful cultivation of "critical care" by creating a sense of *familia* and community. As feminists, we are keenly aware of the ways in which "family" quickly devolves into patriarchy; however, Luperón seemed to provide a kind of culturally congruent environment for these youth who had so recently experienced the trauma of migration, with concomitant familial stresses.

Relationships With Other Students: Trust and Safety

While relationships with teachers, administrators, and staff were clearly significant, the students also described the importance of peer relationships. By and large, students' primary social relationships were with peers they met at the school. In response to questions in the first two years about how they spent their free time, students almost always described outings with family members or time spent socializing, often on the phone, with friends from Luperón. The students in the study talked a great deal about "hanging out" with other Dominicans or Latinos, with whom they felt comfortable. They shared interests in music, school gossip, and most importantly, they could speak to each other in Spanish. During this time, this socializing happened almost exclusively in Spanish. For some students, this pattern continued well into their final year of school, although by then Luperón students were more willing to experiment with English.

However, lurking behind their comments about feeling comfortable with other Latinos were also concerns about safety. Our interview with Fausto illustrated this point:

Interviewer: What would you tell a new kid about life in New York?

Fausto: Here they say that schools are bad, but schools are not bad, what happens is that the great majority of schools here, I mean all schools have their bad part, but in the majority of schools here, what the kids want is to go to school to have fun, to skip classes, get into the bathrooms... they don't want to take classes, what they go for to school is to hang out, but those kids, in their majority, are the ones that you later see on the streets, standing on the corners, and are the ones that later have to beg for money on the subways. I would tell him not to hang out with them... not to not hang out with them, because he is going to be with them at school, but not to let himself be influenced by those who are on the wrong path.

Interviewer: What would you tell him about this school?

Fausto: Well, I would tell him that Luperón would be a good school for him, because if he doesn't know English, well here they help him out, but he has to study English well, and that also, he can't get together with everyone here, because as I told you before, in all schools there are good people and bad people... And if he did come to this school, he would be better than in other places because here he would be among us, because here we are all Hispanics.

(interview, 2006)

Juan had a similar answer:

Interviewer: What would you tell him about this school?
Juan: This is a wonderland here... That it is good, and that here one feels like
                family because almost everyone here is Dominican.

                                                                    (interview, 2006)

Indeed, fights were not common at Luperón, and when they occurred, they were dealt with immediately. The school had a student-run mediation service to arbitrate disagreements: several of the students in our study participated as peer counselors. In fact, the students reported feeling very safe at their school, which they contrasted to what they heard about schools that their siblings, cousins or neighbors attended. Eduardo, for example, warned about a school, as we recorded in fieldnotes:

When asked about the other students at Luperón, Eduardo said that in general they:

> are good people. He continued by saying that the school is very safe, not because there is security but because the students are good. He mentioned George Washington High School is known for having problems with students. He learned about stories from his friends and the news. (field notes, 2006)

In contrast to the insecurity they felt outside the school, the students felt quite safe at Luperón. This is significant because studies have suggested that an adversarial school environment with security threats is linked to boys' declining engagement with school (Qin Hilliard, 2003). Boys, in particular, appear to be vulnerable to becoming recruited into the sort of oppositional cultures that too often pit one ethnic group against another in high schools (Gibson, 1997).

The concentration of ethnic groups in specified schools can be experienced as segregation. However, in this circumstance, the students expressed a strong sense of belonging and connection to their peers and faculty at Luperón. They found the cultural familiarity to be comforting; as reflected in the quotes offered above, that sense of connection contributed to their feelings of safety. As Suárez-Orozco and Suárez-Orozco (2001) note, for some immigrant youth, "the general dissonance in cultural expectations and the loss of predictable context will be experienced as anxiety and an acute disorientation" (p. 72). Instead, the students of Luperón appreciated the opportunity to share humor, cultural references, popular culture and their burgeoning English; students expressed a sense of connection to their peers in this school.

The sense of cultural belonging helped some of the students adjust to life in the United States. Tony, who had graduated from Luperón, eloquently described how the concentration of Latinos at the school helped him adapt to college, as recorded here in our field notes:

> I ask him how he thinks teachers at Luperón helped him prepare for being in any type of situation in life, as he was describing, be it a minority or a majority. He explains how when one comes to the U.S. one experiences an identity crisis, in which you have to juggle values and ideas from your culture and the culture you are inserting yourself into. He says some people lose their culture when inserting themselves in a new one (or think this process needs to take place), and he says this happens because they don't have strong roots in their own culture and they eventually adopt the new culture with greater ease, but by "forgetting" their own. He says Luperón helps students learn about the culture they are coming from, feel pride about coming from where they come from, and about being who you are. (interview, 2008)

The cultural familiarity and pride that reigned at Luperón helped to address the youth's concerns about trust and safety. Unlike the first and second generation immigrant youth in Valenzuela's (1999) study, students at Luperón felt that the school provided precisely the sense of trust, or *confianza*, they needed.

CLOSING THOUGHTS

Luperón's additive approach and its tight identification as a *familia* foster students' academic achievement by valuing the home language and by creating authentic relationships and culturally responsive institutional practices that mediate the multiple vulnerabilities faced by most immigrant newcomers. In the current era in which public education in America has become transfixed on bureaucratic accountability, privatization and increased high-stakes testing, Luperón continues to position strong social relations as integral to engaging and effective learning. This small bilingual, culturally additive, newcomer school sets high standards for students, offers rigorous instruction and provides the critical linguistic and social support necessary within a community of commitment. Luperón provides an important model for what the schooling we develop for increasing numbers of immigrant teens might look like.

Luperón's small size is but one of several critical characteristics, including shared accountability between the school and the community; family-like relations between faculty, staff, and students; and an overall sense of belonging and safety. Many schools in New York City have been "downsized" or chartered as small schools, but critical small schools—those schools like Luperón and others discussed in this volume that engage students and faculty in transformational and democratic educational practices—are part of a literal educational "re-form" quite distinct from the federal government's No Child Left Behind. These schools offer important lessons about additive, culturally- and linguistically-inclusive schooling.

NOTES

1. However, De Jesús and Vásquez (2005) warned that actual graduation numbers may be lower than those reported.

2. Fry (2005) asserts that many of the status dropouts are foreign-born males with previous schooling difficulties who came as labor migrants and may never have sought schooling in the United States. These patterns hold true for Latino immigrants. Specifically, among the Mexican-born population, "21 percent of recent arrivals who do not appear to have had schooling difficulties before migration are dropouts. However, of recently arrived Mexican-born teens who did not keep up in school before coming to the United States, 83 percent are not enrolled in school. About 11 percent of recently arrived Puerto Rican-born youths who stayed on track in Puerto Rico are currently not enrolled in school. Among their counterparts who fell behind in Puerto Rico, 54 percent are out of school" (p. 9).

3. The status dropout rate refers to the percentage of people in a given age range who are not in school and have not completed high school. Some may never have enrolled after immigrating to the United States.

4. Under NCLB, the definition and identification of the so-called "Limited English Proficient" (LEP) subgroup and the measurement of its progress have proven to be problematic. NCLB defines an LEP student based upon lack of proficiency in English, as measured by State assessments. Once they reach proficiency, as measured by tests, they are recategorized, and their scores are not registered in the LEP category (Abedi, 2004; see also Crawford 2004). A student's success in acquiring English in essence reduces scores for the category. Acknowledging this fact, in 2007, the U.S. Department of Education issued a nonregulatory guidance allowing schools to include "former LEP" students within the LEP category for up to two years (USDOE, 2007, p. 10).

5. In fact, the flourishing small schools that drew English dominant students from their home institutions inadvertently stranded those students whose home language was not English in failing and closing high schools with increasingly limited language support, potentially increasing dropout rates among that vulnerable population (Advocates for Children of New York and Asian American Legal Defense and Education Fund, 2009). These charges led the city to require that new schools accept emergent bilinguals, starting in 2007; however, advocacy groups charge that emergent bilinguals are segregated, with 43% of them centralized in just 17 of the 233 small high schools in 2008 (Advocates for Children of New York and Asian American Legal Defense and Education Fund, 2009).

6. The research team included Ofelia García, Ali Michael, César Fernandez Geara, Norma Andrade, Elizabeth Crowell Kim, Carmina Makar, Ivania Espinet, and Natalie Catasús. We gratefully acknowledge their important contributions to this project.
7. For more details on the research methods, see Bartlett and Garcia, 2011.
8. Graduation rates fluctuate, depending on the year in question. In 2007, the official 4-year graduation rate was 67.2%, while the 6-year rate was 76.1%, which reflects the necessity of allowing emergent bilinguals more time to develop academic English.
9. Though we do not use a pseudonym for the school or the principal, all students and teachers have been assigned a pseudonym to protect confidentiality.

REFERENCES

Abedi, J. (2004). The No Child Left Behind Act and English language learners: Assessment and accountability issues. *Educational Researcher, 33*(1), 4-14.

Advocates for Children of New York and Asian American Legal Defense and Education Fund. (2009). *Empty promises: A case study of restructuring and the exclusion of English Language Learners in two brooklyn high schools*. New York, NY: Advocates for Children of New York. Retrieved from http://www.advocatesforchildren.org/Empty%20Promises%20Report%20%206-16-09.pdf on 20 June 2010.

American Community Survey. (2007). Washington, DC: U.S. Census. Government Printing Office.

Ancess, J. (2003). *Beating the odds: High schools as communities of commitment*. New York, NY: Teachers College Press.

Antrop-Gonzalez, R., & de Jesús, A. (2006). Toward a theory of critical care in urban small school reform: Examining structures and pedagogies of caring in two Latino community-based schools. *International Journal of Qualitative Studies in Education, 19*(4), 409-433.

Bartlett, L., & Garcia, O. (2011). *Additive schooling in subtractive times: Bilingual education and Dominican youth in the Heights*. Nashville, TN: Vanderbilt University Press.

Bernhardt, E., & Kamil, M. (1995). Interpreting relationships between L1 and L2 reading: Consolidating the linguistic threshold and the linguistic interdependence hypotheses. *Applied Linguistics, 16*(1), 15-34.

Bialystok, E., & Cummins, J. (1991). Language, cognition, and education of bilingual children. In E. Bialystok (Ed.), *Language Processing in Bilingual Children* (pp. 222-232). Cambridge, England: Cambridge University Press.

Boyson, B. A., & Short, D. J. (2003). *Secondary school newcomer programs in the United States* (Research Report 12). Washington, DC: Center for Research on Education Diversity and Excellence.

Brutt-Griffler, J. (2004). *World English: A study of its development*. Clevedon, England: Multilingual Matters.

Capps, R., Fix, M., Murray, J., Ost, J., Passel, J., & Herwantoro, S. (2005). *The new demography of America's schools: Immigration and the No Child Left Behind Act.* Washington, DC: Urban Institute.

Carson, J. E., Carrell, P. L., Silberstein, S., Kroll, B., & Kuehn, P. A. (1990). Reading–writing relationships in first and second language. *TESOL Quarterly, 24*(2), 245-266.

Conger, D., Schwartz, A. E., & Stiefel, L. (2007). Immigrant and native-born differences in school stability and special education: Evidence from New York City. *International Migration Review, 41*(2), 402-431.

Crawford, J. (2004). *Educating English learners: Language diversity in the classroom* (5th ed.). Los Angeles, CA: Bilingual Educational Services.

Crawford, J. (2008). No Child Left Behind: Misguided approach to school accountability for English language learners. In *Advocating for English learners: Selected essays* (pp. 128-138). Clevedon, England: Multilingual Matters.

Cummins, J. (1991). Conversational and academic language proficiency in bilingual contexts. *AILA Review, 8*, 75-89.

Cummins, J. (2000). *Language, power and pedagogy: Bilingual children in the crossfire.* Clevedon, England: Multilingual Matters.

De Jesús, A., & Vásquez, D. W. (2005). *Exploring the Latino education profile and pipeline for Latinos in New York State* (Policy Brief Vol. 2, No.2). New York, NY: Centro de Estudios Puertorriqueños, Hunter College. Retrieved from http://www.centropr.org/documents/working_papers/
Exploring_Latino_Education_Pipeline_Educati_Brief.pdf

Fine, M., Jaffe-Walker, R., Pedraza, P., Futch, V., & Stoudt, B. (2007). Swimming: On oxygen, resistance, and possibility for immigrant youth under siege. *Anthropology and Education Quarterly, 38*(1), 76-96.

Fry, R. (2003). *Hispanic youth dropping out of U.S. schools: Measuring the challenge.* Washington, DC: Pew Hispanic Cener.

Fry, R. (2005). *The higher dropuot rate of foreign-born teens: The role of schooling abroad.* Washington, DC: Pew Hispanic Center.

Fry, R. (2007). Are immigrant youth faring better in U.S. schools? *The International Migration Review, 41*(3), 579-601.

Fry, R., & Lowell, B. L. (2002). *Work or study: Different fortunes of U.S. Latino generations.* Washington, DC: Pew Hispanic Center.

Fry, R., & González, F. (2008). *One-in-five and growing fast: A profile of Hispanic public school students.* Washington, DC: Pew Hispanic Center.

Gabriele, A., Troseth, E., Matohardjono, G., & Otheguy, R. (2009). Emergent literacy skills in bilingual children: Evidence for the role of L1 syntactic comprehension. *International Journal of Bilingual Education and Bilingualism, 12*(5), 1-15.

Gándara, P., & Contreras, F. (2009). *The Latino education crisis. The consequences of failed social policies.* Cambridge, MA: Harvard University Press.

García, O. (2009). *Bilingual education in the 21st century: A global perspective.* Malden, MA: Wiley/Blackwell.

García, O., & Bartlett, L. (2007). A speech community model of bilingual education: Educating Latino newcomers in the USA. *The International Journal of Bilingual Education and Bilingualism, 10*(1), 1-25.

García, O., & Kleifgen, J. A. (2010). *Educating English language learners as emergent bilinguals*. New York, NY: Teachers College Press.

García, O., Kleifgen, J. A., & Falchi, L. (2008). *Equity in the education of emergent bilinguals: The case of English language learners*. The Campaign for Educational Equity Research (Vol. 1). New York, NY: Teachers College Press.

Gibson, M. A. (1997). Complicating the immigrant/involuntary minority typology. *Anthropology and Education, 28*(3), 431-454.

Gutiérrez, K., & Jaramillo, N.E. (2006). Looking for educational equity: The consequences of relying on *Brown*. In A. Ball (Ed.), *With more deliberate speed: Achieving equity and excellence in education—Realizing the full potential of* Brown v. Board of Education (Yearbook of the National Society for the Study of Education, Vol. 105, Issue 2, pp. 173–189). Malden, MA: Blackwell.

Jaffe-Walter, R. (2008). Negotiating mandates and memory: Inside a small schools network for immigrant youth. *Teachers College Record, 110*(9), 2040-2066.

Kim, J. S., & Sunderman, G. (2005). Measuring academic proficiency under the No Child Left Behind Act: Implications for educational equity. *Educational Researcher, 34*(8), 3-12.

Koyama, J., & Gibson, M. A. (2007). Marginalization and membership. In J. V. Galen & G. W. Noblit (Eds.), *Late to class: Social class and schooling in the new economy* (pp. 87-111). Albany, NY: State University of New York Press.

Logan, J. (2001). *The new Latinos: Who they are, where they are*. Albany: Lewis Mumford Center for Comparative Urban and Regional Research University at Albany. Retrieved from http://www.s4.brown.edu/cen2000/HispanicPop/HspReport/MumfordReport.pdf

López, M. H. (2009). *Latinos and education: Explaining the attainment gap*. Washington, DC: Pew Hispanic Center.

Louie, V., & Holdaway, J. (2009). Catholic schools and immigrant students: A new generation. *Teachers College Record, 111*(3), 783-816.

McCabe, K., & Meissner, D. (2010). Immigration and the United States: Recession affects flows, prospects for reform. *Migration Information Source*, January. Washington, DC: Migration Policy Institute. Retrieved from http://www.migrationinformation.org/Profiles/display.cfm?ID=766

Menken, K. (2008). *English language learners left behind: Standardized testing as language policy*. Clevedon, England: Multilingual Matters.

Monzó, L. D., & Rueda, R. (2009). Passing for English fluent: Latino immigrant children masking language proficiency. *Anthropology & Education Quarterly, 40*(1), 20-40.

New York City Department of City Planning. (2000). *The newest New Yorkers 2000: Executive summary*. New York, NY: Department of City Planning. Retrieved from http://www.nyc.gov/html/dcp/html/census/nny.shtml

New York City Department of Education. (2008). *The class of 2007 four-year longitudinal report and 2006-2007 event dropout rates*. New York, NY: Office of Accountability. Retrieved from http://schools.nyc.gov/daa/reports/The_Class%20of%202007_Four-Year_Longitudinal_Report.pdf

Noguera, P. A. (2003). *City schools and the American dream*. New York, NY: Teachers College Press.

Noguera, P. A. (2004). Social capital and the education of immigrant students: Categories and generalizations. *Sociology of Education, 77*(2), 180-183.

Oakes, J. (2002). *Education inadequacy, inequality, and failed state policy: A synthesis of expert reports prepared for Williams v. State of California.* UC Los Angeles: UCLA's Institute for Democracy, Education, and Access. Retrieved from http://escholarship.org/uc/item/8727d11z

Orfield, G., & Eaton, S. (1996). *Dismantling segregation: The quiet reversal of Brown v. Board of education.* New York, NY: The New Press.

Orfield, G., & Lee, C. (2005). *Why segregation matters: Poverty and educational inequality.* Cambridge, MA: The Civil Rights Project, Harvard University.

Qin-Hilliard, D. B. (2003). Gendered expectations and gendered experiences: Immigrant students' adaptation in schools. *New Directions for Youth Development, 2003*(100), 91-109.

Ravitch, D. (2010). *The death and life of the great American school system: How testing and choice are undermining education.* New York, NY: Basic Books.

Rivera-Batiz, F. (2008). International migration and the brain drain. In A. K. Rutt & J. Ros (Ed.), *International Handbook of Development Economics.* Northhampton, MA: Edward Elgar.

Ruiz-de-Velasco, J. & Fix, M., (with B. Chu Clewell) (2000). *Overlooked and underserved: Immigrant students in U.S. secondary schools.* Washington, DC: Urban Institute.

Short, D., & Boyson, B. (2000). *Newcomer database for secondary school programs in the United States: Revised 2000.* Washington, DC: Center for Applied Linguistics.

Short, D., & Boyson, B. (2003). *Secondary school newcomer programs in the United States.* Center for Research on Education, Diversity & Excellence, Research Report No. 12.

Suárez-Orozco, C., & Suárez-Orozco, M. (2001). *Children of immigration.* Cambridge, MA: Harvard University Press.

United States Census Bureau. (2007). *American Community Survey (ACS).* Washington, DC: U.S. Government Printing Office.

U.S. Department of Education. (2001). *No Child Left Behind Act of 2001.* Retrieved from http://www.ed.gov/nclb/landing.jhtml

United States Department of Education. Office of Elementary and Secondary Education. (2007). *Guidance on regulations regarding assessment and accountability for recently arrived and former limited English proficient (LEP) students* (May 2007). Washington, DC: U.S. Department of Education. Retrieved from http://www2.ed.gov.

Valdes, G. (1996). *Con respeto: Bridging the distance between culturally diverse families and schools.* New York, NY: Teachers College Press.

Valenzuela, A. (1997). Mexican-American youth and the politics of caring. In E. Long (Ed.), *From sociology to cultural studies: New perspectives* (pp. 322-350). Malden, MA: Blackwell.

Valenzuela, A. (1999). *Subtractive schooling: U.S.-Mexican youth and the politics of caring.* Albany, NY: State University of New YMMork (SUNY) Press.

Van Hook, J., & Fix, M. (2000). A profile of the immigrant student population. In J. Ruiz-de-Velasco, M. Fix, & B. Chu Clewell (Ed.), *Overlooked and underserved:*

Immigrant children in U.S. secondary schools (pp. 9-33). Washington, DC: The Urban Institute.

Vernez, G., & Abrahamse, A. (1996). *How immigrants fare in U.S. education.* Santa Monica, CA: RAND.

Walsh, C. E. (1991). *Pedagogy and the struggle for voice: Issues of language, power, and schooling for Puerto Ricans.* New York, NY: Bergin & Garvey.

CHAPTER 6

LEARNING FROM OUR STUDENTS

Recovering the Purpose of Small Schools in an Era Beholden to Standardization

Liza Bearman and Nora Ahmed

INTRODUCTION

Today's dominant discourse in the current debates about urban school reform is rooted in the language of success and failure, competition, accountability and results, and "school turnarounds,"—as evidenced most recently by President Obama's "Race to the Top" program and the dialogue surrounding Davis Guggenheim's 2010 documentary "Waiting for Superman." Yet, the public rarely hears debates about urban school reform that focus on the difference between smaller schools and "critical small schools." While those involved in the creation of smaller schools purport to believe in making schools smaller, more personal and student centered, they frequently lose sight of the interdisciplinary, real world connected, and project-based education that takes place in critical small schools. The latter integrate students' interests and voices into curricula, re-conceptualize teachers' roles from deliverers of knowledge to facilitators of learning,

Critical Small Schools: Beyond Privatization in
New York City Urban Educational Reform, pp. 103–119
Copyright © 2012 by Information Age Publishing

and shift the emphasis placed on robotic student achievement via test scores to student engagement via authentic personalized learning. These schools are rooted in the work of thinkers like Maria Montessori, John Dewey, Ted Sizer, and others invested in making the daily experience of children in school more meaningful and beneficial. This said, as more adults enter the field of "school reform" through newly created educational organizations that place primacy on test scores and use school size as a proxy for success, a growing danger surrounds the use of the language of small schools. Many of these organizations are not considering the practices and relationships necessary to guide the work of critical small schools.

To date, this lack of understanding of what is needed to create a critical small school has created a real conundrum for those who have entered the small schools movement hoping to build upon the decades of work of small school pioneers like Deborah Meier and Sizer from the Coalition of Essential Schools. These harbingers, and many other like-minded practitioners who began this work 40-plus years ago, have put forth a genuine effort to produce truly democratic, personalized, student-centered, relationship-driven, joyful and real-world connected schools— not just small versions of large schools.

Jackie Ancess, Codirector of the National Center for the Restructuring of Education Schools and Teaching (NCREST) at Teachers College (TC), Columbia University combats the notion of "small schools in drag" (Fine, 2005) in a May 2008 Educational Leadership article entitled "Small Alone is Not Enough." In it, she highlights the "unfortunate detour" that the current school reform movement has taken. She writes:

> Sadly, many leaders of small high school reform initiatives do not seem to understand their mission. Threatened by the consequences of high-stakes, standardized test-based accountability, they feel pressured to focus on low-level knowledge and skills that can be quickly and regularly assessed, measured by numbers, and speedily and simply remediated. As a result, many of today's small schools are substantively indistinguishable from their larger counterparts. This current version of small high schools represents quite a detour from the intention of the original small schools movement. (p. 2)

Thus, it appears as if most of the educational terminology that was born in, arguably, a more authentic, deliberate, and small-scale era of critical small school reform, has been *hijacked* or *co-opted* by many of today's school reform initiatives. Examples of recent attempts at smaller school "reform" include the following: considering a "small" school one with 500-plus students and 30-plus students per class with disconnected academic disciplines (versus a truly small school that enrolls less than 400 students, maintains intimate class sizes, and demands integrated, connected and relevant curricula); calling a weekly 50 minute homeroom meeting an "advisory" (versus an advisory group that meets daily and is the root of students' learning experiences); and claiming that "personalization" is illustrated by each student having her/his own laptop (versus detailed personal learning plans guiding students' individual growth).

In sum, Ancess (2008) asserts that small schools, in the tradition of Sizer and others mentioned above, require four critical traits: caring relationships with adults, a unified school community, a strong safety net for students, and intellectually transformative experiences. Sadly, these traits are not at the forefront of the minds' of today's "school reformers." Instead, these individuals are quickly shifting the conversation in dangerous ways, ultimately leaving those of us who believe in critical small schools wondering how "educators [can] recover the purposes of small schools" (p. 1).

This chapter describes one example of an "intellectually transformative experience" (Ancess, 2008, p. 5) that occurred in one small high school. In it, we explore the ways in which a new critical small high school —embedded in a large-school reform effort—committed to a yearlong student centered and student driven project that helped root the students, teachers, and the school more deeply in the school's original mission and vision. Drawing from memory, reflection and field notes written throughout the yearlong process, this chapter, written by the co-facilitators of this endeavor, demonstrates the possibilities and power of generating youth led and produced projects during a time when these processes are sidelined in the name of small school reform.

METHODOLOGY

Ancess (2008) highlights examples of how some small schools, even in this era of school reform, are creating learning environments for students that are genuinely challenging and rigorous, relevant and exciting, and providing "intellectually transformative experiences" that encourage "students to use their minds well" (p. 5). She describes one "student publication project ... conducted at Pablo Neruda Academy, a small New York City high school [where] seniors did their inquiry on small schools and published *Small Schools, Big Questions: A Student-Led Inquiry into High School Redesign* (Student Press Initiative, 2007)." She states:

> The project released potential that had been dormant, convincing students that their voices counted and that they could write.... When students discover that they can be successful in school and produce high-quality, intellectually powerful work, they gain a new level of involvement and sense of expertise. They begin to imagine new possibilities for their future. (p. 6)

As the adult facilitators for this project described above by Ancess, we went on a yearlong journey with our students that resulted in the published book *Small Schools, Big Questions: A Student-Led Inquiry into High School Redesign*. Much has been written and studied about our students' book, including Ancess' "Educational Leadership" article that focused on their text and Dr. Sherrish Holloman's 2009 Teachers College, Columbia University, doctoral dissertation, titled *Writing for Real: A Phenomenological Study of Urban Students' Experiences Writing for Publication*. Additionally, the publication has received interest from a dozen or so schools of education for classroom use with pre- and in-service teachers, filling a void in the literature and research base on the subject of students' perspectives on the small city schools created on their behalf. And, most importantly, we still hear from our students, more than three years later, about the impact the TC Student Press Initiative (SPI) project had on them as college students, employees and human beings.

In this current era of standardized tests, standardized curricula and standardized schools, this chapter seeks to explore the richness and rigor experienced by students at a new small high school in the Bronx who ultimately generated their own individualized, project-based curriculum during their one year partnership with SPI. We will revisit our students' process here via the "traditions in qualitative interpretive research: document analysis, collective memory work, and deep interpretation and reflection" (Lesko, Simmons, Quarshie, & Newton, 2008, p. 1551). Of central focus will be our own recorded observations of the students' roles throughout the preparation and publication of their book, as well as their actual written final product and other artifacts from our journey. We will closely examine the four pivotal experiences that defined much of our students' engagement and experience with us. In so doing, we hope to shed light on the possibilities that still exist in urban small schools today, even though current educational policy that is focused on results, competition, standardization, and accountability poses a great threat to these sorts of coconstructed curricular experiences that create powerful results for students.

We revisit our students' project now to propound the notion that today's small schools must engage students in "intellectually transformative experiences" (Ancess, 2008) if they seek to fulfill their original mandate to alter the academic experiences and future possibilities of youth stereotyped as disadvantaged. Small schools that educate students with scripted curricula and assess them primarily though high-stakes standardized exams "run the risk of being severed from their radical roots and the vibrant movements that birthed them" (Fine, 2005, p. 5). For, as Ancess (2008) writes:

Education will not improve if schools get smaller and otherwise stay the same. This reform is not just about size. It's about making a cultural change in schools and school systems—in the roles, responsibilities, and relationships among educators, students, and administrators.... Perhaps we need to ... look at how schools use their small size to reach kids and get them to use their minds well.... Getting students to use their minds well also means conveying to students that ideas are exciting by providing school tasks worthy of their engagement. All too often, the tasks assigned to students—particularly in schools providing a test-prep curriculum concerned primarily with skills and bits of information—trivialize knowledge, are devoid of ideas, and thus are unworthy of students' engagement. (pp. 51-52)

The following sections of this chapter provide educators, policymakers, researchers, and others with an overview of a project that intended to embrace the voices of youth in the South Bronx by allowing them to take part in creating their own curriculum. The project, in which our students were expected to be researchers and scholars, provided space for them to weigh in on contemporary school reform, which, according to many savvy government officials volleying for space in the popular press, is " 'the civil rights issue of our generation' " (Klonsky, 2010). Students' perspectives are arguably the most important in both the practice and policy arenas and it is our belief that conversations around critical small school reform, including actionable conversations about pedagogy and assessment with tangible examples of authentic, student-led projects like the one detailed below, must include students' perspectives and expertise.

Our students wanted to make sense of the small schools movement in which they were explicitly implicated, yet conceptually not invited to participate in shaping. This is particularly poignant since, as Sizer once put it, "students are the best critics of their own experience" (personal communication, n.d.). And, since the students, rather than us, their teacher-facilitators, charted the course for both the process and the product (i.e., the content and design) of this publication, we ground our current analysis of critical small schools in the importance of student led and produced curricula.

Context

During the 2006-07 academic year, Pablo Neruda Academy (PNA), then in its fourth year as a small architecture-themed public high school created under New Visions for Public Schools' New Century High School Initiative, developed a partnership with TC's SPI. This enabled Nora, a third year English teacher who came to teaching via the New York City Teaching Fellows program, and Liza, a faculty member at Teachers College and PNA's former Literacy Coach from 2003-2006, to coteach a research and writing course about school reform as part of the students' English curriculum. Thus, twenty members of the soon-to-be first graduating class of PNA set out to investigate the small schools movement. Of the 20 seniors who participated in this project, 14 had been at the school since their freshman year (2 of whom were on the school's original design and planning team in 2002); 4 came to the school in its second year in the fall of 2004; and 2 started in the school's fourth year, in the fall of 2006. Table 6.1 provides insight into the student population at PNA during the 2006-2007 academic year.

At the time of this project, PNA was housed inside the Stevenson High School campus, a formerly large failing high school in New York City's Southeast Bronx. However, the school spent its first year (2003-2004) as a program at Lehman High School in the Bronx. In September 2004, the school moved to Stevenson, an "Impact School," designated as such by Mayor Bloomberg for its history of violent activity. Stevenson therefore maintained a significant police presence and metal detectors. PNA was part of the reform effort that sought to replace the large high school with five autonomous new small high schools. Unfortunately, Stevenson's "Impact" designation trickled down to all five of the new small high schools, which included PNA.

CREATING *SMALL SCHOOLS, BIG QUESTIONS:*
THE PROCESS AND PRODUCT

Over the few years we each spent at PNA prior to our SPI work, our students often shared their hopes, fears and anxieties about what it meant to grow up in the Bronx and what it meant to deal with the intangible idea of an academic life within and beyond the invisible fence that frequently keeps the reality of life in the inner city segregated from the rest of the nation. Together and separately, we both often sat and listened to our students inside and outside of formal classes. We realized that these were the "poor Black and Latino kids" that academics and policymakers reference but rarely invite to speak for themselves; these were the kids who read about themselves as being "low performing" and/or "dropouts." But, they were also the constituency that policymakers, particularly in the era of No Child Left Behind, and now, Race to the Top, are presumably trying the most to help. So we wondered: Where do their voices go?

As a result of listening to our students' thoughts and complaints about their experiences in school over the years, we wanted to help them find a way to constructively wrestle with their anger about their labels and their feelings about the thrills and challenges that characterized their collective

Table 6.1.   Demographic Information for Pablo Neruda Academy

Category	Statistic	Number	Percent
Enrollment for the 2006-07 Academic Year	Grade 9	101	29%
	Grade 10	113	33%
	Grade 11	95	27%
	Grade 12	38	11%
	Total	347	100%
Gender	Male	241	69.5%
	Female	106	30.5%
Ethnicity	Black	88	25%
	Latino	251	72%
	White	0	0%
	Asian	7	3%
	Other	3	0.01%
Subsidized Lunch	Free/Reduced lunch	267	77%
ELL (English Language Learners)	Classified as ELL	50	14%
SPED (Special Education)	Classified as SPED	71	20%

experience as the first group of seniors in a new small urban high school. We felt that our students' many stories illustrating their appreciation for their "special" high school experience, coupled with their anxiety about whether or not their new small school was preparing them for college and life beyond, were important to share and worthy of further exploration, especially since New York City and many other urban centers were refashioning large failing schools into smaller learning communities and/or autonomous schools to help reduce the achievement gap. As such, we fashioned an essential question to present to our students—a question we hoped would guide the evolution of the project. In early September 2006, we posed the following question: **How can your perspective fill in the gaps about the small schools movement and help shape it based on your experience as the first graduates of a new small school?**

On September 22, 2006, we formally kicked off the SPI experience with our students. We asked our students to "brainstorm" words associated with their experience as students in a new small school. Some of the words they listed included "mistake," "disorganized," "alternative," "low-budget," "united," "small classes," "projects," "portfolio," "hands-on," "community," "internship," "feels like jail," "teacher retention," "bad idea," "crowded building," and "optimistic." How revealing (although not entirely surprising!) these words were to us. We wondered how we would be able to harness such strong, insightful and complicated feelings about the experience of being the first graduates of a new small high school in order to effectively create an avenue through which our students would gain new skills and knowledge, actually *enjoy* exploring the subject, *and* become better writers and published authors.

We wondered if our students—attending one of five new autonomous high schools in a converted large high school building—even knew this was happening outside of their school. Within Stevenson, which was now known as the Stevenson High School Campus, the five small schools were, namely, PNA, Bronx Guild (a Big Picture Company partnered school), School for Community Research and Learning (a Good Shepherd Services partnered school), Millennium Arts Academy and Gateway School for Environmental Research and Technology. We quickly learned that most (if not all) of our students had no idea that the process of creating PNA, including the phase-out and break-up of Stevenson into the aforementioned autonomous small schools, was happening elsewhere in the Bronx, New York City and beyond. We thus had to reimagine the SPI curriculum that we had initially mapped out in June. The students, of course, led the way.

What resulted was an attempt by us both, within our student led SPI curriculum and within the students' regular English curriculum taught by Nora (of which SPI was a part), to catch them up on the movement in which they were situated so deeply. We introduced them to the history of education in the United States and to the birth of the small schools movement in New York City in the 1980's with graduate level reading materials, current popular press articles and PowerPoint presentations. We shared with our students a map from New York City's New Visions for Public Schools, illustrating in great detail the new small schools existing in the City as of January 2006. Our students poured over that map, marveling at all of the once-traditional high schools that were now, like their school, all converted to small schools with unique names and specific themes. This immediately gave them a sense of belonging to something much larger than themselves and, in a certain way, validated the past three years for them in ways we could not have anticipated. They did not feel so alone in this "experiment," as they often called their experience at PNA. This was one of many transition points that occurred during the *Small Schools, Big Questions* project.

In hindsight, we have now realized that the "process" of our SPI project, the inquiry-based student directed methodology, was as significant as the final "product," the publication. Moreover, throughout our work on this project from June 2006 to May 2007, there were some important experiential and pedagogical decisions made predominantly by our students that deeply impacted us, the students, and the production of *Small Schools, Big Questions*. These include our students':

1. Desire to host academic experts and New York City Department of Education (NYCDOE) officials;
2. Creation of their own essential question, which guided their independent inquiries;
3. E-mails to and from experts in the urban education field; and
4. Visits to other restructured formerly large school buildings in New York City.

Hosting "Experts" in the Field of Urban Education

In November 2006, an article appeared in the *Harvard Educational Review* titled "Implementing Small Theme High Schools in New York City: Great Intentions and Great Tensions" by Jackie Ancess and David Allen. The article focused in large part on PNA. Unbeknownst to us, the research had been done during the 2005-2006 school year. We both read the 15 page single-spaced article and decided to share it with our students. The students' reactions were overpowering.

While reading the article, it finally dawned on our students that this movement was real, and that it was not something that their teachers made up for them under the guise of just trying to get them to do work void of purpose (which was, sadly, generally how they interpreted their educational experience at school). Since September, about half of our students had come fully on board with the project, while the other half remained resistant. After reading this article, they were now mostly all ready to shift gears and move past their stagnant place of interrogation and resignation. Immediately, our students began asking important, burning questions about what was written in the *Harvard Educational Review* article, how, why and for whom. They started articulating very specific concerns about their experience in a new small school, as all they had studied over the past few months began to coalesce. Our students were fully engaged with this academic text. While it contained some of the most sophisticated language our students had ever encountered, they took ownership of their own learning in a way neither of us had ever seen them do prior to this experience. It was clear that it was relevant to their lives.

Our students were asking questions that only led to more questions, including one about whether or not Ancess and Allen might be interested in discussing the article with them. Luckily, due to the authors' relationship with the school, a date was set for them to visit PNA and meet with our students. In preparation for the visit, we worked with the students to fine-tune their critical reading and critiquing skills.

When Ancess and Allen (2006) came to PNA, our students were ready. And, for the first time in relation to this project, we saw them all sit and sound like scholars for two whole hours. They even stayed 45 minutes after the end of the school day—on a Friday no less! They questioned their guests and, in the process, they started asking investigatory questions about specific details surrounding the inception of the small schools movement.

Our students' questioning continued into the next year. We knew there was much more to learn, so we took our cues from them. For example, our students became very interested in the notion of Empowerment Schools (the newly formed school governance structure in the New York City school system) and wondered where they might learn more. Accordingly, we contacted Sanda Balaban, Chief of Staff for Empowerment Schools. We also contacted Eric Nadelstern, Chief Executive Officer of Empowerment Schools for the NYCDOE, and one of the early pioneers of the small schools movement that began in the 1970s. Nadelstern was also Superintendent of the Bronx Office of New Schools in 2002 when small schools like PNA were first planned and implemented.

Like Ancess and Allen before them, Balaban and Nadelstern were more than willing to participate in our students' inquiry around small schools. They spent an hour and a half with us at PNA in early February. As with our previous visitors, our students were prepared. They read the article appearing in the January 1, 2002 edition of *Phi Delta Kappan* by Gil Schmerler about Nadelstern, titled "One Man's Continuing War Against Recentralization: A Long Struggle for School Autonomy," and learned more about the history and structure of the current Empowerment School Initiative. Additionally, during Balaban and Nadelstern's visit, we photographed, videotaped and audiotaped their interaction with the students as we had done during Ancess and Allen's visit in December. We then proceeded to use these transcripts as research documents in our SPI class.

Creating Essential Questions

Around the time of the crucial visits of Ancess, Allen, Balaban, and Nadelstern, as our students processed and synthesized the various materials and experiences that occurred during the past few months, our students began to identify specific areas of interest they wanted to individually probe more deeply. Accordingly, they began to group themselves into categories such as "school funding," "sharing school space," and "assessment." With our support, they each developed an essential question that would serve as their "research question" for the duration of the project. We encouraged each and every one of them to *really* focus on their essential question throughout their exploration of the small schools movement. As the weeks wore on, our students created categorized research questions and solidified their small groups according to topic, which guided the evolution of the rest of our journey. Some examples of our students' individual essential questions were:

1. If these new schools are changing the way we learn, then how come tests haven't changed yet?
2. Should education be the same as it was in the nineteenth century now that we are in the twenty-first century? Should small schools like PNA have their own curriculum and not have any standardized tests?
3. Who would think small schools would be successful in a huge Impact school building?
4. Regardless of certain impoverished conditions at PNA, do we as students really have a right to complain when we have teachers that are dedicated to helping students and students dedicated to tormenting those teachers?
5. Are principals and teachers forced to lower standards of high school work in order to have an 85% graduation rate?
6. How are small schools preparing students when they do not offer a lot of opportunities like different types of classes?
7. Should teachers in new small schools teach one subject or should they have the education to teach two subjects?

The pivotal visits of Ancess, Allen, Balaban and Nadelstern helped shape our SPI project in many ways. Our students finally started to connect the dots and understand why asking questions is such an essential part of what it means to be informed about a topic. As a follow up to their experience with our visitors, our students read many articles related to education in preparation for the writing of their "Mastery Statements," a component of their required end of semester portfolio, which focused on themselves as learners and their educational experience at PNA. The students were presented with conservative traditional views of education in addition to more liberal constructivist views. They read the likes of John

McWhorter, Shelby Steele, Pat Buchanan, Roland S. Martin, Pedro Noguera, Jonathan Kozol, Roger Schank, Alfie Kohn, and Nora Ahmed's June 2004 piece for graduate school titled *Education within the Age of Urbanization and Progressivism: Politicizing a Nation of Thinkers,* which cited such thinkers such as John Dewey, Noam Chomsky, Diane Ravitch, Gloria-Ladson Billings and others. Our students' interests, skills and ideas expanded as they chose to expose themselves to more information.

Dialogue With Experts via E-Mail

As this project took on a life of its own, the students began to internalize the notion that one question leads to more questions and no definite answers. This, to us, was true inquiry based learning. The students saw that when they asked people to come and speak with them, they were listened to. As such, when we proposed that they write letters to experts in the field of the small schools movement to learn even more from primary sources, they latched onto the idea of researching a person and a topic.

This led us to wonder who, in the world of small schools, might be interested in engaging in a dialogue with our students around their research questions. We prepared detailed biographies of multiple "experts" in the field of urban education for our students to read, including academic researchers, professors, small school principals (past and present), activists, and policymakers. From that list, each student chose one "expert" with whom s/he desired to connect. Due to issues of geography and resources, we decided to create a way for our students to engage in "e-mail conversation" with their chosen "expert" around their research question. Our students subsequently engaged in more research around their topics and even created a detailed "wiki" site for that purpose. As the students became more informed about their topics, they began a lengthy letter writing and revision process. Finally, in February, these letters were sent out via e-mail to the students' chosen "experts," including but not limited to:

- **Deborah Meier:** Founder of Central Park East Secondary School (CPESS) and Boston Arts Academy (BAA);
- **Jeannie Oakes:** At the time the Presidential Professor in Educational Equity and Director of the University of California at Los Angeles' (UCLA) Institute for Democracy, Education & Access (IDEA);
- **Pedro Antonio Noguera:** Professor in the Steinhardt School of Education at New York University, Executive Director of the Metropolitan Center for Urban Education, and Codirector of the Insti-

tute for the study of Globalization and Education in Metropolitan Settings; and

- **Elliot Washor:** Cofounder of Big Picture Learning, a global school development organization working to create innovative and personalized schools.

By late February the field participants had responded and we presented our students with the e-mails personally addressed to them. They proceeded to silently and diligently read the responses to their questions. Our students were thrilled and honored that these very important people "out there" took the time to respond to them with seriousness, depth and sincerity. We were equally heartened and grateful that the "plan" had worked out.

Our students' SPI book quickly took shape and they soon took complete control of the book and the inherent learning that played such a crucial role in the process of creating a collaborative publication. By this time, the students had also clearly defined their SPI groups in alignment with the way the students envisioned their chapter titles, which are, namely: Small Schools and Learning; Small Schools and Facilities; Small Schools and Assessment; Small Schools and Teachers; Small Schools and Funding; Small Schools and Standards; and Small Schools and College. Our students engaged in the revision of their writing for final publication, collaborated to create their book's title, came up with individual chapter headlines, designed each chapter's artistic theme, and chose the student artist for the book's cover. Despite the many students who remained at a more investigatory stage, other students became true historians, conducting research at home, staying with us for hours on end at TC to perfect their chapter art, writing and rewriting their reflections on the movement, and never ceasing to ask subquestions related to their essential question.

Visiting Other New Small Schools

In addition to the impact of the e-mail correspondence with the field experts, we pursued opportunities for students to interact with other small schools and their students. We spent an entire school day in late February 2007 visiting other small schools in New York City, including the Julia Richman Education Complex (JREC) in Manhattan. JREC was restructured in the early 1990's from a large failing high school into four autonomous small high schools, an elementary school and a school for autistic children. Since JREC's success largely informed the practice and policies guiding today's critical small schools movement, our students received a tour of JREC from Urban Academy students and spent time discussing their research questions with Ann Cook, the Codirector of Urban Academy and the New York Performance Standards Consortium. We also ate lunch with Louis Delgado, the Principal of Vanguard High School, one of the other small schools at JREC, and some of his students.

Later that day, we arrived at the Morris High School Campus in the South Bronx, which was also once a deeply troubled large high school. Morris began its restructuring in 2002 and is now home to five autonomous small high schools. At Morris, after touring the entire campus and visiting the five small schools residing therein, our students met with the founding principal of one of the five new small schools in the building to discuss their research questions. For the remainder of the afternoon at Morris, our students each paired up with a student from three of the five small schools on the Morris campus. Our students were given the opportunity to compare and contrast their experience at PNA with students from other small schools in an Impact building that had gone through a similar conversion process as the one that took place at Stevenson. Our students thus had an experience that most students never get: The opportunity to take a day off from school to visit other schools to compare their experiences with those of other students in a similar restructuring process. Our students' ability to talk about and listen to each other's feelings regarding their own school's redesign process was remarkable. They became the true experts at this stage, speaking with knowledge and authority about topics they had heavily researched and, now, owned.

CONCLUSIONS

Hearing others discuss and write about "successful" projects with students frequently makes teachers, all of whom struggle with curriculum and engagement at times, feel like imperfect educators. The process we engaged in was not easy, and we did encounter significant glitches for which the space in this chapter does not allow (e.g., gaining the students' "buy in," the entire process of revising student writing for publication, and maintaining our momentum amidst all of the other pressures on our students' lives inside and outside of school). In actuality, the moment we decided to work on this project, we knew that it would resemble the opening of Pandora's Box. And, in many ways, it was. Not only was implementing a student-led curriculum challenging and chaotic for multiple reasons, but moving our students—many of whom opposed academic research and writing—*from* a very resistant place of angry complaints and hopelessness to an informed and intellectually charged place, was extremely challenging and, at times, an overwhelming task to envision executing. Throughout our time together, we saw our students shift back and forth between multifaceted roles. We saw them behave as interrogators, observers, critics, commentators, investigators, explorers, questioners and inquirers. They transitioned from digesting to sharing, from reflecting to writing, from revising to re-revising, from responding to listening and from thinking they have all the answers to pursuing different viewpoints and, ultimately, they continued questioning their own experience. They learned how to formulate research questions; seek both primary and secondary sources; crosscheck their data; analyze their findings; draw conclusions; and make recommendations based on their research.

Throughout our time together, we were transparent with our students about our commitment to allow them to truly navigate this project. We were invested in their capacity to really look at the labels society places upon them, to interrogate what it means to grow up in the inner city, and to take ownership over what it means to be a part of a school change initiative designed to combat the dismal graduation rates and other statistics plaguing their schools. They knew we respected them and thus embraced the fact that we wanted them to analyze how they felt about their educational experience and speak about it to academics, policymakers, students and adults from other small schools and other interested parties in the education field. We realized we were asking students to do an extremely metacognitive and emotional activity that many adults either are unable to do or completely avoid: the notion of examining one's own experience while living it. Hence, we understood why there were times when the students seemed resistant to the whole process. After all, we were asking students still in the process of struggling to acquire a high school diploma, students who had yet to complete college applications and pass all their Regents Exams (New York State's subject specific graduation exit exams), to weigh in on a national dilemma—urban school reform—with social, political and economic significance. Our students constructed a bridge between the "ivory tower" and the "real world," between "theory" and "practice," and between themselves and "school reformers" with the publication of *Small Schools, Big Questions*.

IMPLICATIONS FOR SMALL SCHOOL REFORM

Revisiting the experience that we had with a group of new small high school students in the South Bronx in 2006-2007 allows us to provide a palpable illustration of the kind of student-led and student-generated work that small (and, we would argue, all) schools should and can do to create lasting and "intellectually transformative experiences" (Ancess, 2008) for students, rooted in kids' own lives and supported by solid relationships between adults who know students well. We hope, too, given the increasingly quantitative measures by which the United States currently judges student—and school—success, that we have adequately underscored the extreme danger that accompanies looking at youth and education through scripted curricula and standardized test scores, resulting in the impossibility of carving out critical experiences for students like the one we describe here. As Beers, Robert, Probst, and Rief (2007) put it:

> [We need students who are prepared to enter their adult lives capable of] ingenuity, imagination, and empathy, those who are willing to take risks and work cooperatively. We should be preparing students for such a world, yet the politicization of education has resulted in a different agenda where a prescribed assembly-line curriculum seemingly asks only that students pass a test. The current focus on high-stakes tests produces students who can answer multiple-choice items but have lost the interest and agility to ask probing questions, to conceptualize our new world. (p. xii)

Imagine if those currently responsible for the very high-stakes decisions to standardize and mechanize our nation's schools tried to recover the purpose of critical small schools by listening to students describe the kinds of experiences they have in school when they are actually learning and growing. They would hear very powerful testimonies about what works best for students and why. This sort of attention to student voice and to the student experience should fuel critical small school reform policy.

REFERENCES

Ahmed, N. (2006). *Education within the Age of Urbanization and Progressivism: Politicizing a Nation of Thinkers* (Fordham University, Master of Science and Teaching Education Portfolio).

Ancess, J. (2008). Small Alone is not enough: How can educators recover the purposes of small schools? *Educational Leadership, 65*(8), 48-53.

Ancess, J., & Allen, D. (2006). Implementing small theme high schools in New York City: Great intentions and great tensions. *Harvard Educational Review, 76*(3).

Beers, K., Robert, E., Probst, R. E., & Rief, L. (Eds.). (2007). *Adolescent Literacy: Turning promise into practice.* Portsmouth, NH: Heinemann.

Fine, M. (2005). Not in our name. *Rethinking schools, 19*(4), 11-14.

Holloman, S. (2009). Writing for real: A Phenomenological Study of Urban Stu-
    dents' Experiences Writing for Publication (Doctoral Dissertation, Columbia
    University, Teachers College, New York, NY).

Klonsky, M. (2010, July 16). *Re: Spouting clichés*. [Mike Klonsky's SmallTalk blog].
    Retrieved from http://michaelklonsky.blogspot.com/2010/07/
    spouting-cliches.html

Lesko, N, Simmons, J., Quarshie, A., & Newton. N. (2008). *The Pedagogy of mon-
    sters: Scary disturbances in a doctoral research preparation course.* New York, NY:
    Teachers College Record.

Schmerler, G. (2002). One Man's Continuing War Against Recentralization: A
    Long Struggle for School Autonomy. *Phi Delta Kappan, 83*(5), 370-374.

CHAPTER 7

FREEDOM FROM HIGH-STAKES TESTING

A Formula for Small School Success

Martha Foote

INTRODUCTION

What does the phrase "small schools" really mean? Is it merely about size or does it additionally encompass other important educational aspects? Just as the phrase "progressive education" has countless meanings dependent on the perspectives of the speaker and listener, "small schools" resonates differently among its many purveyors and audiences. One knows very little about a school labeled "small" until deep digging occurs and answers are unearthed.

Unquestionably, a school that is small in size is not necessarily a "critical small school." To earn that distinction, a small school must focus on active learning and critical thinking, which is facilitated by curricular and pedagogical freedom, especially from the constraints of high-stakes state tests. Using field observations, teacher and student interviews and an analysis of college transcripts, I examined the New York Performance Standards Consortium (the Consortium)—a group of schools that has both this focus and the accompanying freedom—and the college perfor-

Critical Small Schools: Beyond Privatization in
New York City Urban Educational Reform, pp. 121–133
Copyright © 2012 by Information Age Publishing

mance of its graduates. I assert that it is this curricular and pedagogical autonomy that has allowed the schools to immerse their students in deep, critical thinking, an educational approach that not only engages these students at the high-school level, but also prepares them for college work. As such, the Consortium schools are an example of *critical*—and success-ful—small schools.

CONTEXT: THE RISE OF SMALL SCHOOLS IN NEW YORK CITY

As is examined throughout this volume, myriad definitions of "small schools" are abundantly in play in New York City. Several waves of school reforms have been producing small schools since the 1970s, yet the term now frequently refers exclusively to the Gates-funded schools of the last decade, spearheaded by Mayor Michael Bloomberg and former Schools Chancellor Joel Klein. While the Bill and Melinda Gates Foundation warned America in the early 2000s that its large, impersonal high schools were failing children and inducing dropouts, Bloomberg and Klein embraced this message and received tens of millions of dollars from the foundation to break down existing large high schools into several smaller high schools with roughly 350-500 students each. This top-down approach led to the formation of over 200 new small high schools in New York City, linked by their size and bureaucratic genesis (Bloom, Thompson, & Unterman, 2010).

To connect these schools to the neighborhoods in which they were situated, community groups and educators were invited to submit proposals for creating these new theme-based small schools; however, the true impetus came from Bloomberg and Klein as they enacted their reform to restructure existing large high schools. As a result, while a few of the new schools took advantage of their small size to foster more supportive teacher-student relationships and develop a close school community, many simply replicated the impersonal large-school structures—top-heavy administrations, punitive security measures, large class sizes—that they were replacing. Aside from the similarity in size and origin, however, there is another crucial link among these Gates-funded and Gates-inspired small high schools. They must all prepare their students to take five state standardized tests: the New York State Regents exams in English language arts, math, science, global history and United States history. These exams loom large in the life of New York City high school students as the state not only requires passage of all five exams for the awarding of a high school diploma, but the city also threatens school closure when it deems students' passing rates are below par. With such high-stakes placed on these exams, school curricula inevitably centers around them. Furthermore, as the exams necessitate so much specific factual knowledge, a transmission model of pedagogy—lecture, note-taking, Regents-prep textbook readings—is typically used to convey the requisite information to students. The result is a tightly regulated, content-heavy, top-down approach to teaching and learning regardless of each school's theme (McNeil, 2000).

Though these Gates-funded New York City schools may be small in size, their curricular and pedagogical focus on the state's graduation exams precludes their inclusion with "small schools" as defined by the progenitors of the original small schools movement, Ted Sizer and Deborah Meier. When Ted Sizer (1984) and Deborah Meier (1995) described their vision of "small schools," it was never enough for a school to be merely small in size with a close community of supportive teacher-student relationships. It was imperative that deep, critical thinking occurred in classes with students probing essential questions through active and engaged learning. However, when high-stakes standardized tests are the currency of schooling, these tests dominate the life of the classroom (Lipman, 2004; Nichols & Berliner, 2007; Perlstein, 2007). Not only do students need to pass them to graduate, teachers need their students to pass them so that their schools will remain open and their jobs will continue. There is little to no room for active learning, as students must prepare for exams that demand the memorization of decontextualized bits of content knowledge and formulaic essay writing.[1] Though the new Gates-funded high schools in New York City are small in size, they are not truly "small schools" in the original sense of the term as the demands of the high-stakes state exams precludes the kinds of in-depth and critical learning that Sizer and Meier stipulate. For schools to be "small" in this manner, or in other words, be *critical* small schools, they must be free from high-stakes tests and their inherent curricular and pedagogical restrictions. One such example is the group of "small schools" that comprise the New York Performance Standards Consortium.

THE NEW YORK PERFORMANCE STANDARDS CONSORTIUM

The New York Performance Standards Consortium is a group of 28 small high schools based primarily in New York City.[2] Demographically, the Consortium schools are representative of the NYC public high schools, though there is a very slight variation between them. Specifically, the Consortium in aggregate has a slightly higher percentage of African-American and Latino students (71.95% vs. 71.87%), English language learners (12.7% vs. 12.3%), students with special needs (14.3% vs. 13.0%), and students who qualify for free or reduced lunch (64.2% vs. 63.6%). Its students, on average, also score lower on the eighth grade state tests in math and English language arts (2.71 vs. 2.76 out of 4.50) before entering the Consortium high schools.[3]

These "small schools" were founded at various time periods, beginning in 1971, by educators and community leaders seeking to address gaps and inequities in their local education systems through making meaningful change. Some founded schools, such as Rochester's School Without Walls, for example, to serve disaffected students on the verge of dropping out. Others designed schools, for example, International High School at LaGuardia Community College, for recent immigrants still learning English. Even more schools were spurred by a desire to provide an alternative—El Puente Academy in Brooklyn and Fannie Lou Hamer Freedom High School in the Bronx are two examples—to the traditional high school in poor and neglected neighborhoods. Despite all these purposes, however, the schools' founders shared many of the same goals. They designed their schools to be small in size so that (1) students could be well known, academically and personally, by their teachers so they might receive as much support as possible; (2) strong and close-knit school communities could be developed; and (3) structures such as schedules, advisories and class times could be creatively and flexibly implemented to meet student need. Furthermore, all these schools had the professional freedom to develop curricula, pedagogy and assessments that best suited the needs of their students. This autonomy enhanced the teaching culture of the schools as staff had the opportunity to delve into foundational questions of learning and instruction and decide among themselves which approaches made the most sense for their particular context. Overwhelmingly, the schools chose inquiry-based methods by which students could take an active role in their learning and investigate questions and problems profoundly—often those of their own choosing.

The schools' assessments also reflected and supported this approach of deep, critical thinking with such performance measures as essays, research papers, long-term projects and presentations being the gauge by which a student's achievement and progress could be more fully evaluated. Whether pulling initially from Sizer's and Meier's work or not, these schools developed in line with their vision of "small schools" in terms of relationships, community, structures and academic approach.

This diverse group of schools came together as a single body in 1998 as the new state graduation requirements of five Regents exams began to take effect. Calling themselves the New York Performance Standards Consortium, the band of schools decried these new mandates as harmful to the teaching and learning practices that were integral to their schools' missions and helped ensure their students' success. Using an existing state education variance that allowed these schools to employ their own systems of performance assessment in lieu of the then-optional Regents exams, the Consortium eventually won its case to extend this variance, excepting the English language arts exam, to cover the new state requirements. To this day, the state continues to honor the variance, instead permitting the Consortium's requisite four performance assessment tasks: an analytic literary essay that compares at least two works of literature, a social studies research paper, an extended science project or original experiment, and an applied mathematics project.

Ann Cook, cochair of the Consortium, maintains that the schools in the Consortium would be "irreparably compromised" without their variance from the New York State Regents exams (interview, March 18, 2009). This variance, she insists, provides the academic freedom that the Consortium schools need to serve their students well. Without it, schools would have to teach to the state tests; with it, schools can teach their students in a meaningful and engaging manner that encourages analysis and critical thinking. Moreover, the Consortium upholds the state learning standards with each school having documented how its courses and curricula are aligned with the learning standards in English language arts, math, science and history. The enormous difference is that instead of preparing their students for the state tests, individual schools have the autonomy to develop courses designed to grab their students' attention and spur inquiry and exploration, courses such as Supersize Us: America's Foreign Policy as a Superpower, Science of DaVinci, and Facing Today: Urban Identity and Change—each found at a different Consortium school. Through these types of classes, students develop skills found in the state's learning standards, for example, writing, discussion, research, analysis and critical thinking, among others, which they also need to complete the four performance assessment tasks. As the tasks were specifically designed by Consortium members to simulate the kinds of work that college students face, they make sure that Consortium graduates are also preparing for college-level work.

Several mechanisms developed by the Consortium maintain the performance tasks and ensure their value and reliability as assessment tools. First, each task has a detailed rubric that all Consortium schools must employ to guarantee that the same criteria are being used to assess student work. Second, at least two teachers in a school assess each student's finished work so that the grade is not the sole judgment of just one individual. Third, each task's rubric is reviewed by a group of teachers and principals every few years to determine whether the rubric truly addresses the important criteria for that particular task or if changes are necessary. Fourth, the Consortium conducts a moderation study every year with teachers from all of its schools to make certain that each school agrees on the kind of work that merits the four different levels of achievement—outstanding, good, competent and needs revision—in the four different tasks. Fifth, each task comprises an oral presentation with reviewers external to the school to ensure the quality of the students' work. Finally, the Consortium also has a Performance Assessment Review (PAR) Board that oversees its system of assessment. Consisting of veteran educators and researchers, like Michelle Fine, Linda Darling-Hammond and retired principals of Consortium schools, the PAR Board ascertains that each Consortium school is properly implementing the performance assessment tasks, as well as verifies that student work meets the Consortium's standards. In this age of accountability, the external reviewers are essential for helping the Consortium maintain the public trust in the quality education that its schools are providing.

Consortium teachers, especially those who have taught in Regents-based high schools, greatly appreciate the curricular freedom of their critical small schools. One such teacher, Rob, described the initial feeling of working at a Consortium school:

> Teaching with the Regents and everything else after a while you realize you're in a box and the box is pretty small. And my first perception [of teaching at this Consortium school] was oh my God they opened up the box. My first perception was I can stand up and the next one was I can move outside the box. And it was freeing…. I could create my own curriculum and a certain amount of autonomy and feeling responsible that if something didn't work, I could take a certain amount of responsibility because I'm creating my curriculum. I could also find the kids' interests. (interview, June 11, 1999)

Another teacher, Nathaniel, compared his teaching at a Consortium school with teaching to the Regents test mandates:

> I think it's a damn shame that that sense of autonomy, that ability to create your curriculum with high standards has to be thrown out every place by something that I think is artificial. It takes out the creativity of teaching and you're teaching to the test. (interview, October 20, 1999)

Another teacher, Amy, described the differences in preparation between the Regents Exams and teaching at a Consortium school:

> At my school, I teach students what a thesis is, and how to write thesis papers, because that's what they'll have to do in college. But the Regents tests have them do things like write an essay using a 'critical lens' that has nothing to do with college work. (field note, February 8, 2001)

All these statements point to the freedom that Consortium teachers have to create their own curricula—curricula that they believe better serve their students than Regents-driven courses.

RESEARCH ON THE CONSORTIUM SCHOOLS

While it is vitally important that teachers in the small schools of the Consortium enjoy their work and feel a sense of autonomy and professionalism, it is even more critical that the schools in which they work are successful. To gauge this success, I examined several indicators: 4-year graduation rates, 5-year graduation rates, dropout rates, college-going rates and attendance. On all these measures, the students at Consortium schools outperform students at non-Consortium New York City public schools. The Consortium schools' four-year graduation rate is nearly 10 percentage points higher at 68.6% compared to NYC's 59.0%. Its 5-year graduation rate is 76.0%; NYC's is 66.1%. The dropout rate in these schools is less than half of NYC's: 5.3% versus 11.8%. Finally, the attendance rate shows a slight difference at 87%; NYC's is 85%.[4]

As strong as the performance of a school may be, success at the high school level should not be sufficient information to examine the overall effect of a high school's program—it is also necessary to look at the college performance of a school's graduates to determine whether they have been adequately instructed to continue their academic pursuits. This question of how Consortium graduates perform in college is especially important in the context of "small schools" as the Consortium claims that its educational approach of deep, critical thinking and inquiry-based learning combined with its performance-based assessments—made possible by its variance from the state's graduation exams—prepares students for college.

To make this determination, I invited all 28 Consortium schools to participate in a college performance study over a 2-year period. Those schools that agreed asked their graduating seniors to sign a release form granting me permission to obtain their college transcripts. The first year, 18 of the 28 schools agreed to participate. The second year, 15 of the 28 schools agreed, including 13 of the original 15, for an overall school participation rate of 59% over the two years. The average participation rate for each school's seniors was 74%. The schools' population, i.e., race and poverty level, of the participating schools closely approximated the Consortium's demographics as a whole.

Each round of signed release forms was sent to colleges approximately 18 months after the students had graduated from high school. Of the 967 forms in total that were sent, colleges were able to produce 666 transcripts, for a return rate of 69%. When a transcript was not available, colleges typically gave one of three reasons: no enrollment record (due to the inevitable change in college plans between high school graduation and college matriculation), insufficient data on the senior release form to locate the student in the college database (especially true for large universities) or a hold on the transcript for internal institutional reasons. Only one college refused to recognize the release form.

Once collected, the 666 transcripts were analyzed and coded for GPAs, number of credits counted toward GPAs, certain college descriptors (i.e., college governance and selectivity levels as determined by Barron's Guide) and current enrollment status. To increase reliability, individual GPAs were weighted against the number of earned credits. Statistical analyses were then run to determine the percentages of students attending 4-year colleges and universities, 2-year colleges, and vocational or trade programs; 4-year college selectivity-level enrollment rates; average GPAs; and persistence rates into a second year of college (for those students in the study who had matriculated within one year of high school graduation).

Results of the study support the Consortium's contention that its schools' graduates are prepared for college-level work. Of the 666 students whose transcripts were obtained, 77% enrolled in 4-year colleges and universities. Only 19% enrolled in 2-year colleges and 4% enrolled in vocational or trade programs. Of those enrolled in 4-year colleges and universities, the vast majority—83%—attended institutions ranked "competitive" or better, and more than half attended those ranked "very competitive" or better (see Table 7.1). The average GPA for students in the study was 2.6 out of 4.0 (approximately a B-) for up to three semesters of college work. For students in 4-year institutions, the average GPA was 2.7. For students in 2-year colleges, the average GPA was 2.2. Significantly, the ACT—the nonprofit organization that produces the college admissions ACT exam and conducts research on college academic success—defines college readiness as the ability to earn at least a C, or 2.0, in college-level courses (Lewin, 2003). This definition supports the Consortium's assertion that its schools' graduates—who averaged a B- in the study—are prepared for college work.

Table 7.1.   Percentage of Consortium Graduates Attending 4-Year Colleges and Universities as Ranked by Barron's Guide Profiles

College and University Rank	Percentage of Graduates
Most Competitive	7%
Highly Competitive	14%
Very Competitive	30%
Competitive	32%
Less Competitive	14%
Noncompetitive	2%
Specialized	1%

For those students in the study who matriculated in college within one year of high school graduation and whose enrollment into a second year could thus be determined, there is a robust persistence rate. For all such students, 78% enrolled in a second year. Of those attending 4-year institutions, 84% enrolled in a second year. Of those attending 2-year colleges, 59% enrolled in a second year. These rates surpass the national averages in which 73% of students in 4-year institutions and 56% of those in 2-year colleges persist into a second year of college. To date, there has been no comparable study of New York City schools' graduates.

WHY THE SUCCESS?

All these results indicate that the schools in the Consortium do prepare their students for college-level work as their graduates go on to primarily competitive colleges where they earn solid GPAs and persist in their studies. But why is that the case? What exactly do the Consortium schools do to prepare their students for college academics? The Consortium contends that beyond the small-school structures that allow schools to know their students well and give them the support they need to succeed, it is the focus on college-level skills in classes and on the performance assessment tasks that prepares their students for college. This focus is a direct result of the variance from the state testing mandates that gives Consortium schools the academic freedom to teach and assess in ways that engage, motivate and prepare their students for college work. When Consortium schools' graduates who are currently attending college are interviewed and asked what occurred in their high schools that prepared them for college, they reply with three consistent responses: the emphasis on writing; the focus on speaking confidently in class through oral presentations and class discussions; and learning to develop an argument or thesis and support it with evidence. These responses uphold the Consortium's contention that it is the schools' focus on college-level skills, as exemplified by its performance assessment system, which helps prepare students for college.

Writing

Graduates of the Consortium schools constantly speak of the emphasis on writing at their high schools and how this emphasis put them in good stead in college. One graduate, Jamal, stated: "My high school taught me how to write better essays, how to structure them better. I have a lot of friends in college who struggle with their writing, but I have no problem at all" (interview, June 24, 2010). Lea, another graduate, described a similar college experience: "Writing the papers for the performance assessment tasks prepared me for college. When I got to college, I could write a 30-page paper while my classmates were saying they never wrote more than eight pages" (interview, July 21, 2010). Another graduate, Melody, also spoke of the value of the performance assessment tasks in improving her writing:

> High school prepared me mostly with writing. We worked on writing skills doing the performance assessment tasks. I'm now prepared for longer essay tasks. College has a lot of writing assignments, so the work I did on the performance assessments gave me a lot of support for doing those. (interview, December 18, 2008)

The Consortium schools' graduates saw that their school's emphasis on writing, both for classes and the performance assessment tasks, prepared them well for the writing demands of college.

Presentations and Discussions

Aside from writing, many graduates of Consortium schools speak of the benefit of oral presentations and class discussions in preparing them for college. One graduate, Zora, who had attended a Consortium transfer high school, described her experiences with oral presentations as preparation for college:

> When I went to my [Consortium] high school, I had to do a Power Point presentation on my [performance assessment for science] and a presentation on my [performance assessment for social studies]. It was the first time I'd ever spoken in front of a large group, and I really improved. I learned how to make sure my body language was good and that my words were accurate. It was like college, where you have to gather information, write a paper, and then present. (interview, January 22, 2010)

Another graduate, Brian, enumerated several ways his high school prepared him, including presentations: "I had a lot of essay-writing, the performance assessment tasks, and the oral presentations. I just took a public-speaking class in college, and I had experience and confidence from high school" (interview, December 19, 2008). When asked how her high school had prepared her for college, Eliza, another graduate, explained that she was really good at writing and discussion:

> I'm really good at the classes that are paper- and discussion-based.... At my high school, they made class discussion the class environment; it was really

comfortable there. So I usually feel more confident in the discussion-based classes—I have a comfort zone that comes from my high school experience. (interview, July 27, 2010)

As these quotes show, these graduates saw the focus on oral presentations and class discussions in their high schools as useful preparation for their college classes.

Developing an Argument or Thesis and Supporting it With Evidence

Aside from writing, class discussions, and oral presentations, Consortium school graduates consistently describe being taught to develop an argument or thesis paper and supporting their point with evidence as good preparation for college. When asked how her high school prepared her for college, one graduate, Jessica, explained:

> I'm a government major in college and we write a lot of papers. In high school I learned how to write a really good thesis paper and persuasive essay. Some papers at high school were even longer and more complicated than I've written in college. (interview, November 26, 2008).

Alex, another graduate, described how his high school prepared him: "When I first started writing at my high school, I had to explain better and put in evidence to support my point, and I got the hang of it" (interview, June 25, 2010). Another graduate, Bobby, explained,

> When I transferred to my high school, I needed help with writing, to be able to put 'good points' together. I learned how to support my argument and to put all my ideas into a fluid whole. It strengthened my essay writing and you need that for college. (interview, April 20, 2010)

As these quotes indicate, these graduates learned in high school how to write an argument or thesis paper and support it with evidence, a skill that prepared them for college work.

CONCLUSION

Small schools alone cannot improve education; however, they do provide opportunities for innovative structures that promote supportive teacher-student relationships and a strong learning community. Nevertheless, small schools that are subject to state education mandates such as standardized graduation exams, can be severely hindered in reaching this goal. If testing demands predominate, student needs may not be met and teachers may have difficulty exercising their professional judgment and autonomy to create classes and schools that are fully responsive to their communities.

Yet, when small schools are exempt from state graduation tests, conditions are ripe for these schools to become "critical small schools." Curricula can be rich, in-depth and engaging and the types of school assessments used can promote college-level work. The New York Performance Standards Consortium operating under a testing variance provides just such an example. Consortium students, despite their disadvantages upon entering high school, stay in school, learn to think deeply and critically, and graduate prepared for college, where they earn solid GPAs and persist into a second year. They can write, discuss, present, and develop and support their theses. Because of the Consortium's testing variance, these students have been taught the skills to succeed in college—and they do.

NOTES

1. Several New York State Regents exams have been critiqued by independent panels of experts (see http://performanceassessment.org/consequences/ccritiques.html/).
2. There is one Consortium school in Rochester and one in Ithaca.
3. Statistics found and derived from: NYCDOE (2009): 2008-09 Progress Report Measures for high schools; NYCDOE (2010): 2008-2009 Progress Report Measures for schools for transfer students; NYCDOE (February 2010): School register data, found at each school's NYCDOE website; NYSED (April 2010): NYStart Accountability and Overview Reports for each school; NYSED (2010): Public School Total Cohort Graduation Rate and Enrollment Outcome Summary—2008-2009 School Year All Students; NYCDOE (March 2010): New York City Graduation Rates Class of 2009 (2005 Cohort).
4. See Note 3 above.

REFERENCES

Barron's Profiles of American Colleges: 25th Edition, 2003. (2002). Hauppauge, NY: Barron's Educational Series.

Bloom, H. S., Thompson, S. L., & Unterman, R. (2010). *Transforming the high school experience.* New York, NY: MDRC.

Lipman, P. (2004). *High stakes education.* New York, NY: RoutledgeFalmer.

McNeil, L. M. (2000). *Contradictions of school reform: Educational costs of standardized testing.* New York, NY: Routledge.

Meier, D. (1995). *The power of their ideas.* Boston, MA: Beacon Press.

Lewin, T. (2003, August 20). High school seniors weak in math and science tests. *New York Times*, B-8.

Nichols, S. L. & Berliner, D. C. (2007). *Collateral damage*. Cambridge, MA: Harvard Education Press.

Perlstein, L. (2007). *Tested*. New York, NY: Henry Holt.

Sizer, T. (1984). *Horace's compromise*. Boston, MA: Houghton Mifflin.

PART III

BEYOND THE SPHERE OF
SCHOOLING: STUDENTS NAVIGATING
POSTSECONDARY TRANSITIONS

This final section explores what happens to students after their departure from these critical small schools. Even after students have graduated or left the schools, their experiences in these schools continue to inform the decisions they make and their ability to follow through on those decisions. These chapters both examine some of the processes within the schools which facilitate the transition, such as applying to college, as well as follow students into their post secondary experiences to examine how these schools have impacted many of their life choices and behaviors outside of schooling.

- In what ways have critical small schools realized their distinct and unique missions?
- What seem to be the main obstacles for students both within and beyond their critical small schools? Why do these obstacles exist?
- How can critical small schools build upon the research presented here to move towards more equitable and socially just spaces?
- How can we use research on small schools to challenge current trends in mainstream educational policy?

CHAPTER 8

REDEFINING SUCCESS

How CPESS Students Reached the Goals That Mattered

Alia R. Tyner-Mullings

I wanted my parent's approval ... I found education interesting and exciting and I engaged it in those terms. I thought education would create opportunities my family didn't have. My father said if you want to grow up and not live in public housing, pay attention in school.

—Chancellor Joel Klein,
New York City's school chancellor (Berger 2007)

INTRODUCTION

In 2007, while "selling" a pilot program to New York City families which would provide monetary incentives to elementary and junior high school students, Chancellor Klein shared his own motivations for achievement in school. In this quote, Klein emphasizes the importance of having clear goals in schooling. He was taught to recognize the importance of schooling as a path to a better future. However, the goals of schooling are not as clear cut for many of the students within the public school system. Pierre Bourdieu (1977) theorizes that the structure of education is often benefi-

Critical Small Schools: Beyond Privatization in
New York City Urban Educational Reform, pp. 137–165
Copyright © 2012 by Information Age Publishing
All rights of reproduction in any form reserved.

cial to those in the dominant group while preventing those with little access to dominant cultural, social and economic capital from achieving any kind of social mobility. In public schools, this is manifest through the imposition of invisible pedagogies (Bernstein, 1975) and a focus on testing and discipline. In contrast, most private schools have the opportunities to emphasize critical thinking and creative learning.

As a response to the shortcomings of public education and the lack of quality educational options available for low income and minority children, alternative schools began to emerge during the school choice movement in the 1970s (Fliegel, 1993; Sullivan, 2003). On the national level, the term "alternative school" refers to schools for students who are not allowed to attend or are unable to function in traditional high schools. These schools include General Equivalency Diploma (GED) programs, night school or "seat time" (where students receive credit for attendance) schools. However, Mary Anne Raywid (1999) sorts alternative schools into three categories: those that change the student, those that change the school experience, and those that change the school system.

This research is concerned with small schools that use an alternative approach to assessment, curriculum, pedagogy and/or school structure; those schools that in Raywid's (1999) taxonomy "change the school experience" or "change the school system." These types of alternative schools are not merely small schools; nor are they necessarily schools for individuals who cannot function in traditional school environments. Rather, they are small schools established with the specific mission of creating a particular educational environment. These schools, what we term "critical small schools," are distinct from both other alternative schools and schools that are simply small. These schools attempt to reframe the goals of education and create new educational paths which challenge the goals of the traditional system. Through goals concerning social mobility and the pursuit of knowledge, the pedagogical structure and philosophy of New York City's critical small schools aim to educate low-income and minority students to become public intellectuals and democratic citizens.

This chapter will explore these alternative educational goals through an analysis of survey and interview data from former teachers, students and administrators of one of the first critical small schools in New York City, Central Park East Secondary School (CPESS). Additionally, organizational documents and events from CPESS are used to examine the goals of the school in its early years and the effectiveness of CPESS in achieving those objectives. While many of the public alternatives to traditional education have turned to specialized schools and the more privatized charter options, CPESS, like other schools in this volume, found ways to provide quality education to underserved students from within the existing system. Understanding how this is done, and the strengths and weaknesses of this model, offers the opportunity for high levels of educational attainment to students who have not previously had access to it.

CONTEXT

Central Park East Secondary School (CPESS) began in 1985 as a joint effort between Deborah Meier and Ted Sizer, two educational innovators. CPESS encompasses grades seven through 12 and was organized into three divisions—Division 1, Division 2 and the Senior Institute—composed of two grades each.

CPESS became an influential educational model in the 1980s and into the 90s as the school graduated its first class in 1991. The school boasted impressive statistics in the poorly performing New York City school system with a 90% graduation rate in the 1990s, compared to the city's rate of 55%. Even more striking was that between 85 and 95% of graduates went to college (Chicago Public Schools, 2003). This can be compared to national college enrollment rates of 39, 33 and 29% for White, African American and Hispanic graduates, respectfully, during the same period (Carter & Wilson, 1991).

Unlike the specialized high schools which recruited high performing students from the junior high schools in New York City, CPESS did not require an exam for consideration or entry into the school. However, students interested in CPESS did have to select it.[1] When asked if there was a particular type of student for which CPESS was best suited, Meier explained:

> I don't know that anything works for everybody … you know, in the lower grades, we used to say the school's designed to be right for everybody who wants to be here. But if there's a family that doesn't, then we're putting the kid in between. If the family thinks this is a stupid way to educate kids, then a kid feels torn. So there's always that dilemma about what do we mean by "it's right for everybody?" I think there's nothing in the model itself that I can say, "Well, this is the kind of kid it doesn't work with." I once had a theory that it didn't work for con artists. Because we were so dependent on interpersonal relationships that a kid that was very clever at conning himself, we wouldn't know how to handle. Because we were always accustomed to trusting … and it doesn't matter if the teacher has to look him straight in the eye and say, "Well, I don't care how charming and wonderful and sweet you are, this is the rule and I can't change it." So it is possible there are kids who need some rigidity. But I wouldn't know how to recognize that kid. But I can see a parent saying this school has too much room for flexibility, and my kid is always figuring out how to use that as an excuse. (interview, March 3, 2007)

CPESS was based on what Bryk, Lee, and Holland (1993) term voluntary communities, school situations where students and teachers work together to create a community in which both groups are willing participants. According to Meier, she used open classrooms and a flattened hierarchy to allow students to "come out feeling very intellectually and personally powerful, both to shape their own lives and to influence the world around them" (interview, March 3, 2007). Although not the only attribute, small size was critical to implementing the voluntary community. As such, CPESS contrasted with the comprehensive high schools that were attended by most public high school students and the specialized high schools that were only attended by a minority of students. Enrollment at CPESS was between 500 and 600 students. This, in itself, made it one of the smallest public high schools in the city. However, there were a variety of other ways—such as the divisions and class groupings called "houses"—that CPESS' faculty and staff endeavored to make their small school even smaller. Additionally, the school used alternative pedagogical methods such as performance-based assessment, which included completing 14 portfolios for graduation, and in-class projects referred to as exhibitions.

CPESS Population

In 1996, the *Annual School Report* recorded 340 students at the high school level of CPESS. The school was 5.5% White, 41.5% Black, 50% Hispanic and 2.9% other. According to the *Report*, 77% of students were eligible for resource room services, indicating the need for academic assistance outside of the daily classroom services. In addition, 42.5% of students received free or reduced fee lunch in 1995, a measure of the size of a school's low-income population that is often used in public schools (Division of Assessment and Accountability, 1996).[2] In addition, the *Report* listed 21 high school level teachers at CPESS, 90% of whom were fully licensed and permanently assigned to the school. Sixty-four percent of the teachers had taught for more than five years and 92% had at least a master's degree (Division of Assessment and Accountability, 1996). Approximately 65% of teachers were White, 20% Black, and 10% Latino. The staff was 63% female.

METHODOLOGY

In order to fully examine the ability of CPESS to reach its goals, I collected data from a variety of sources to examine the origins of the school, its structure and functioning, the students it created, and the future of this school and others like it. These questions required the use of a variety of methodological approaches, including document analysis, surveys and interviews. This type of triangulation[3] is appropriate when one methodological strategy will not adequately address the research questions.

Data Collection

I administered a survey to former CPESS students and conducted interviews with both teachers and students. I also analyzed public documents, including school reports, websites and media reports. The survey included 78 students, and I conducted open-ended interviews with 21 students, 8 teachers and 1 administrator. In addition, I attended several events sponsored by alternative and critical schools in New York City which had historical ties to CPESS.

Participants

Out of the 78 students who responded to the survey from the graduating classes of 1991 to 1995, 63% were female; 13% were White, 40% Black, and 22% Latino. The average age of the former students at the time of the survey was 30 and they currently identify as 2% poor, 41% working class, 50% middle class and 8% upper middle class. The teacher sample was 63% male and 75% White. The average age of the staff at the time of the interviews was 53 and they had taught at CPESS for a mean of 11 years. Seventy-five percent of the teachers in the sample currently classified themselves as middle class and the remainder, upper middle class.

Inside/Outside

In ethnography, practitioners often allude to the insider/outsider perspective or status (Naples, 1996). This refers to the status of the researcher and research subjects in reference to the group being researched and the distinct viewpoints this generates—each with its own strengths and weaknesses and each with a distinct contribution to the research. As a graduate of CPESS, I enjoy status as insider who spent 6 years in the school and graduated with the class of 1994. That I was privy to insider knowledge added ease to interviewing because respondents could use terms such as "advisory," "portfolios" and "humanities" without having to explain what they meant. They could speak freely about their experiences and not be restricted by my level of understanding. My insider status also facilitated my recruitment of respondents. According to teachers and former students, the fact that I was an alumna of the school generated trust and encouraged the view that I and my research were legitimate.

I also have an outsider status. As a member of the class of 1994, I remain an outsider to the other graduating classes,[4] and while some respondents from these classes remembered me, many did not. Several students began their responses with "I don't know if it was like this when you were there..." and "things might have changed later but..." placing me in the role of outsider.

I also played both roles as I interviewed teachers and administrators. Because I had never taught at CPESS, I was an outsider to their occupational position. Nonetheless, I did have some knowledge of their experiences, having taught at one of the high schools that used CPESS as a model. I believe that my position as a former student of the school also facilitated my relationships with teachers and administrators. They seemed to transfer the level of trust shared by members of the CPESS community to me as a researcher. The CPESS faculty and staff appeared to be very open and honest, sharing stories and observations with me that seemed to demonstrate their belief in my trustworthiness and the importance of the research.

I am aware that my position as both insider and outsider could potentially lead to bias. The nature of this project tends to engender strong feelings either in support of or against the school. Recognizing my positionality, however, forced me to be aware of and control for my biases while presenting multiple viewpoints, many of which differed from my own. The survey allowed me to capture the distinct viewpoints and experiences of a large group of people while the interviews provided an opportunity to explore those differences.

THE NEW DEFINITIONS OF EDUCATION

The Cardinal Principles of Education—a report written in 1918—developed a framework which became the foundation for the goals of most high schools. It stated that the purpose of schooling was to "develop in each individual the knowledge, interests, ideals, habits, and powers whereby *he will find his place* and use that place to shape both himself and society toward even nobler ends"[5] (Ballantine, 2001, p. 136). Critical and alternative small schools in New York—CPESS among them—have reexamined these goals of education and embodied new ones. Implicit in their goals are three general principles that embody the mission critical small schools were designed to accomplish: to create public intellectuals, to create democratic citizens and to prepare students for the "next step." The remainder of the chapter examines how well this school enacted these principles.

Putting the Public in Intellectual

According to Max Weber (1946/1958), intellectuals are a "group of men (sic) who by virtue of their peculiarity have special access to certain achievements considered to be 'culture values,' and who therefore usurp the leadership of a 'culture community' " (p. 176). Former CPESS students recognize both the community aspects of intellectualism and its more basic attributes concerning the constructive use of knowledge. When asked how they interpreted the mission of the school, 40% of students interviewed used words like "teach us to use our minds well" and "encourage critical thinking":

> I think, simply put, it would be to make independent, responsible thinkers. I think it was sort of drilled into us over and over again that we could engage with anything that we wanted to but then, along with that, there was a very clear sense of having a duty to yourself and to the community around you. You know to think thoughtfully and ethically. Yes, we didn't talk much about ethics but I kind of felt like that was behind everything that we were doing. —Kenneth Edward,[6] alumnus[7] (interview, April 21, 2006)

Teachers provided similar descriptions of the school's goals:

> Well, I think the official goals were the ones I actually took seriously, which were to create people who could use their minds well. And using the mind well was defined by imbuing the Habits of Mind. —Dan Patton, Humanities (interview, March 8, 2007)

Educators view these objectives as contrasting sharply with goals that have been characteristic of traditional schools. Public schools have traditionally needed to prepare students to pass standardized tests and therefore must focus on the coverage of particular discrete aspects of curriculum. Ted Sizer (1984) describes the goals of more traditional schools as "simply a listing of what the *teachers* will do, what 'things' the kids will be 'exposed' to" (p. 6). Conversely, a catch phrase several teachers at CPESS used was "we teach students, not curriculum." One student noted that a humanities class "started [him] off ... as an intellectual person in the school" (Bryan Ornell, alumnus, interview, May 11, 2006).

In examining some of the principles of CPESS, Meier explains what being an intellectual required of both teachers and students:

One was that teachers had to be generalists and know students and not see themselves as only devoted to their particular academic discipline. And that they were interested in how kids and adults thought—intellectual life in general. And they happened to have specialized in one particular field, but they were interested in the life of the mind, if you want. Because one of Ted Sizer's principles was that the purpose of the school is to help young people learn to use their minds well. And he didn't mean it just academically or in any particular academic [discipline], but the idea that we have intellectual capacities that are normally not tapped, and that all human beings have such intellectual possibilities. (interview, March 3, 2007)

What CPESS administrators and teachers mean by intellectual training includes inculcating pedagogical tools such as the "Habits of Mind" which promote the evaluation of evidence and its significance, encourage students to be critical thinkers and teach them to use their minds well. While many popular and academic definitions of an intellectual include a value judgment, the pedagogy at CPESS applied a definition closer to that found in the dictionary. *Webster's Ninth Collegiate Dictionary*, for example, defines an intellectual as an individual who is "given to study, reflection and speculation" and "engaged in activity requiring the creative use of intellect" while the *American Heritage New Dictionary* defines an intellectual as "a person who engages in academic study or critical evaluation of ideas and issues." These definitions encompass the intent of the Habits of Mind that all CPESS students were encouraged to implement in their school and homework everyday. They also include an emphasis on the student's voice. When asked if he remembered the Habits of Mind, alumnus Shane Rayburn explained:

[The Habits of Mind were] sort of similar to the who, what, when, why and how's but it was about perspective and who's perspective it was about. What's the evidence? It was about who said what and why did they say it and their perspective on the subject matter was based on what facts. You know what I'm saying? How did that person come about thinking like that? Who is this person? Why is this person acting like this? What factors contributed to that? What's your evidence? (interview, April 17, 2006)

Only 16% of students interviewed could specifically name the Habits of Mind, yet 74% of students could describe what they were and felt that the Habits of Mind were so ingrained that while they could not necessarily name them, they felt they used them every day. One student expressed this dramatically

[If I hadn't attended CPESS,] I think I would have been a cold-hearted bastard that saw the world in this one-dimensional, limited perspective as opposed to one who uses the "Habits of Mind" to sort out things about the world around me. —Bryan Ornell, alumnus (interview, May 11, 2006)

Beyond the imposition of the "Habits of Mind", the attention to alternative cultural and curricular arbitraries at CPESS contributed to students' ability to become intellectual. Pierre Bourdieu's analysis concludes that schools which strongly emphasize traditional arbitraries also limit their students' ability to question those arbitraries. What is taught in those schools is often considered "objective truth" (Bourdieu & Passeron, 1977, p. 29). In contrast, teachers in critical small schools must continually justify their curriculum choices, and students learn the importance of questioning and may use it to criticize the school in their requests that curriculum be explained and interrogated. Bryan Ornell continues:

> I remember at one point, [three of us] were actually very dissatisfied with the level of educational returns of mathematics or certain subjects. We felt that it was deficient and it needed more … so we actually half-way had some kind of semi-movement that lasted all of two weeks or whatever to kind of change that. (interview, May 11, 2006)

The development of voice as part of the definition of intellectuality was promoted by other aspects in the CPESS curriculum. The openness of CPESS' exhibition and portfolio processes encouraged students to realize their creativity in the presentation of their work. When asked about the portfolios of work students completed for graduation, students emphasized the importance of the opportunity to tailor their work to their interests:

> I also liked that for my fine arts portfolio I put in stories that I had written over the course of high school and that basically each of my portfolios was kind of individually tailored to me. —Joy Vernon, alumna (interview, April 13, 2006)

Former students report carrying that creativity into their later education and careers, making creative decisions about their schooling and occupations based on distinct elements of their human capital and individual personalities. Rather than allowing traditional fields and majors to dictate their path through education, some former students found more creative solutions to satisfy their diverse interests. Kenneth Edward explained that the opportunity to play sports at CPESS was the first time he was able to combine his brain and his body in one activity and explained how this had an effect on his career as a massage therapist:

> I was interested in finding more of a balance between my mind and my body, and the combination of the mind, the body and the spirit is something that

is particularly intriguing to me and massage was like a very concrete way to talk about all three things and to experience all three things. —Kenneth Edward, alumnus (interview, April 21, 2006)

Much of the criticism of contemporary intellectuals takes issue with the academy because of the distance it puts between mainstream society and the "ivory tower." The idea of the public intellectual is an attempt to address this issue. Richard Posner (2001) has defined a public intellectual as "a person who, drawing on his intellectual resources, addresses a broad though educated public on issues with a political or ideological dimension" (p. 170). A public intellectual uses language that is understood by the educated public to educate those outside of academia.

Explicit in the goals of CPESS is that its students develop into public intellectuals. At CPESS, the public aspect of this was centered on working towards change in the community. The administration at CPESS, and other critical small schools, emphasized the importance of service work to their students. One teacher explained:

I think that the norm of "You should serve society in some good way." I think that was a strong message that came through. But I think also there was an understanding that there was a real diverse spectrum of ways to do that. You're supposed to serve your community, but you can do that in a number of ways. —Chiara Salvatore, Math/Science (interview, March 17, 2007)

The school's community service program placed 12 to 16 year-olds in positions to try to make a difference in their communities and in their schools. Through this program, students began the process of the integrating their intellectual abilities and service work—creating a public intellectual orientation for each student. For instance, one former student, Ramon Quesada, suggested that this contributed to the way in which he engaged with and viewed his own community:

I think it's important to have students engage in some [community service] ... some form of contributing to your community, whatever that is, whether it's the school community, whether it's the local community, whether it's the greater New York community.... So I think community service is a huge, huge, huge thing ... if I did a school, I would try to make the placements as meaningful as possible. —Ramon Quesada (interview, May 15, 2006)

Many students echoed this sentiment. CPESS deliberately made this part of the curriculum and culminated the experience with a portfolio. Including a portfolio about their internship forced students to consider subject from an academic perspective, present their work and often led them to integrate it with other subjects/portfolios. An early innovation in the school was an internship seminar which gave students the opportunity to discuss their placements. The seminar, portfolios and discussions that happened in advisories assisted students in concretizing the relationship between their intellectual work and their service to the community. If nothing else, community service and internship seemed to provide the students with valuable work experience which made their job and college applications stand out from others. Former principal and school founder, Deborah Meier elaborated that she originally:

> thought the idea was nice, that people should have some practical skills.... They should know how to type and answer the phone—they should know how to do things so that they could, if necessary, get a job. (interview, March 3, 2007)

Students' experiences with community service often stimulated their interest in work that could become their occupations. For example, Julia Juarez said her dream job would be

> The hospital. I guess in labor and delivery [because] I like helping people and I like being able to make people feel comfortable because in that environment it's not the easiest place for people to feel comfortable and I just like to care for people. —Julia Juarez, alumna (interview, March 3, 2007)

At CPESS, she was given the opportunity to participate in internships and community service at both hospitals and elementary schools and she went on to become a teacher's aide at an elementary school.

CPESS seems to have been effective in providing an intellectual base for their students. Thirty-nine percent of those interviewed said that the most important thing they took away from CPESS is their critical thinking skills; and 90% of those surveyed said that they gained the skill of critical reading, 88% said they learned analytic thinking and 85.7% said critical thinking was learned at CPESS, at least "a little."[9] One student admitted he did not perceive the importance of all of CPESS' lessons but still, like his classmates, felt that:

> Project work is high-level stuff, critical thinking, developing that kind of understanding is, to me, very high-level stuff. It's very hard. You don't even get that at college, for most people. —Ramon Quesada (interview, May 15, 2006)

Students also appeared to have received the message on the importance of service learning. While only 25% of survey respondents stated explicitly that they were currently involved in community-based organizations, 67.2% said they had been actively or sometimes[9] involved in community service outside of a school environment since graduating from high school. Former students have developed socially conscious clothing lines or started low-cost summer camps. Ninety-two percent rated helping others who are in difficulty as either very important or somewhat important in their lives and 35% of students surveyed were involved in the traditional helping professions that include teaching and medicine. Nationally, approximately 23% of employed persons 16 years of age or older are involved in the helping professions[10] (U.S. Census, 2006-2008). As Shane explains, students took what CPESS gave them and shared it:

> I was into being intelligent. I was into being smart. I was into being street smart.... So, CPESS gave me the essential questions to out think anybody, since I was a street hustler.... I was around grown adults but I was outthinking them. I was teaching people on the streets how to read. I was teaching homeless guys how to count, how to read.... The skills that I had at CPESS, I gave away because they gave me more than grown men had and I had to share that with them. —Shane Rayburn, alumnus (interview, April 17, 2006)

Despite this individual describing himself as a drug dealer and hustler, he was also an intellectual who shared his knowledge with people he met in his everyday interactions who did not have access to it. While perhaps not entirely using his knowledge for the betterment of others, it does seem that he identifies as a kind of public intellectual as he used his CPESS developed skills to teach people on the street. The CPESS model seems to extend beyond traditional definitions of public intellectuals to include service work and a role in transforming society. The intellectuals it attempted to produce are more in keeping with Antonio Gramsci's (1999) notion of organic intellectuals who emerge from the working class, are aware of their subordinated position and seek to resist the reproduction of social hierarchies.

Citizen of the Planet

The second most popular interview response (14%) when students were asked the mission of the school was "creating effective and productive citizens." According to Meier and other teachers, CPESS expected its students to expand on public intellectualism and become part of a citizenry that would cultivate cooperation and encourage change.

> The stronger students could, by explaining material to kids in their group who didn't understand it, achieve a greater mastery of it. Maybe achieve some kind of fulfillment from having clarified stuff for the other, weaker

students. And also learn what it is to be a good citizen, helping other people along. —Chiara Salvator, Math/Science (interview, March 17, 2007)

In examining citizenship, many researchers are interested in the ways in which people are excluded from participating as citizens in their societies ("American Civil Liberties Union," 2006; Marshall, 1965; The Sentencing Project, 2007). More relevant to this study is that minorities have historically been denied access to several rights of citizenship. Marshall identifies three types of rights: civic rights, political rights and social rights. While slavery and incarceration have restricted the largest number of African Americans from exercising their political rights though voting, immigrant status and restrictive voting practices have, even as recently as the presidential elections of 2000 and 2004, kept the voices and views of many minorities from being heard. Though all born or naturalized citizens of the United States over 18 legally have the right to vote, their ability to take advantage of this and other citizenship rights varies greatly.

Few former students spontaneously commented on their political beliefs or leanings during their interviews, although two students did name a political community when asked to name the communities of which they were a member. Survey respondents, however, indicated their civic involvement by their high levels of participation in particular activities. Ninety percent of former students surveyed had participated in at least one of the following activities: boycotts, protests or demonstrations, union volunteering, political party volunteering, contributing to political campaigns or signing or creating a petition. Seventy percent had participated in at least two activities and 56%, three or more.

How former students utilize their political rights can be demonstrated in voting behavior. Eighty-one percent of those surveyed said that they voted in the 2004 presidential election and 68% voted in the 2005 local election. This participation compares favorably to the national voting rates reported by the United States Census—58.3% of eligible voters voted in the presidential election and 42.3% in the local election (U.S. Census, 2004). Sixty-six percent of former students rated values such as influencing political structure as very important or somewhat important[11] to them, 84% gave influencing social values the same rating and 54% of former students similarly ranked becoming a community leader. Eighty-seven percent said the same about keeping up with current events, all characteristics that would be required of a knowledgeable citizenry.

Social citizenship or social rights (also referred to as socioeconomic rights) are one of the clearest demonstrations of inequalities in citizenship status. These are the differences in the resources to which different groups in society have access. Six percent of former students cited economic difficulties as one of the reasons why they were unable to complete their college educations and 5% discussed problems in balancing school and work (and often family) as leading to a longer than average road to their first postsecondary degree. Antonia chose to leave her large, public university because "It got too expensive and difficult all around!" (Antonia Huerta, alumna, interview, November 27, 2006). Similar to most public schools, CPESS functioned within a system of unequal social citizenship structures and despite all the advantages of CPESS, low-income minority students still had to struggle with the societal inequalities they encountered in other institutions.

During her 2007 interview, Deborah Meier described visiting a school in the Bronx where she found that most students had never been out of the borough, a situation that was not unique. Students all over the city have similar perspectives on the narrow boundaries of their world. Ellen Donald, a former Humanities teacher, recalled her observations of the same phenomenon:

> People don't leave the Bronx, they don't venture out. The beauty of being in East Harlem was, you could literally walk over to that garden over on Fifth Avenue, and you'd be transported to another world, that showed you something else other than black top and high rises. And that was really essential, being able to hop on the bus and go down to the Metropolitan [Museum of Art]. (interview, March 22, 2007)

At CPESS, teachers encouraged their students to understand the vastness of the world and to discover their part in it—to understand how an event occurring half-way across the world could affect them. Bryan Ornell expressed this global perspective well:

> I would say the benefit of the school is that a graduate out of that school cannot say that they don't have a basic foundation of how to operate in the world on a theoretical level.... A CPESS education prepares you for that. It prepares you for being around those different people and taking into account how they live their lives, how you want to live your life. It teaches you how to be a citizen of the world ... I think CPESS was designed to make better citizens of the planet. (interview, May 11, 2006)

Several other students discussed the importance of a global perspective in their school years and in their later lives and how, without CPESS, they would have "looked at the world a little differently" (Claire Sebastin, alumna, interview, November 20, 2006). This global perspective includes a sense of openness to others' ideas, which 74% of respondents said they learned at CPESS, and getting along with people who are different which 80% of respondents said they learned at CPESS.

Meier asserted that the student's ability to see herself as part of a community larger than her immediate neighbors is important. Most students named New York as one of their communities but also included communities based on race, education, interests and ideology. Clearly, the students had an opportunity to leave their homes and see other parts of the city, state and country—to develop an eye that could see beyond the East, Hudson and Harlem Rivers and to make connections between their world and the world around them. This global perspective helped them acquire skills and values key to the mission of many critical small schools and essential to becoming more democratic citizens. For example, 70.8% of students surveyed said they learned leadership in CPESS, 52.1% said they learned to be adaptable, 60.4% said they developed self-confidence and 69.4% said they learned the importance of helping others.

Taking the Next Step

Eleven percent of students interviewed thought preparation for the next step was the mission of the school and that teachers and staff attempted to provide students with the opportunity to do anything they choose after leaving the school, including a myriad of post-secondary options including school, work and family. Teachers also emphasized the importance of preparing students for their next step whether it was college, employment, family or simply exhibiting an alternative perspective on the world:

> [The mission was] To help kids get into college. To expand them into seeing things that were beyond the scope of many high school students in East Harlem at the time. To teach kids to think, to use all of the tools that they had they may not have even been aware of. To get kids to be able to become as much as they wanted to be. To open up a new world to them. To be able to get them to use their minds, expand horizons, use Habits of Mind. —Rod Timothy, Other (interview, March 20, 2007)

> I think we also communicated to kids the fact that, "we know some of you are not going to go to college. Not necessarily because you can't, maybe some of you because you can't, but also because it's not in the cards for you and maybe it's not what you want and that's okay. These habits of mind will still serve you," and I think we made that pretty clear. —Jim Geneva, Math/Science (interview, December 1, 2006)

The teachers agreed that it was CPESS' expectation that all students attend college—part of the graduation requirements was to take the 'entrance' exams and apply to a number of City University of New York

(CUNY) and State University of New York (SUNY) schools. The reality, however, was that not all students were able to attend an institution of higher learning. Despite the efforts of CPESS' faculty and staff, students still had to confront the unequal socioeconomic structures of the larger society after leaving CPESS. Recognizing this, preparation for the next step included options beyond college.

All in the Family

Although better parenting was not an explicit goal of CPESS, a few students remarked that CPESS had an effect on the ways in which they communicated with others and that this extended to family relationships:

> Communication is something that I learned from CPESS, like I said, the teachers there, the entire relationship between student and teacher was, was so accommodating that it rarely made a student feel oppressed or being led rather than guided, you know what I mean? ... I pretty much use the same concepts that CPESS kind of teaches its students [with my step-children], you know, "you can call me by my first name. We're friends. You're welcome to tell me anything you want to tell me. You can talk to me about it without fear of reprisal or of judgment..." and the kids really love that because a lot of times they'd rather talk to me than talk to their mom or talk to their father. —Vincente Ortega, alumnus (interview, April 6, 2006)

The flattened hierarchy of the school structure led to many students comparing the school to a family. The respectful nature of the relationships cultivated at CPESS, specifically in advisories—the small family-like group of which each student was a part—might be more easily transferred to family than those from other, more hierarchical and less communal educational experiences:

> I thought it was pretty cool. We were all family in our advisory ... I felt that they pushed each other for the most part.... They definitely looked out for each other, big time. And I'm not talking physically, in fighting, I'm talking about "you better get that done because [the teacher's] seriously gonna get in your face" or whatever it was, because they knew what my expectations were of them and if somebody was slacking off, they were able to check each other and I found that very admirable of them to do as the year went through. —Elias Boston, Math/Science (interview, April 2, 2007)

In describing their experiences, several students expressed appreciation for the relationships they formed and found modeled in the school. The values of community, cooperation and family came out in several of the student surveys and interviews, as well as other examples within this volume. Rafique graduated from a large, public university and described the close relationship he had with a teacher at CPESS:

[One teacher] was like an extended family member. He played a strong role in my social development outside of the home ... and, in some ways, knows aspects of me better than my family. —Rafique Coleman, alumnus (interview, May 29, 2007)

As much of the research in this volume has mentioned, the use of family relationships in alternative education was essential to the functioning of the schools. While this structure broke down the often adversarial relationship between teacher and student within the school, students were also able to apply those same methods to dealing with other hierarchical relationships in their lives outside of school.

Working Hard for the Money

A survey of 1,040 corporations and managers supports the importance of a liberal arts education to success in the work place. The research found that almost half of the employers surveyed preferred graduates from liberal arts colleges because of the quality of their communication skills as well as their "ability to understand people, [their] appreciation of ethical issues, and [their] leadership skills" (Galaskiewicz, 1990, p. 559). CPESS students were attractive to potential employers because the scope of the curriculum at CPESS was similar to that at a liberal arts college. Kenneth describes CPESS as a school where:

They were giving us a liberal arts education, I think, with the hope, anyway, that we would go to, well, that we would be able to do whatever we wanted but that we would be prepared for a liberal arts education in college. —Kenneth Edward, alumnus (interview, April 21, 2006)

CPESS students were also attractive to potential employers because of the work experience they had from internships and community service:

Outside of the internship, I wouldn't have had the opportunity to be in a hospital and see different procedures done and learn about different procedures. I wouldn't have had an opportunity to be able to work with kids and that actually gave me a decent amount of experience so that when I went for my first job, I got it. —Julia Juarez, alumna (interview, March 3, 2007)

Some students' portfolios were specifically directed towards preparing them for the world of work. The internship portfolio allowed for reflection on the work done over the course of the year and gave students an opportunity to think about work and its importance for them. Additionally, students were both positive and negative about their practical skills and knowledge portfolio, but they all recognized that completing it provided them a level of training for their later life experiences:

> You had practical skills and knowledge portfolios where basically they gave you a list of possibilities where you came up with things that you might actually use in life so I remember one of the things that I did I think was finding an apartment or something and actually going through it—figuring out how you would get a loan and where you would look for an apartment, and another thing was doing your taxes, and so you had to go through them: explain a tax form and stuff. —Joy Vernon, alumna (interview, April 13, 2006)

CPESS also maintained connections to an outside vocational program (Co-Op Tech) in which students could choose to participate and learn skills such as the use of drafting tools for architecture.

Sixteen percent of students surveyed did not go on to college following CPESS—they went directly into the workforce or the military. Their reasons for this choice ranged from family obligations to finances. Those who joined the workforce, however, reported that they appreciated the additional skills they learned through community service, internships and the practical skills and knowledge portfolio. While all teachers would say their efforts were focused on getting students into college, there was also recognition that college was not the goal of all students and teachers at CPESS did provide a space for students who chose to end their formal education, temporarily or permanently, after high school.

The College Way

> I've always said that if CPESS had its own college, I would have had the perfect educational experience. I felt that CPESS prepared me for life … not necessarily for college. —Joy Vernon, alumna (interview, April 13, 2006)

Most of the students' complaints about their CPESS experience can be placed in this category. According to the data collected here, 95.8% of former CPESS students applied to college, nearly all were accepted and 89% of survey participants began college. However, sustainability in college proved to be more of a challenge than may have been expected. One of the most significant problems, as discussed earlier in this chapter, is that after spending between 2 and 14 years in an alternative educational program, students had to return to or for many students enter for the first time, the type of traditional educational institution that CPESS had socialized them to resist. Similar to findings in other chapters in this volume (see Hantzopoulos; Bloom), many former students and teachers from the first five graduating classes referred to a culture shock in the process of moving from the sheltered, nurturing CPESS environment into college.

I feel like one of the weaknesses of CPESS was that the curriculum was so dissimilar than what you would expect at a standard high school that it put their students at a disadvantage when they finally did move on to college, which of course was the goal of the school. —Frank Huerta, alumnus (interview, June 22, 2006)

The culture shock of students moving from CPESS, and similar schools, to other educational opportunities led to almost all the former students reporting difficulties in two general areas of college: math and science and study skills. Students explained that while they often found math to be interesting in CPESS classes, most felt that they did not receive the fundamentals of math and therefore were forced into remedial or supplementary math classes:

I think it was a wonderful place, and a wonderful world for us to be in at CPESS. It allowed us to be free and create knowledge. But we had to go out in the real world. We had to compete with students from traditional high schools. We had to compete with these other schools. And it was great that we were able to explain our process and all that. But when I was at school, I didn't know—it was difficult. That first year was kind of difficult because I wasn't used to taking tests.... And so I think that although it was great that … I learned how to play poker, I learned how to Yahtzee. It didn't help me with the SATs. And so a lot of us … from that first class took remedial math when we got to college. Took some remedial basic sciences when we went to college […] Because we hadn't learned the regular way of doing things. Again, everything was so creative. I'm so glad I know how to play poker, but when it came to me taking statistics in college, I was behind. —Olivia Wright, alumna (interview, April 22, 2006)

This could be attributed to the "less is more" philosophy which may have produced students who were very proficient in some areas and were not at all familiar with others. As described in the Coalition of Essential Schools common principles:

The school's goals should be simple: that each student master a limited number of essential skills and areas of knowledge. While these skills and areas will, to varying degrees, reflect the traditional academic disciplines, the program's design should be shaped by the intellectual and imaginative powers and competencies that the students need, rather than by "subjects" as conventionally defined. (Coalition of Essential Schools, 1998)

Colleges tended to expect general "subject" knowledge from their students rather than the "intellectual and imaginative powers and competencies" that CPESS tried to offer. For example, if one were to examine the topics covered in the lowest level math class at CUNY's Hunter College—

symbolic logic, sets, number systems, relations and operations and topics in probability and statistics—it is likely that CPESS students would have come in with knowledge of only one or two of these topics and therefore would have to take this course (Mathematics and Statistics Department, 2006). A more advanced class with topics such as introduction to matrices and vectors, systems of linear equations and linear programming with applications, however, might be a course with which a CPESS student would be more familiar. In order to enter that course, though, a student would have to have taken and passed a much lower level course. Thus, while students were equipped with applicable math skills, many of them struggled when it came to more basic mathematical concepts.

It seems that for the majority of the former students of CPESS, math in college was difficult. Students spoke highly of their general analytic skills, but few were positive about their attempts to extend their use of the mathematical skills taught at CPESS to other educational experiences.

CPESS students, however, did make educational choices that included the sciences. Three survey respondents majored in the sciences (including physics, neuroscience and chemistry) and four others studied economics and computers. All seven of them currently have math or science occupations. Two of these students had the advantage of supplemental educational programs or tutoring, but the others mastered these skills without that access.

Overall, fewer students were negative about science education. Students who discussed it tended to place it with math in their criticism. Only two students spoke specifically about their issues with the science program on their survey—primarily that it was lacking—but both of these students went on to pursue science careers. They were the most affected by problems in the school's science education, as well as capable of overcoming them.

Finally, students commented on their deficiencies in study skills. They had trouble taking notes or tests because this was not required in CPESS classes. In discussion-based classes, jotting down a few words here and there was often more than sufficient. Lecture-based classes, which tend to predominate at lower level college courses especially at the larger schools, required more detailed notes—a skill that was, at the least cultivated, if not developed in other high schools. Some students reported that their discomfort with the lecture format also made them uncomfortable asking questions to clarify their notes or going to see the professor after class.

Few students mentioned problems with essay or short-answer tests in their classrooms—73.5 and 57.1% respectively said they learned these skills at CPESS—but complaints about standardized tests were second only to complaints about mathematics. The number of students who said that CPESS should have given more standardized tests was surprising.

Most students advocated for both tests and portfolios—if for no other reason than to ensure that students were prepared for the tests they would someday have to take to move on to further steps (SAT, GRE, GMAT).

The students' complaints about the gaps in their education were not unique to critical small schools. Math, especially, tends to be a problem in many schools, especially those in low-income and minority areas. However, students in other schools often have more exposure to lecture based classrooms and high-stakes exams and therefore, when they must face these experiences in college, students are better prepared. For some of the teachers at CPESS, learning about the problems their students faced in these areas once they began college led to a reconsideration of their course structure. For others, they acknowledged that CPESS was different but also that it was meant to be:

> I was annoyed that we started getting feedback from graduates that kids couldn't do lecture courses. They weren't really habituated to listening to lectures. I think some senior institute teachers started doing that. I was like, "This is wrong!" It's hard enough to get kids to use their mind, I don't think we should have colleges dictate to us what we consider to be the needs of our kids. —Dan Patton, Humanities (interview, March 8, 2007)

> When a lot of kids say "my math skills were lacking", they were doing that based on what happened to them after they left. Right?... The unfortunate thing is that if you're doing new stuff with kids, the rest of the world has not necessarily caught up and they are still testing them according to ways that we don't think were accurate or fair.... So, I'm aware of the struggle a lot of kids had when they went into the "real world" because we were basing our math curriculum on things that were going on at the time in the late 80s, early 90s ... when they got out, they were hit with a lot of tests that involved a lot of jargon, a lot of terms that they were not used to knowing—although, if they knew what the terms meant, they would understand what it was. They're also forced to take classes with teachers in college that were not necessarily teaching in the most up-to-date manner, doing a lot of lecturing, doing a lot of going from the book and that's another thing. Our students were not used to working out of a textbook, they were not used to doing that.... But kids when they left my class were stronger in math then they were when they came in ... [In college,] they were being confronted with basically standardized tests which, as you know, we didn't give at Central Park East, we had a variance. So, I would say, yes, we did not prepare you for the way math is taught outside of our school. Sorry. —Jim Geneva, Math/ Science (interview, December 1, 2006)

Students who went to small, liberal arts colleges seemed to fare better overall than those who went to other types of colleges. Many of those who were able to attend small colleges selected them for their CPESS-like qualities. Students commented on their size, their openness and their seminar classes—all which resembled the learning environment to which they were accustomed:

> I went to [a small school] so the class sizes were small, similar to CPESS. We had discussions. There were some classes that were more structured and less alternative but in essence [it] was very much like attending an alternative high school. —Kimberly Hawthorne, alumna (interview, December 6, 2006)

Some students who began their post-secondary educations in large schools found they felt more at home, learned more and were more likely to graduate from the small school they transferred to than those students who remained in larger public universities. Forty-nine percent of former student respondents did not finish at their first school and 69% of them began their post-secondary education in large schools.

> [At CUNY] there were some classes that were more hands-on than the others. There were quite a few classes where we were just basically taking notes the whole time. The teacher didn't speak to us as much as it was just taking notes the whole time and they would tell us what we needed to do or what had to be done. [After leaving CUNY] I went to [a smaller school] for a while. And that seemed more like the CPESS experience. The classes were a lot smaller and there was more interaction between us and the teachers there, and I did really well there. —Julia Juarez, alumna (interview, March 3, 2007)

Other students succeeded in larger schools. Most of those large schools were within driving distance of the city and several students said that proximity to New York City was one of the things that they liked about their college experience. These students also found themselves in schools that, while usually majority White, had enough diversity to allow the students to be comfortable. Students who attended larger schools complained about the size of the school and the classes but most reported that they were able to find enclaves in their schools to make them feel smaller. Syracuse University, for example, is a school of 19,000 students that many CPESS students attended (12.8% of those surveyed who attended college in this survey); and 60% of those who attended, graduated from the school. According to teachers and students, it was the support system available at Syracuse that helped many students through the transition. This included both the in-school support and the relationship CPESS had with the school, which led to a small community of CPESS students attending the school at any particular time. Students also found that there was a population of minority students at the school which contributed to their comfort on campus. For those students who reported that Syracuse did not work well for them, the large size and the weather seemed to be their biggest difficulties.

When students were asked about the advice they were given about their college choices, there was a mixed response. Some students reported that their advisors did their best not to unduly influence their advisees in any way. This led to some students feeling that their institutions were poorly chosen:

> You know, I got into Oberlin. Going to Oberlin versus [a less prestigious school], which no one knows, right? I think adults should have said that specifically. Your résumé will have more cache, if you went to this school. It may not matter to you. At the end of the day, you may not want to be in Ohio, blah, blah, blah, but there is a serious tier system in the colleges. —Ramon Quesada (interview, May 15, 2006)

Other students commented on the value of the college advice they received and the usefulness of the advisory trips in allowing them to think about and visit colleges. Additionally, CPESS helped low-income students find and request college application fee waivers and provided free or low cost Princeton Review SAT preparation, asking only that, those who could afford it, pay a percentage of the program cost to supplement those who could not.

A major latent function (or dysfunction)[13] of this alternative model is that it created students who adapted better to small liberal art colleges. Most of the students, however, were not able to attend these schools, primarily due to a lack of funding. It was also the case that in the context of diminishing social services, balancing school, home and work became very difficult for some. Most students ended up in large public universities because they were less expensive and more convenient for students who had other obligations, allowing them to save money and assist their families by living at home.

Despite these and other issues, CPESS students did graduate from college, 48% of surveyed students who went to college obtained their bachelors degree in four years and 83.9% in six years or less. Twenty-one percent obtained a master's degree and 7.2% continued their educations beyond that level.

Breaking the Cycle

A subtext of this discussion of the goals of critical small school is the effect of this model on Black and Latino students. Twenty-five percent of interviewed students felt that the mission of the school was to provide a quality, alternative education for an underserved population. Frank Huerta explains his view of CPESS's mission: "I think [it was] to address some of the serious problems with our public school system, especially in regards to how it services students of color." Other students added that CPESS intended to "break the cycle," "provide opportunities" and "create a successful school atmosphere."

The analysis of dropout rates is one of the most frequently used measures to assess minority groups' success in education, though the use of some measurements of dropout rates have been found to be problematic,[14] at best. Nevertheless, the high school graduation rates of Black and Latino students are significantly lower than those of their White counterparts. The national graduation rate at the high school level for Black and Latino students has been reported as various points between 50 and 75% with the rate for Whites students ranging between 10 and 30% higher than their Black counterparts (Hale, 2001; Mishel & Roy, 2006).

Given this, the successes of Central Park East Secondary School are remarkable. Nearly all CPESS students from the early years of the school graduated and began college. While they did not all finish college, their rate of success far surpasses that of Black and Latino students nationally. Based on data collected in *The Journal of Blacks in Higher Education*

> black students who earn a four-year college degree have incomes that are substantially higher than blacks who have only some college experience but have not earned a degree ... and blacks who complete a four-year college education have a median income that is now near parity with similarly educated whites. (The Journal of Blacks in Higher Education, 2006)

Disparities in socioeconomic structures are difficult to overcome and some educational researchers have argued that schooling alone will not necessarily lead to larger societal changes (see Anyon, 1997; Coleman et al., 1966). It is important, however, to attend to the effectiveness of any model that attempts to combat these socioeconomic issues and can assist in addressing some of the income disparities present in society for these students, especially when that model has led to a social movement for educational change (Anyon, 2005).

CONCLUSION

Similar to Robert Merton's social adaptation category of "rebellion," CPESS teachers and administrators were not only interested in rejecting many of the means and goals of traditional education but replacing them with others. This is not an easy task—trying to implement an educational rebellion from inside a public secondary school. These schools must function within the state's traditional educational system all the while trying to produce an alternative to it. The practices of the educators at CPESS were intended to lead "[men and wo]men outside the environing social structure to envisage and seek to bring into being a new, that is to say, a greatly modified social structure. It presupposes alienation from reigning goals and standards" (Merton, 1957, p. 211). While wide-spread transformations are not easy, the school sought to create graduates who would have the abilities to work within the structure and, at the same time, to change it.

The students of the school—mostly low-income, urban, and minority students—applied to, were accepted and attended colleges at higher rates than similar students nationwide. In their postsecondary classrooms, former CPESS students tended to feel comfortable expressing their viewpoints in discussion and writing papers. In college, some of the problems they recounted, such as financial difficulties and family, school and occupational role conflict, were similar to those of their counterparts from other public high schools. Perhaps unlike their traditional school counterparts, however, they struggled more in lecture courses that emphasized standardized tests and memorization.

While this may lead some educators to question the value of a CPESS education, many CPESS teachers and administrators assert that it should be the schools that value memorization, lectures and standardized tests that should be open to question. Despite the number of CPESS alumni who did not finish college, *a number still lower than similar students from other schools*, CPESS enrolled more students in higher education, thereby providing more of them with an opportunity to stay and graduate. Furthermore, CPESS teachers felt they had given the students the tools necessary to become public intellectuals who used their knowledge to change the larger world and citizens who recognized the importance of democratic values and the responsibilities of citizenship.

External constraints also limited social mobility. While students were able to attend college, occupational and economic inequalities posed challenges that kept some students from graduating. Those students who were able to break away from the more traditional types of schools in their later schooling seem to have been the most successful, but others were also able to use their alternative educations to adapt to those more traditional institutions.

Finally, despite some of the problems Central Park East Secondary School confronted, the school proved to be a space within which students who are overwhelmingly underserved by the urban public school system could be educated and prepared for productive participation in life outside of school. It contributed to a dialogue on urban education and was at the forefront of a social movement to address some of the inequalities inherent in the educational system. While clearly, the recent proliferation of critical small schools has not produced large scale economic equality or equivalent social mobility for low-income and minority students, the emergence of these schools and their alternatives to traditional educational goals continues to reduce the disparities in educational access and to create individuals who can comprehend and compete in the quickly globalizing world around them.

NOTES

1. Students were given a form on which they ranked their top high school choices. At the time, if they choose not to use this method, they were assigned to their neighborhood school.
2. This is the first year for which the Division of Assessment and Accountability report was available for Central Park East Secondary School.
3. Triangulation is the process of using more than one method to gain a more nuanced explanation of a phenomenon (Bickman & Rog, 1998).
4. Since the school utilized heterogeneous groupings, I shared classes with both the class of 1995 and the class of 1993.
5. Italics mine
6. All teacher and student names are pseudonyms. However, because of the nature of the school, Deborah Meier's name has not been changed.
7. Each respondent is identified as a teacher or alumni. The students are all former students. Teachers, if it will not compromise their identities, are categorized as either a math/science teacher, a humanities teacher (which includes all teaching positions which are not math science) or other (non-teaching positions).
8. The categories are "a little," "a lot" or "not at all."
9. The categories are "actively," "sometimes" or "never."
10. As the U.S. Census uses occupational categories, the percentage is approximate based on combining the general categories within which professions such as teaching, medicine, counseling and therapy can be found.
11. The categories are "very important," "somewhat important" or "not important at all."
12. Robert Merton examines social institutions and their functions (or beneficial consequences) and dysfunctions (or negative consequences). Those that are manifest functions are intended and the latent functions are unattended.
13. Dropout rates are measured in a variety of ways, and, in reporting the rates, it is not always made clear which methodologies are used. Dropout rates can be measured through self-reported survey responses, the percentage of 17-year-olds with high school diplomas as well as data reported by the school about who drops out. Even school-reported data, however, can be unclear because schools define who is a dropout differently. Some schools will claim that if students attain a GED, they are not to be counted as dropouts. Other schools attempt to track what happens to students once they leave the school. This can be a costly and difficult process and is therefore not often implemented (Greene & Forster, 2003; Kaufman & Chapman, 2002). Dropout rates are also frequently measured by counting

those students who begin high school and do not finish. This measure misses students who leave before the ninth grade, a relatively common occurrence if schools have required standardized tests in eighth grade (Kaufman & Chapman, 2002; Kozol, 1991).

REFERENCES

American Civil Liberties Union of Florida says Gov. Bush's task force overlooks impact of felon disenfranchisement. (2006). *Press release.* Retrieved from http://www.aclu.org/votingrights/exoffenders/25372prs20060426.html

Anyon, J. (1997). *Ghetto schooling: A political economy of urban educational reform.* New York, NY: Teacher's College Press.

Anyon, J. (2005). *Radical possibilities: Public policy, urban education and a new social movement.* New York, NY: Routledge.

Ballantine, J. H. (2001). *The sociology of education: A systematic analysis* (5th ed). Upper Saddle River, NJ: Prentice-Hall.

Berger, J. (2007). Some wonder if cash for good test scores is the wrong kind of lesson. *The New York Times.* Retrieved from http://select.nytimes.com/gst/abstract.html?res=F6091FFB38540C7B8CDDA10894DF404482&fta=y&incamp=archive:article_related

Bernstein, B. (1975). Class and pedagogies: visible and invisible. In A. H. Halsey, H. Lauder, P. Brown, & A. S. Wells (Eds.), *Education: Culture, economy, society* (pp. 59-79). Oxford, England: Oxford University Press.

Bickman, L., & Debra, J. R. (1998). *Handbook of Applied Social Research Methods.* Thousand Oaks: SAGE.

Bourdieu, P., & Passeron, J. (1977). *Reproduction in education, society and culture,* (2nd ed.) London: SAGE

Bryk, A. S., Lee, Valerie E., & Holland, Peter B. (1993). *Catholic schools and the common good.* Cambridge, Massachusetts: Harvard University Press.

Carter, D. J., & Wilson, R. (1991). *Minorities in higher education* (10th annual status report, 1991). Washington DC: American Council on Education. Office of Minorities in Education.

Chicago Public Schools. (2003). *Small schools get results.* Retrieved from http://smallschools.cps.k12.il.us/research.html

Coalition of Essential Schools. (1998). *The CES common principles. Elementary and Secondary School Inclusive.* Retrieved from http://www.essentialschools.org/items/4

Coleman, J. Campbell, E., Hobson, C., McPartland, J., Mood, A., Weinfeld, F. & York, R. (1966). Equality of educational opportunity (Eds.), *The structure of schooling* (pp. 120-136). Mountain View, CA: Mayfield.

Division of Assessment and Accountability. (1996). Annual school report Published by New York State Education Department.

Fliegel, S. (1993). *Miracle in East Harlem: The fight for choice in public education.* New York, NY: Random House

Galaskiewicz, J. (1990). Liberal education and the corporation: The hiring and advancement of college graduates by Michael Useem [review]. *Contemporary Sociology, 19*(4), 558-560.

Gramsci, A. (1999). *Selections from the prison notebooks of Antonio Gramsci* (Q. Hoare and G. N. Smith, Eds.). New York, NY: International Publishers.

Greene, J. P., & Forster, G. (2003). Public high school graduation and college readiness rates in the United States. *Education Working Papers, 3.* New York, NY: Center for Civic Innovation at The Manhattan Institute.

Hale, J. E. (2001). *Learning while black: Creating educational excellence for African American children.* Baltimore, MA: The Johns Hopkins University Press.

The Journal of Blacks in Higher Education. (2006). Black student college graduation rates inch higher but a large racial gap persists. *The Journal of Blacks in Higher Education.* Retrieved from http://www.jbhe.com/preview/winter07preview.html

Kaufman, P., & Chapman, C. D. (2002). *Dropout rates in the United States: 2000.* Washington DC: National Center for Education Statistics.

Kozol, J. (1991). *Savage inequalities: Children in America's schools.* New York, NY: Crown

Marshall, T. H. (1965). Citizenship and social class. *Class, citizenship, and social development. Essays by T. H. Marshall.* New York, NY: Anchor Books.

Mathematics and Statistics Department. (2006). Mathematics and statistics. *Hunter Course Catalogue.* New York, NY: Hunter College

Merton, R. K. (1957). *Social theory and social structure.* New York, NY: Free Press of Glencoe.

Mishel, L., & Roy, J. (2006). *Rethinking high school graduation rates and trends.* Washington, DC: Economic Policy Institute.

Naples, N. A. (1996). The outsider phenomenon. In C. D Smith & W. Kornblum (Eds.), *In the field: Reading on the field research experience* (pp. 139-149). Westport, CT: Praeger

Posner, R. A. (2001). *Public intellectuals: A study of decline.* Cambridge, MA: Harvard University Press

Raywid, M.A. (1999). History and issues of alternative schools. *The Education Digest, 64,* 47–51.

The Sentencing Project. (2007). Felony disenfranchisement. *The Sentencing Project. Research and Advocacy for Reform.* Retrieved from http://www.sentencingproject.org/IssueAreaHome.aspx?IssueID=4

Sizer, T. (1984). *Horace's compromise: The dilemma of the American high school.* Boston, MA: Houghton Mifflin.

Sullivan, L. (2003). How East Harlem hatched a model for public school choice. *Philadelphia Public School Notebook 11*(4). Retrieved from http://www.thenotebook.org/fall-2003/03856/how-east-harlem-hatched-model-public-school-choice?page=2

U.S. Census. (2004). Voting and registration in the election of November 2004. Retrieved from http://www.census.gov/population/www/socdemo/voting/cps2004.html

U.S. Census. (2006-2008). S2401. Occupation by sex and median earnings in the past 12 months (in 2008 inflation-adjusted dollars) for the civilian employed population 16 years and over. *American community survey.* Retrieved November 20, 2010 from http://factfinder.census.gov/servlet/STTable?_bm=y&-geo_id=01000US&-qr_name=ACS_2008_3YR_G00_S2401&-ds_name=ACS_2008_3YR_G00_

Weber, M. (1958 [1946]). *From Max Weber: Essays on sociology,* HH Girth & C. Wright Mills (eds.). New York: Oxford University Press.

CHAPTER 9

WILLIE RIVERA THOUGHTS

Critical Small Schools and the Transition to Higher Education

Janice Bloom

INTRODUCTION

When the movement to create critical small schools began in New York City in the 1980s, its central goal was to serve urban low-income students and, as Deborah Meier (1995) writes in *The Power of Their Ideas*, "to demonstrate how all children could meet high standards of intellectual achievement within a public school setting," (p. 15). From the beginning, these high schools set out to close the gap in college matriculation, judging themselves based not just on the number of students they could graduate from secondary school, but on how many continued on to higher education. In the decades since then—as indicated by a flood of new programs, studies and initiatives, including President Obama's 2009 "American Graduation Initiative"—the importance of higher education in creating equal life opportunities has only become clearer.

In the years since they began, critical small high schools in New York City have had major successes with getting first generation students to college. From the first crucial leap of conceptualizing college matriculation as their responsibility, to the networks of college counselors and advisory programs

Critical Small Schools: Beyond Privatization in
New York City Urban Educational Reform, pp. 167–188
Copyright © 2012 by Information Age Publishing
All rights of reproduction in any form reserved.

that now help students through the college search and application process at quite a few of the critical small schools, the movement has created and continually adapted a powerful set of structures for supporting students through this difficult transition. In many ways, they pioneered the college-preparatory work with low-income students that Obama is now calling for, long before others were attending to it.

At the same time, critical small school educators have encountered repeated challenges in pursuit of their goal. In the mid-90s, when I began my teaching career at one of the original small high schools in East Harlem, my colleagues and I believed that in order to reach the goal of getting all of our first-generation students to college, all we needed to do was provide them with a first-rate education—as Meier (1995) notes, following "in the tradition of many of New York's independent private schools" (p. 16). When I moved to teaching 11th grade at a critical small school on the Lower East Side that was just graduating its first class, my colleagues and I realized that we needed to begin talking to our students about college applications in their *junior* year, rather than waiting until they were seniors. Despite these adjustments, we continued to find that our students struggled with the transition to college in ways we didn't anticipate. One colleague captured our bewilderment in an e-mail titled, "Willie Rivera Thoughts."[1]

> I ran into Willie Rivera at the Harlem Children's Society Science fair on Saturday. When I asked him, "Well, how's it going?" (meaning in college), he said he didn't go to Hofstra, dropped out (without penalty) and plans to take computer tech courses at DeVry. He still hopes to complete a four-year college and become, eventually, a doctor. I was rather shocked because, as I told him, in terms of basic raw intelligence and good work habits he is one of the strongest students I've taught here. I'm sure he got good recommendations, had a strong GPA, AND the excellent summer experience working in the Harlem Society intern program two summers ago. So what I don't understand is: WHAT HAPPENED? (personal communication, October 19, 2002)

In this chapter, I look at the successes of New York City's critical small schools in getting their students to college; I also attempt to understand what prevented Willie Rivera from following the higher education pathway he set out upon, despite what appeared to his teachers to be a most promising start. Having written elsewhere (Bloom, 2007) about the ways that academics, policymakers, and educators too often "misread" first-generation students' struggles to access higher education, I attempt here to spell out some of the crucial cultural, social and economic capital that are required to make well-informed higher educational choices in the twenty-first century, and to think about the school structures necessary to provide these resources to first-generation students. Many of New York City's small schools have gone a long way towards putting these structures into place, but there is more they must do.

RESEARCH SETTING AND METHODOLOGY

From 2002-2004, I followed the paths of a group of high school seniors at three critical small schools in New York City as they made their way towards graduation and beyond.[2] While a great deal of research has been done, especially in recent years, in the arena of college "choice" "transition" and "access," only a fraction of these studies have included ethnographic data on the transition to higher education. None of these studies have been done in small public high schools; instead, they have focused mostly on large, traditional public schools (see Knight, Norton, Bentley, & Dixon, 2003; McDonough, 1997; Roderick et al., 2008; Tierney & Colyar, 2006) or on private schools (see Avery, Fairbanks, & Zeckhauser, 2003; McDonough, 1997). Thus, there is a lack of understanding of how the structures and belief systems of small schools in New York City are succeeding—or not—in meeting the needs of first generation-college going students in their transition to higher education.

In order to capture this kind of fine-grained ethnographic data, this article focuses in on one of these schools, Tower High School, where research was conducted from 2003-2004. Importantly for the purposes of this chapter, Tower has a greater racial and economic balance than many public schools—including small schools—in New York City, which made it possible to watch the college application process for students from a range of social classes and ethnic backgrounds and to compare their experiences (see Table 9.1). Though Tower is now larger than most other schools that belong to this reform movement,[3] it has held onto many of the defining structures and goals (e.g. untracked classes, an "advisory" system which endeavors to ensure that all students and families are known well by at least one adult in the school, graduation by performance-based assessment) that characterize them. From September 2003 to June 2004, I did participant observation at Tower in two "advisory" classes[4] where students (all of them seniors) were focusing on applying to college. I attended these classes at least once a week, listening and taking notes as well as occasionally leading full class discussions or helping individual students. I also followed six students much more closely,[5] conducting focus groups and individual interviews with them on an ongoing basis over the course of the year and through the following summer.

Table 9.1.   Statistics for Tower High School (2003-2004)

Category		Statistic
Number of students		1003
Number of seniors		215
Racial/ethnic background of students	Black	18%
	Latino	28%
	White	45%
	Asian/Other	9%
Percentage of students qualifying for free lunch		36%
Graduation rate[a]		85-90%
Percentage of seniors accepted to and planning to attend 4-year colleges[b]		91%

a. This figure varies depending how it is calculated (4 years vs. 5 years to diploma, and whether students who graduate with a GED instead are counted).
b. Based on data compiled by the Tower college office.

In order to complete the picture of students' college application process, I interviewed their parents, Tower's college counselor, principal and a range of teachers several times over the course of the school year. Finally, I administered two surveys to a larger cohort of the seniors (one in December, one in June), making it possible to see how common or unique individual students' experiences and perspectives were within the context of the school as a whole.[6]

In addition to recording the rich details of students' journeys to college, this research resulted in an overview of how the school structured students' transition to college. Thus, I documented what pieces of the process Tower did or did not help students with, what messages were transmitted to students (both formally and informally), how the school interacted with families around college, and how administrators and teachers thought about this aspect of their work. All of these were then set in the larger context of access to college in the twenty-first century.

COLLEGE ACCESS IN THE TWENTY-FIRST CENTURY

The college-going outcomes that my colleagues and I were wondering and worrying over in the mid-1990s fit into much larger national patterns that were coming into increasingly sharp focus just as I began my teaching career. Despite aspirations by almost all students and their parents towards higher education at the end of the twentieth and beginning of the twenty-first century (Adelman, 2002; Choy, 1998; Kinzie et al., 2004; Rosenbaum, 2001; Venezia, Kirst, & Antonio, 2003), there is little question that access to higher education continues to be stratified across race and class lines.

An extensive body of research traces the growing difficulties low-income students face in paying for college, as college costs have skyrocketed, real income for poor and working class families has fallen, and state and federal governments have retreated from need-based financial aid over the past 20 years (Carnevale & Rose, 2004; Gladieux, 2004; Heller, 2005; Kane, 1999; Mumper, 1996; Paulsen & St. John, 2002). Fears of taking out loans and the complexity of applying for financial aid create additional barriers for first-generation college-going students (Bloom, 2007; Carnevale & Rose, 2004; Dynarski & Scott-Clayton, 2006; Kane, 1999; King, 2004).

Structural lack of access to adequate academic preparation for low-income students of color has also been extensively documented in K-12 settings, and more recently by those examining the "pipeline" to higher education (Haycock & Huang, 2001; Nieto, 1992; Oakes, 1985; Venezia, Kirst, & Antonio, 2003). Recent studies by the Social Science Research Council (2005) and the Pathways to College (2004) network catalogue a daunting list of academic barriers that these students face, including tracking and differences in academic programs, lack of access to good teachers, lower expectations and higher dropout rates.[7]

Lack of access to sufficient college counseling is an additional barrier for low-income students of color, particularly in urban areas (Knight et al., 2003; McDonough, 2004, 2005; Perna et al., 2008). Both the American Counselor Association and the American School Counselor Association recommend a maximum counselor-to-student ratio of 1:250; while the national average is 1:513, one study of the largest U.S. cities (which have the greatest concentrations of low-income students of color) found that the average high school counselor-to-student ratio in these cities was 1:740 (McDonough, 2005).[8]

Finally, a great deal of research over the past several decades points to the effects of access to "dominant" (Carter, 2003) cultural and social capital on the college choice process for students across social class. This type of "cultural capital" includes an understanding of the landscape of college and the college application process on the part of both parents and students; Bourdieu (1986) theorizes that the acquisition of cultural capital often happens, "in the absence of any deliberate inculcation, and therefore quite unconsciously" (p. 245). "Social capital" describes access to social networks that can connect students to college-related information and opportunities in informal ways (e.g., visiting friends on a campus, neighbors who know someone who works at a university). It has become increasingly clear that access to these kinds of knowledge and networks impacts both the experience and outcomes of students' transition to higher education.

For example, many researchers note that while poor and working class parents offer emotional support and encouragement in applying to college, they are often unable to help their children with the specifics of the process (Bloom, 2007; Gandara, 2002; Hagedorn & Fogel, 2002; Knight, et al., 2003; McDonough, 1997; Mehan, Villanueva, Hubbard, & Lintz, 1996; Stanton-Salazar, 1997, 2001; Terenzini, Cabrera, & Bernal, 2001; Tierney, 2002). Terenzini, Cabrera, and Bernal articulate what this looks like as it plays out differently across social class in students' "college choice" process, noting,

> In general, more affluent students, compared to their less well-off peers, tend to rely on several sources of information, are more knowledgeable about college costs, are more likely to broaden the search to include a wider geographic range, tend to consider higher-quality institutions, and have parents who planned and saved for college. (pp. 8-9)

More recently, Roderick et al. (2008) document very similar patterns, and argue that they result in "constrained enrollment" or college "mismatch" for many first generation students, as lack of sufficient information leads students to either enroll in institutions that are less selective than those for which they are qualified, or fail to enroll at all. They point out that the barriers that lead to constrained searches exist at numerous points throughout students' college search and application process.

> First, many students simply lack the information and guidance on what kinds of colleges they may be eligible to gain admission to and how to determine what college would be a good fit. Second, many students do not apply to multiple colleges or look at a broad range of institutions. Third, even the most motivated students constrain their college options, because they do not understand financial aid, lack guidance on how to manage college finances, and do not apply for financial aid in a timely manner that maximizes their awards. (p. 85)

This is the case regardless of students' academic qualifications. Carnevale and Rose (2004) note that the number of students from low-income backgrounds who are academically prepared for BA attainment (including at the most selective colleges) is far larger than actually attends; fully 31% of these students with high test scores did not attend any postsecondary institution at all (p. 136). In a broad survey of students in Chicago public high schools, Roderick et al. reached a similar conclusion, finding that "the most qualified students were just as likely to not enroll in college or enroll in a college far below their match (37%) as they were to enroll in a very selective college (38%)" (p. 73).

Thus, from the "macro" of economic policies that constrain students' access to secondary education, to the "micro" of what your aunt and neighbor know about the SATs and Pell grants, low-income, first-generation college-going students across the country face a daunting set of barriers to higher education.

College Access Successes in New York City's Critical Small Schools

Through their vision of school structure, New York City's critical small schools have already addressed some of the major barriers described in the college access literature. What is this vision of school structure, and how does it address issues of college access? First, unlike the majority of public high schools around the country, many of New York City's small high schools do not track their students into differing academic levels based on ability. Instead, informed by Jeannie Oakes' (1985) *Keeping Track: How Schools Structure Inequality*, the earliest small schools purposely worked to create multi-age, heterogeneous classrooms at every grade level. The New Century High Schools Initiative (founded in 2000) required new schools that it opened to accept students with a range of academic abilities, and to create environments that were not tracked by ability. While some of these schools (including Tower) have added "Advanced Placement" classes for seniors or created some tracking in specific subjects (most notably math), a recent study of 14 new small schools in New York City noted that they are academically untracked, and offer college preparatory curriculum to *all* of their students (Huebner, Corbett, & Phillippo, 2006).

Second, the inclusion of a system where students meet regularly in an "advisory" or "family group" goes a significant way towards addressing the lack of access to college counseling that has been well documented in low-income urban schools. This system, which the Institute for Student Achievement describes as "distributed counseling," creates an institutional mechanism so that every student will be known well by at least one adult. So, for example, at Tower, advisory was a non-academic class that met four times a week for 35 minutes, and consisted of a faculty member and small group of students (15-20); this grouping stayed together throughout students' 4 years at the school, so that faculty could become well acquainted with students' families, interests, and academic history over time. Each year at

Tower, advisories focused on issues central to students' developmental, social and emotional needs: in ninth grade, they might talk a great deal about adjusting to high school, while in the second half of junior year and much of senior year, the school expected advisory to be devoted to the college search and application process.

This structure is an attempt to put in place what Stanton-Salazar (1997) refers to as "institutional support", which he defines as: "(1) The provision of funds of knowledge, (2) bridging, or the process of acting as a human bridge to gatekeepers, (3) advocacy, (4) role modeling, (5) the provision of emotional and moral support, and (6) evaluative feedback, advice and guidance" (p. 11). Stanton-Salazar notes that the structures of traditional public schools often preclude the provision of this kind of institutional support, arguing that, "Teachers and counselors may at moments take on aspects of parents and mentors, yet their support remains fundamentally conditional.... The established social order in schools does not allow the consummation or formalization of long-term committed relations" (pp. 18-19). However, the "established order" of small schools formally and intentionally creates just these kinds of long-term committed relationships between advisors and students and their families.

These relationships, and the time set aside to nurture various developmentally appropriate projects each year, translated into significant college counseling for students at Tower. Junior advisories began focusing on the college process extensively in the second half of the school year; senior advisory classes were given over almost exclusively to the college search, application and decision process for the entire year. In one of the senior advisories I observed, students took part in group discussions about their concerns about college, worked in the computer lab to research colleges and find and print out college applications, met with the advisor individually for a full period three times over the course of the year to track their progress (and many more times outside of class if they needed help), and discussed how to decide where to attend, their fears about college life and financial concerns.

Far from pro forma, these conversations occurred in the context of long-lasting connections between advisors and students (and the group of advisees, who had also been together for 4 year) and with students' families. Thus, schools like Tower have already achieved the "better high school structures and supports for students in the college search, planning, and application process," (Roderick et al., 2008) for which the most current college access research is calling.

Finally, data on New York City's small schools shows that, overall, these structural reforms are paying off in terms of decreased dropout rates and increased college-going. Several studies showed the small schools that opened in the 1980s and 90s posting impressive graduation and college-going rates for low-income youth of color (Ancess & Ort, 1999; Gladden, 1998; Sares, 1992), and more recent research reiterates these findings (see Bartlett & Koyama, Foote, Hantzopoulos, Shiller, Rivera-McCutchen, Tyner-Mullings, this volume). One large-scale study found that small high schools are posting graduation rates 6.8% higher than other New York City high schools (68.7% vs. 61.9%) (Bloom, Thompson, & Unterman, 2010); another recent study of the New Century High Schools found that 81% of seniors at these schools applied to college, and of those who applied, 85% were accepted to two or four year institutions (Huebner, Corbett, & Phillippo, 2006). Tower's numbers for graduation and college going rates were especially impressive, with between 85-90% of students graduating, and 91% of graduates accepted to and planning on attending 4-year colleges.

What Critical Small Schools Still Need to Do: Understanding and Replicating the Resources It Takes to Get to College

Critical small schools' structural reforms appear to be paying off in both higher graduation rates, and higher college application and acceptance rates. At the same time, both research data and extensive anecdotal evidence from small schools around the city attest to a continued gap in getting students to actually matriculate *into* a college—even those who, at graduation, have been accepted to and are planning to attend institutions of higher education. What happened to Willie Rivera, and is continuing to happen to his peers, despite the best efforts of their small high schools?

Part of the answer is related to larger macroeconomic realities; the rising cost of college, the falling value of real income for the middle and working classes, shifts in state and federal financial aid policy that have decreased the amount of college costs that low-income students receive help with. It is important to recognize that addressing these issues must be undertaken through larger social and political change—that schools *cannot* fix everything.

But another part of the answer is connected to the ever-increasing complexity—and expense—of the college search and application process, and the degree to which high schools provide first-generation students with the resources to successfully navigate these difficult waters. Fifty years ago, when far fewer students went on to higher education, applying to college was relatively straightforward. As greater percentages of students began to attend, both the number of colleges and the complexity of the application process expanded tremendously (Kinzie et al., 2004). Understanding the landscape of more than 3,000 colleges across the country, and what schools are looking for in their applicants, now takes increasing stores of knowledge, time and social connections; in order to be prepared, students and families need to begin earlier, and spend more money for things such as test prep, visits to campuses and filing applications; in order to be able to pay for college, families need to fill out more forms, submit more papers and apply for more scholarships than ever before. And these are things that high schools can, and should, be helping first generation students and their families navigate.

What my research at Tower revealed, however, was that while the school's existing support structures worked quite well for middle class students and families in these areas, they failed to adequately provide for the needs of working class families and students, most of whom were encountering the extensive complexities of the college search and application process for the first time. This did not appear to be because Tower's staff didn't *care* about these students, or did not *want* to help them and their families; rather, it was because teachers and counselors were most often *themselves* middle class, and therefore were acting on unconscious assumptions about what kinds of financial resources, and cultural and social capital, their students had available to them.

What kind of resources—in the form of cultural, social and economic capital—*do* middle class families bring to bear on the process of accessing higher education in the twenty-first century? Burns (2004), McDonough (1997) and Sizer (2002) all find that middle class parents provide concrete administrative, editing, and problem-solving help with their children's school work; my own research found that they did the same with the college application process, bringing their stores of cultural capital to bear on its complexities. One young woman explained, "My dad's been helping a lot. He gets the applications offline, and I fill it out on paper. Then he puts it in online." Another middle class student concurred, "My dad's helped—for a lot of stuff I don't understand, he does. Even with him helping me, I feel like I can't get it right sometimes." Another student's mother admitted somewhat sheepishly:

> I was kind of like, oh God, you know, I've got to fill out this application this weekend. And it would make me some weekends mad at Nathaniel, because it's like I'm up at 6am doing the Oberlin application and he's asleep "till eleven or whatever. And I would mention it to friends, and they were like, 'Oh, yeah, I know.' " (interview, February 24, 2004)

Additionally, as Lareau (2000) and Horvat, Weininger, and Lareau (2003) note in relation to elementary school children, middle class parents are often embedded—through both their careers and residential locations—in networks of professionals who can provide instrumental help with various concrete parts of the process. These kinds of networks provide advice, help set up interviews or otherwise negotiate access to institutional actors on college campuses for middle class seniors. One father who came into the Tower college office referenced his extensive use of his family's social networks in a conversation with Ms. Bart, the college counselor:

> Amy is interested in Sarah Lawrence, Vassar, Columbia, Bard and Columbia as her top choices right now. Vassar is her first choice—we have a friend in the building with a son there. She's going to visit Bard next week, a woman who interns where my wife works is in the office there. And we have an in at Sarah Lawrence—a woman in our building is on the board there. She's writing a letter for Amy. (field notes, October 3, 2003)

At the school, I also watched as middle class parents engaged in what Stanton-Salazar (1997) refers to as "instrumental actions" on behalf of their children's college search. Many felt comfortable coming in, calling and e-mailing teachers and college counselors with questions throughout the course of students' senior year (and sometimes as early as freshman year of high school). At a meeting with 11th grade teachers at the beginning of the school year, Ms. Bart warned, "The knob gets turned pretty hard this year with parents—you'll be getting a *lot* of email."[9] Based on observations of who "dropped by" the college counseling office often (as opposed to waiting for a scheduled appointment), middle class children confidently utilized this resource as well.

Finally, middle-class parents rely on their economic resources. Above and beyond the cost of college itself, the middle-class parents I spoke with were able to take for granted having disposable income available to meet the many costs of the application process: taking tests, paying for application fees, planning visits to college campuses.

J. Bloom:	So, how has the whole application process been this fall in terms of what you expected? Has it been harder, or easier?
Middle-class parent:	It's all online now, so that makes it a lot easier. The only difficult part was handing over my credit card every five minutes…. And also, the deadlines are all different. Mostly I figure, you know, he's got it under control. It's just when he comes to me the day before and says, "Oh mom, can you FedEx this tomorrow? It has to be out"…

(Interview, January 29, 2004)

While handing over her credit card "every five minutes" to pay for college application fees (this young man applied to eight colleges, at a cost of $40 to $75 each)—and paying an extra $30 to send an application by FedEx the day before it was due—was an annoyance, it was perceived as simply part of the process by this family.

All of these examples indicate the myriad kinds and extensive amount of dominant cultural, social and economic capital that middle class families bring to bear as their children navigate the complexities of the college application process: researching and visiting schools; finding and filling out applications; editing essays; dealing with the costs of college. Families act as experienced Sherpas, accompanying their children on their climb between institutions: guiding the way, carrying some of the heaviest loads, catching them when they stumble.

As they make their way through the college application process, these kinds of resources are much less likely to be available to young people who are one of the first in their family to attend college. Their families are far less likely to be embedded in networks that can provide help with these tasks (See Horvat, Weininger, & Lareau, 2003; Lareau, 2000; Stanton-Salazar, 1997); nor do they and their families have the same sense of comfort in asking for this help from institutional school actors (see Lareau, 2000; Stanton-Salazar, 1997). And, as noted earlier, poor and working class parents—the majority of whom did not attend college themselves—are rarely able to offer the very specific kinds of administrative help to their children that middle class parents are, for a range of reasons.

William, a working class student who was one of the six that I followed at Tower, offered a poignant reflection on this in a follow-up interview conducted once he was in college.

William:	It's easy to put off things that you are not exactly ready for. You're going to put it off in your mind because you're going to say, Oh, I'll get to that eventually; really saying, I'm scared to pieces trying to do this thing.
J. Bloom:	What was scary about it?
William:	Well, knowing that with other experiences I had more guidance from my parents. But with this experience it was a little different because a lot of things I had to do on my own—applying to colleges and writing my letter to send out and things like that. It was like, Wow, I'm doing this on my own. And then people telling you that these next four years can make or break you and stuff like that. That's a lot of stress to put on someone coming out of high school.
J. Bloom:	That makes sense. Your mom did help with some of this. When I talked to her a while back, she knew what schools you were applying to....
William:	Oh yeah, but in terms of some of the things that I had to do, I realized that she wasn't going to be able to help me because she was just as out of the loop as I was; with finding out prices of schools and things like that.

(Interview, January 15, 2005)

Another working class student struggled similarly, though her circumstances were different. She came from a family that had been upper-middle class in their native Ecuador, but was struggling financially and in other ways here (her father, an architect, did not speak English and had been unable to find anything but blue collar work in the United States). In an interview, her mother commented specifically on their lack of access to a rich trove of college-related social capital, and how it impacted her ability to help her daughter either get into college, or even understand how the process worked in a new country:

> We don't have American friends. I work in the morning, my husband works in the evenings, and we do not socialize with other families, other American persons. We are just close to my mother, my sister and brother, no one else … so sometimes I think it is just a little harder to learn more. About this country, about how things are. Because even if you read, you don't—it's not like someone who is giving you advice or suggesting because of an experience—it's not the same. It's not the same. (interview, March 9, 2004)

There were also other important resources that working-class parents didn't have at their disposal that impacted their children's college searches. One was time: as Ms. Howell, William's advisor noted,

> It's not like William's parents aren't supportive, they totally are. But they don't have time to help him. (interview, March 27, 2004)

William's mother expanded on the ways that this had been the case throughout his school career.

> When I was doing my undergrad, I was going to work, running to get William afterschool, sometimes having to take him to a babysitter. Then, go back to the babysitter to get him, then go home after school. Because in between I had to go to school. (interview, March 10, 2004)

> I was doing my internship, doing my job, going to school, coming home, trying to read a bit, then turn around next day and do the same thing. In the meantime, William, he's suffered throughout this—because I just felt that I should have been home. (interview, March 10, 2004)

Struggling to get a degree herself while holding down a full-time job, William's mother did not have the same kind of time that middle class parents did (as seen above) to provide concrete help with college applications, take William to visit college campuses or call Tower's college counselor with questions about the process.

Working-class parents also lacked access to some of the resources that money could buy to help with college applications. For example, regular and reliable computer access had been an issue throughout William's high school career. His mother explained that she had often brought him to Fordham with her when he needed to use a computer.

> If he needs something done for his school, and at one point we had problems with, we didn't have a computer ... we would come here [to Fordham] and he would get on the Internet here, and he would do his schoolwork here. (interview, March 10, 2004)

By senior year, she had used a loan to buy a computer: however, the family still did not have a printer, or reliable access to the Internet. The major impact this had on the seemingly simple task of gathering application forms can be seen in the following field note I wrote during a day at Tower:

> My date to meet William to help him find and print some college applications. We go upstairs to the computer lab, and sit down in front of two computers, but one of them doesn't work. We move across the room to another set, William signs in, and I suggest that we go to Google and put in "Lafayette College," the one he had said he wanted to start with.
>
> When we get to the Lafayette page and click on admissions, we both sit there for a minute: it's not immediately clear where to get the application. It takes a few minutes of clicking around to find the right page, which takes us to the Common Application, which Lafayette uses. But when it goes to the page, nothing comes up on the screen. I tell him to go back to the Lafayette supplement—still nothing. We realize that perhaps Adobe Acrobat hasn't been enabled on the computer. Ten minutes later, after consultation with a teacher who is staffing the lab, we access Acrobat, then go back and click on the document. Sure enough, it works! Finally we have the common application up on the screen.
>
> We hit print. Nothing comes out. We wait a minute—still nothing. The teacher comes over and says, "Don't hit print again." So we go back and sit down and wait. Nothing. The teacher comes over and fiddles with the computer. "You should go to the tech room, I know that printer is working," she tells us. I'm not sure what to do. I look at my watch - the period will be over in 15 min—this has taken ½ an hour already and we've gotten nowhere. I can't quite believe how hard it was to get these applications. And here I thought we'd be able to get all of them in one period. The websites aren't that clear; the technology screws up; it takes a LOT of steps to get this done. I decide to use my adult privilege to go down to the college office and print the Common Application out on Ms. Bart's computer; this enables William to leave with at least one of the applications he needs. He hung in through a bunch of these steps, but on his own how would he have been able to accomplish anything? (field notes, November 3, 2003)

Thus, at multiple steps along the way, William and his family ran into hurdles that families with middle class resources—such as working computers and printers in their home—sailed over without even noticing. Lack of other resources that many middle class families take for granted, like credit cards or small amounts of disposable income for unexpected expenses, continued to pose problems for William as the year continued. For example, when Ms. Howell conducted individual meetings to check in with students after Christmas break, she was surprised to find that William had not completed his applications by the January 1 deadline.

William:	Um, I didn't send out the Lafayette one yet.
Ms. Howell:	When was it due?
William:	January 1. I'm late on that. Because it turned out I needed a fee waiver. I need to give a tax return or something to Ms. Bart. It was like $50—it was too much money, so....

His family's lack of a credit card also proved to be a problem. In February, he approached me to ask:

I have a question. I need to send my SAT scores to the schools, but I'm having trouble because if you could send cash or a money order it would be okay, but you can't, you have to use a credit card. And I don't think my mom has a credit card right now. (field notes, February 11, 2004)

Over the course of his senior year, all of these small but important financial difficulties added up to a significant set of challenges for William, challenges that his middle class peers did not need to confront.

Thus, in terms of access to a range of important resources—knowledge about the landscape of higher education, college-related social capital, a certain level of disposable income—the college application process is experienced in very different ways by students from working and middle class backgrounds. How, then, can schools begin to level the playing field, and create more equal access to college for students from a range of social class backgrounds?

First, in order to *address* these inequities, schools need to *understand* them. In an institution that requires college and eventually masters degrees of all its employees, it is far too easy for schools to assemble staffs who come predominantly from middle class backgrounds, and thus had access to the wealth of resources named here when they applied and went to college themselves. It may be difficult for these staffs to forsee the spots where their working class students will stumble: to imagine the texture of life without a computer or credit card, to understand how bewildering the application process is if others who have gone through it themselves cannot walk you through it.

Without this knowledge, it is far too easy to read students' struggles as a failure of compliance, or simply as mystifying. For example, discovering William had missed the January 1 application deadline for Lafayette, Ms. Howell exclaimed:

> I don't understand! William turns in all of his work on time—it's never an issue. I just don't get it ... it's weird. I don't know what to do. (field notes, March 20, 2004)

While Ms. Howell was extremely sympathetic, and aware that William's family did not have the same set of circumstances as some of his more well-off peers, she also struggled to anticipate—or know how to help with—the many problems he seemed to keep running into throughout his senior year.

Ms. Bart, the college counselor, was similarly baffled, and often frustrated. William came up in our conversations several times throughout the year:

> I don't understand: he gets good grades, doesn't he? (field notes, November 9, 2003)

> I just don't get what's up with him. I know he's a good student, but he just doesn't seem very on top of things. (field notes, January 12, 2004)

> I worry—he doesn't seem to understand what to do, I don't know what the problem is. And if he needs this much hand-holding, what's going to happen when he does go to college? I just worry sometimes with the amount of hand-holding we do here. (field notes, March 29, 2004)

I heard similar sentiments echoed by other teachers at Tower, and more widely by middle class teachers and counselors at other schools in the wider study. In order to be truly helpful to their working class students, educators need to understand much more explicitly the resources that applying to college in the twenty-first century requires, and the ways that access to those resources exist—or do not exist—in the worlds of students from different backgrounds.

Second, armed with this understanding, schools serving working class students need to create structures that *replicate* the dominant cultural and social capital available to middle class students in their college search and application process. They need to begin in ninth grade to help students and families understand the landscape of college, rather than assuming that they already understand it; throughout high school, they need to provide experiences that will build families' and students' college-related capital, exposing them to and facilitating conversations with a wide range of actors in the world of higher education (e.g., recent graduates. professors and

administrators, professionals who can talk about how their college education connects to their work); in 11th and 12th grade, they need to provide
specific and individual administrative help with each piece of the college
application process, and concrete resources such as computer access, ways
for students to visit campuses they hope to attend, and help with getting
waivers for college application and test fees. All of these resources are indis-
pensible if students are to conduct a thorough, well-informed and successful
search for a postsecondary path that makes sense for them.

CONCLUSION

In its 25 year history, the movement for critical small high schools in New
York City has put in place an important set of institutional beliefs and
structures. These include (1) the removal of academic tracking and creation of educational structures that support high expectations for academic performance by all students, (2) the creation of college-going
cultures that create and support student expectations for college attendance, and view the transition to college as the work of high schools, and
(3) "advisory" or "family group" systems that seek to ensure that all young
people are known well, and that school staff are connected to families and
students' worlds outside of school. All of these practices are cited in current research on college access as exactly what is needed to support first
generation college students in their transition to higher education.
Therefore, New York City's critical small schools serve as important models for schools around the country in how to re-invent their work on college access *within* high school institutions.

At the same time, while most of New York City's critical small schools
are experiencing above-average success with college access, they often are
not—as my colleague articulated so poignantly in his e-mail—meeting
the much higher standards that they set for themselves. If Willie Rivera's
hard work to get academically ready for college (and his teachers' hard
work to help him) is not paying off in college enrollment and persistence,
then these schools are not succeeding in the mission they set for themselves. What the research in this chapter suggests is that, in order to
achieve this mission, critical small school educators must become more
aware of the multiple cultural and social capital, and financial, resources
that middle class families utilize to propel their children through the college search and application process—and of the ways in which so many of
these resources lie out of reach of first-generation students.

In doing so, educators must tackle the hard work of sorting out their own,
often unexamined, assumptions about higher education; they must separate their own experiences of the transition to college from their students';

as I argue elsewhere (Bloom, 2007), they must take care not to mis-read students' aspirations, motivations and actions based on their own lives.

And then, since as many researchers point out, schools are an important source of social and cultural college-going capital for low-income students (McDonough 1997, 2004; Mehan et al., 1996; Tierney, 2002; Tierney & Venegas, 2006), critical small schools must take the next step of *leveraging* the structures that they have in place to order to replicate for working class students the college-going resources that middle class families and students take for granted. In this way, they can create the "enabling conditions" (Fine & McClelland, 2006) that are necessary for a successful transition to college in the twenty-first century. These efforts are already underway at several networks of small schools,[10] but they must be shared and spread, and incorporated more deeply into the fabric of each school's work. As we all recognize, Willie Rivera deserves no less.

NOTES

1. All names in this article (of individuals and of schools) are pseudonyms.
2. Support for the research in this article came from the Spencer Foundation Social Justice and Social Development in Education Studies Training Grant; writing was also supported through grants from the Spencer Foundation and the ASHE/Lumina Foundation for Education.
3. Though it began with a similar size and student body profile to many of the other small critical high schools (that is, under 400 students, predominantly low-income students of color), for a range of reasons, by the time this research was done, Tower was considerably larger and more racially and socioeconomically diverse than many other schools in the movement.
4. The purpose and structure of advisory will be explained in greater detail in a later section of the chapter.
5. In choosing these students, I attempted to have a balance of males and females, and students from different racial and socioeconomic backgrounds. I enlisted the advisors' help in identifying students who might be interested in participating and who would help to achieve this balance; following McDonough (1997), I defined "middle class" by looking at whether or not both parents had bachelor's degrees and were employed in professional occupations. Of the seven students I approached about interviewing them and their parents, six agreed to participate. The six included one African American male (working class) and two White males (both middle class), one White female (middle class) and two Latina females (both working class). It is difficult not to notice the overlap of race/ethnicity and social class in even this very small sample; however, it is broadly reflective of the demographics of Tower's population, and of course, of larger societal patterns in this country. Scholars examining class processes note that race and class are heavily confounded in the United States (Conley, 1999; Lareau &

Horvat, 1999; Oliver & Shapiro, 1997). Lewis (2006) writes, in relation to her ethnographic work, "It is impossible to separate the realities of class from those of race" (p. 179), and I found these two factors similarly difficult to untangle in this research. In this study, however, I sought to attend particularly to cultural capital *as it related to social class*, though there were many points at which it seems likely that race/ethnicity played an important role as well. Future research might seek to explore in greater depth the intersections of race and class in the transition to college for first-generation students.

6. Overall, within the three schools, I did 32 sets of observations, conducted 12 focus groups and 13 interviews with parents and school staff, and collected 127 surveys.

7. New York City's critical small schools were created in order to counteract exactly these kinds of structural barriers.

8. This is another structural barrier that New York City's critical small schools have endeavored to break down; many have much smaller ratios, with a college counselor working with senior classes of less than 100 students.

9. Lareau (2000) also notes this confidence and sense of entitlement in dealing with school personnel with middle class parents interfacing with elementary schools.

10. Both Urban Assembly and the Institute for Student Achievement have created substantial programs that put in place the kind of "enabling conditions" described above.

REFERENCES

Adelman, C. (2002). The relationship between urbanicity and educational outcomes. In W. Tierney & L. Hagedorn (Eds.), *Increasing access to college: Extending possibilities to all students* (pp. 35-63). Albany, NY: State University of New York Press.

Ancess, J., & Ort, S. (1999). *How the campus coalition schools have re-imagined high school: Seven years later. Executive summary.* New York, NY: National Center for Restructuring Education, Schools and Teaching. Teachers College, Columbia University.

Avery, C., Fairbanks, A., & Zeckhauser, R. (2003). *The early admissions game: Joining the elite.* Cambridge, MA: Harvard University Press.

Bloom, J. (2007). (Mis)reading social class in the journey towards college: Youth development in urban America. *Teachers College Record, 109*(2), 343-368.

Bloom, H., Thompson, S., & Unterman, R. (2010). *Transforming the high school experience: How New York City's new small schools are boosting student achievement and graduation rates.* New York, NY: MDRC.

Bourdieu, P. (1986). The forms of capital. In J. G. Richardson (Ed.), *Handbook of theory and research for the sociology of education.* New York, NY: Greenwood Press.

Burns, A. (2004). The racing of capability and culpability in desegregated schools: Discourses of merit and responsibility. In M. Fine, L. Weis, L. P. Pruitt & A.

Burns (Eds.), *Off white: Readings on power, privilege and resistance* (2nd ed.) New York, NY: Routledge.

Carnevale, A., & Rose, S. (2004). Socioeconomic status, race/ethnicity, and selective college admissions. In R. Kahlenberg (Ed.), *America's untapped resource: Low-income students in higher education* (pp. 101-156). New York, NY: The Century Foundation.

Carter, P. (2003). "Black" cultural capital, status positioning, and schooling conflicts for low-income African American youth. *Social Problems, 50*(1), 136-155.

Choy, S. (1998). *College access and affordability: Findings from the condition of education 1998* (No. NCES 1999-108). Washington, DC: National Center for Education Statistics, U.S. Department of Education.

Conley, D. (1999). *Being black, living in the red: Race, wealth, and social policy in America*. Berkeley, CA: University of California Press.

Dynarski, S., & Scott-Clayton, J. (2006). *The cost of complexity in federal student aid: Lessons from optimal tax theory and behavioral economics* (Working paper No.12227). Cambridge, MA: National Bureau of Economic Research.

Fine, M. & McClelland, S. (2006). Sexuality education and desire: Still missing after all these years. *Harvard Educational Review, 76*(3), 297-340.

Gandara, P. (2002). Meeting common goals: Linking K-12 and college interventions. In W. Tierney & L. Hagedorn (Eds.), *Increasing access to college: Extending possibilities to all students* (pp. 81-103). Albany, NY: State University of New York Press.

Gladden, R. (1998). The small school movement: A review of the literature. In M. Fine & J. Somerville (Eds.), *Small schools, big imaginations* (pp. 113-137). Chicago, IL: Cross City Campaign for Urban School Reform.

Gladieux, L. (2004). Low income students and the affordability of higher education. In R. Kahlenberg (Ed.), *America's untapped resource: Low-income students in higher education* (pp. 17-57). New York, NY: The Century Foundation Press.

Hagedorn, L., & Fogel, S. (2002). Making school to college programs work: Academics, goals and aspirations. In W. Tierney & L. Hagedorn (Eds.), *Increasing access to college: Extending possibilities to all students* (pp. 169-193). Albany, NY: State University of New York Press.

Haycock, K. & Huang, S. (2001). Youth at the crossroads: Facing high school and beyond. *Thinking K-16. Education Trust, 5*(1), 3-22.

Heller, D. (2005). Can minority students afford college in an era of skyrocketing tuition? In. G. Orfield, P. Marin and C. Horn (Eds.), *Higher education and the color line: College access, racial equity and social change*. Cambridge, MA: Harvard University Press.

Horvat, E., Weininger, E., & Lareau, A. (2003). From social ties to social capital: Class differences in the relations between schools and parent networks. *American Educational Research Journal, 40*(2), 319-351.

Huebner, T., Corbett, G. & Phillippo, K. (2006). *Rethinking high school: Inaugural graduations at New York City's new high schools*. San Francisco, CA: WestEd.

Kane, T. (1999). *The price of admission: Rethinking how Americans pay for college*. Washington DC: Brookings Institution Press.

King, J. (2004). *Missed opportunities: Students who do not apply for financial aid*: United States: American Council on Education.

Kinzie, J., Palmer, M., Hayek, J., Hossler, D., Jacob, S., & Cummings, H. (2004). *Fifty years of college choice: Social, political and institutional influences on the decision-making process* (No. Volume 5, Number 3): Indianapolis, IN: Lumina Foundation for Education.

Knight, M., Norton, N., Bentley, C., & Dixon, I. (2003). The power of black and Latina/o counterstories: Urban families and college-going processes. *Anthropology & Education Quarterly, 35*(1), 99-120.

Lareau, A. (2000). *Home advantage: Social class and parental intervention in elementary education* (2nd ed.). Lanham, MD: Rowman & Littlefield.

Lareau, A., & Horvat, E. (1999). Moments of social inclusion and exclusion: Race, class and cultural capital in family-school relationships. *Sociology of Education, 72*(1), 37-53.

Lewis, A. (2006). Whiteness in school: How race shapes black students' opportunities. In E. Horvat & C. O'Connor (Eds.), *Beyond acting white: Reframing the debate on black student achievement* (pp. 176-199). Lanham, MD: Rowman & Littlefield.

McDonough, P. (1997.) *Choosing colleges: How social class and schools structure opportunity.* Albany, NY: State University of New York Press.

McDonough, P. (2004). *The school-to-college transition: Challenges and prospects.* Washington, DC: American Council on Education. Center for Policy Analysis.

McDonough, P. (2005). Counseling matters: Knowledge, assistance, and organizational commitment in college preparation. In W. Tierney, Z. Corwin, & J. Colyar (Eds.), *Preparing for college: Nine elements of effective outreach* (pp. 69-87). Albany, NY: State University of New York Press.

Mehan, H., Villanueva, I., Hubbard, L., & Lintz, A. (1996). *Constructing school success: The consequences of untracking low-achieving students.* Cambridge, England: Cambridge University Press.

Meier, D. (1995). *The power of their ideas: Lessons for America from a small school inHarlem.* Boston. MA: Beacon Press.

Mumper, M. (1996). *Removing college price barriers: What government has done and why it hasn't worked.* Albany, NY: SUNY Press.

Nieto, S. (1992). *Affirming diversity: The sociopolitical context of multicultural education.* New York, NY: Longman.

Oakes, J. (1985). *Keeping track: How schools structure inequality.* New Haven: Yale University Press.

Oliver, M., & Shapiro, T. (1997). *Black wealth/white wealth: A new perspective on racial inequality.* New York, NY: Routledge.

Pathways to College Network. (2004, February). *A shared agenda: A leadership challenge to improve college access and success.* Washington, DC:Institute for Higher Education Policy.

Perna, L., Rowan-Kenyon, H., Thomas, S., Bell, A., Anderson, R., & Li, C. (2008). The role of college counseling in shaping college opportunity: Variations across high schools. *The Review of Higher Education, 31*(2), 131-159.

Paulsen, M., & St. John, P. (2002). Social class and college costs: Examining the financial nexus between college choice and persistence. *Journal of Higher Education, 73*(2), 190-235.

Roderick, M., Nagaoka, J., Coca, V., Moeller, E., Roddie, K., Gilliam, J., & et al. (2008). *From high school to the future: Potholes on the road to college.* Chicago, IL: Consortium on Chicago School Research at the University of Chicago.

Rosenbaum, J. (2001). *Beyond college for all: Career paths for the forgotten half.* New York, NY: Russell Sage Foundation.

Sares, T. (1992, April). *School size effects on educational attainment and ability.* Paper presented at the annual meeting of the American Educational Research Association, San Francisco, CA.

Sizer, N. (2002). *Crossing the stage: Redesigning senior year.* Portsmouth, NH: Heinemann.

Social Science Research Council Project. (2005, Fall). Transitions to college: From theory to practice. *Questions that matter: Setting the research agenda on access and success in postsecondary education.* Brooklyn, NY: Social Science Research Council.

Stanton-Salazar, R. (1997). A social capital framework for understanding the socialization of racial minority children and youths. *Harvard Educational Review, 67*(1), 1-34.

Stanton-Salazar, R. (2001). *Manufacturing hope and despair: The school and kin support networks of U.S.-Mexican youth.* New York, NY: Teachers College Press.

Terenzini, P., Cabrera, A., & Bernal, E. (2001). *Swimming against the tide: The poor in American higher education.* New York, NY: The College Board.

Tierney, W. (2002). Parents and families in precollege preparation: The lack of connection between research and practice. *Educational Policy, 16*(4), 588-606.

Tierney, W., & Colyar, J. (2006). *Urban high school students and the challenge of access: Many routes, difficult paths.* New York, NY: Peter Lang.

Tierney, W., & Venegas, K. (2006). Fictive kin and social capital: The role of peer groups in applying and paying for college. *American Behavioral Scientist, 49*(12), 1687-1702.

Venezia, A., Kirst, M., & Antonio, A. (2003). *Betraying the college dream: How disconnected K-12 and postsecondary education systems undermine student aspirations.* The Bridge Project, Stanford Institute for Higher Education Research.

CHAPTER 10

WHEN CULTURES COLLIDE

Students' Successes and Challenges as Transformative Change Agents Within and Beyond a Democratic School

Maria Hantzopoulos

INTRODUCTION

Nestled in two small, run-down corridors of a larger public high school facility in Manhattan, Humanities Preparatory Academy (Prep) is surprisingly unassuming. At first glance at its cramped physical space, not many would suspect that this school maintains very high graduation and college acceptance rates for the youth who come through its doors. Originally designed as a "mini-school" program within a larger school for students who were underserved and potentially at risk for "dropping out"[1] the founders sought to create a school culture that both rigorously engaged this population and prepared them for college. The program gradually expanded and, four years later in 1997, with the financial and technical support from New Visions for Public Schools,[2] Prep became an autonomous public school. While the school now serves a more heterogeneous population than at its founding as a program (it educates both students

Critical Small Schools: Beyond Privatization in
New York City Urban Educational Reform, pp. 189–212
Copyright © 2012 by Information Age Publishing
All rights of reproduction in any form reserved.

who have struggled academically and those who have experienced academic success), it maintains a distinct learning environment that attempts to engage all students "by personalizing [their] learning situations, by democratizing and humanizing the school environment, and by creating a 'talking culture,' an atmosphere of informal intellectual discourse among students and faculty" (Humanities Preparatory Mission Statement, n.d.). Thus, by constructing a radically alternative educational environment rooted in democratic principles, this school presents itself as a "critical" small school that ostensibly provides a transformative and libratory experience for its students with repercussions beyond the sphere of schooling.

The purpose of this chapter is twofold: to both (1) provide descriptive narratives of the structures, pedagogies and processes within and beyond the classroom that the school community attributes to its successes, and (2) illuminate some of the challenges facing students and teachers while enacting democratic and socially transformative approaches to schooling. While I argue that these structures and processes support the academic socialization and achievement of these youth, I also focus my analysis on the ways that students and alumni make meaning of the school's core values and mission, mindful of how these beliefs are internalized, processed, and negotiated in their everyday life experiences.

Based on ethnographic research conducted between 2005-2008, including student, alumni, and staff interviews, participant observation, anecdotal surveys, and text analysis, I argue that Prep engages youth academically through intentionally creating a culture of care (through strong-student teacher relationships), a culture of respect (though operationalizing the school's core values), and a culture of questioning (through a thematic, culturally-relevant, inquiry and project-based curriculum).[3] This comprehensive approach to school culture, in turn, encourages democratic participation, "collective" critical consciousness, and a commitment to social change. It also helps socialize students academically, giving them a platform from which to think about the world differently and imagine alternatives for the future. As a result, many of the practices at Prep, like the other schools presented in this volume, are informative for the broader critical small schools movement.

A closer look at the experiences of current students and alumni, however, indicates that they also encounter barriers to their sense of "voice" and their agency to affect change when confronted with external "realities" within and beyond the school. Thus, while the school does manage to create a more humanizing and democratizing environment, alumni and students also describe brushing up against values antithetical to those that the school promote, and in some cases, feel Prep sheltered them from figuring out ways to navigate these circumstances. Despite these perceived imitations, I also illuminate how young people circumvent these barriers when confronted with these obstacles by negotiating their agency to their advantage. By exploring through their own experiences how students make meaning of the school's values, both when they are easily assimilated and when there is more evident tension, this chapter provides keen insight into the complexities of enacting an educational program that emphasizes liberation, transformation and social justice. It not only calls into question how the school might prepare students to negotiate these tensions when they arise, but also raises broader questions about the extent to which education can be transformative when larger structural inequalities exist.

BACKGROUND ON HUMANITIES PREPARATORY ACADEMY

As one of the original, "critical" small schools, Prep is simultaneously a typical and an atypical high school in NYC. Demographically, the school serves a student body that spans the socioeconomic, racial and ethnic spectra of New York City. During part of my fieldwork in 2006-2007, the student body identified as 40% Latino, 38% Black, 12% White, 6% Asian, and 4% other. Twelve percent were enrolled in special education, which is slightly above the city average of 11%. This percentage did not include students who had been decertified from special education status, but still received auxiliary services from the school. Approximately 54% of the population at the time qualified for free and reduced price lunch (FRPL is often used as an indicator for the level of poverty in a school), though the administration of Prep does not believe that this is an accurate measure because high school students often do not return the requisite forms, opting instead to skip lunch or eat off campus. Overall, the school is successful as measured by graduation and college acceptance rates. For example, the school has averaged 91% to 100% college acceptance rates since it opened in 1997, while the city-wide rate had not risen above 62% during that same period (Performance Assessment, 2010). The dropout rate is consistently under 4%, as opposed to the city rate of 19.9% (Performance Assessment, 2010).[4]

From the outset, Prep has remained unwavering in its commitment to student-centered education, critical pedagogy, and the school's core values of peace, justice, democracy and respect for humanity, intellect, truth and diversity (Humanities Preparatory Mission Statement, n.d). According to most teachers interviewed and much of the institutional literature, these aspects are not only included explicitly in the school's mission, but also are intentionally woven into classroom and school community practices. For instance, teachers (and students) explicitly use the core values by integrating them into classes, using them as benchmarks for community norms, and awarding students at end term ceremonies for their commitment to them. School governance also reflects such commitments as the structure is flattened and democratized, so that staff, parents, and students are invited to create and shape school policy and practices. While there is a principal at the school's helm, most teachers hold administrative roles, allowing for shared-leadership and consensus-based decision-making. According to most teachers interviewed, this allows for innovation in curriculum design and scheduling, and contributes to teacher "buy-in" (see Hantzopoulos, 2009).

The school is also one of few public high schools in New York City with heterogeneously grouped classes so that there are no prerequisites based on grade levels or ability for students to take most classes.[5] Students therefore choose classes based on interest and meet with an advisor to ensure that their choices fulfill both the state distribution requirements and student-set academic goals. Instead of the Regents' based standardized high-stakes testing used in the New York system, Prep supports a holistic form of assessment known as performance-based assessment (PBA), which resembles the college or graduate level thesis system. Over the course of a year, a student works on an individualized project in a particular subject area. While the projects are student-generated and self-directed, the student is mentored by a teacher until she is ready to present her final work. When the student is ready to present, a panel of two teachers and an outside evaluator[6] use a common rubric to determine whether or not the student needs to revise and re-present her work or if she is ready to move on to another project. This type of assessment has allowed for the creation of student- and teacher-generated courses that reflect thematic approaches; it is not uncommon to find courses like The American Dream, Math and Social Justice, or Water in the catalog. These types of assessments are also seen as a way to foster democratic and inquiry-based learning (Meier, 2004) since students, ideally, generate projects around their own interests and questions they have about the world. Moreover, the classes that students take, which also act as preparation for PBAs, reflect thematic and inquiry-based learning (see Foote, this volume, for more on this).

In addition to project-based assessment, the school has other structures that support learning, critical dialogue, and democratic participation, such as advisory, town meeting and the fairness committee. Advisory is a daily class period of 15 students in which they discuss issues relevant to their lives, receive academic support, develop leadership skills, and build community with other members of their group. On a typical day, one could walk into an advisory and see a workshop on college readiness; in another, a heated discussion about the pay-scale of female athletes; in another, an emotional exploration about the causes of relationship abuse.

Town Meetings,[7] weekly whole-school gatherings at which students and teachers discuss a myriad of personal, community, school-wide, national, and global issues, often build and expand upon the themes explored in Advisory. Topics are selected by students in their advisories and, each week, a different Advisory facilitates the discussion or debate around the selected issue. Like advisory topics, Town Meeting agenda items range, but this space is often used by students to discuss school policies (like the bathroom or lateness policies) as well as explore larger "world/local issues" like environmental racism, political prisoners, and military recruitment in schools. Often, guest speakers are invited to come to the town meetings.

Finally, the fairness committee is an integral structure that is unique to the school. Often framed as a form of "restorative justice,"[8] it is a mechanism through which students can discuss with one another, and with teachers, violations of the community's core values, as well as brainstorm alternatives and solutions to these dilemmas. Examples where a teacher or student might be taken to the fairness committee include inappropriate language, missing class, and vandalism. When a committee is convened, they are encouraged to ask questions, listen to all parties, and help uncover what transpired. The structure emphasizes process and real dialogue over product and fixed outcome, so the end result is sui generis to each particular committee meeting (see Hantzopoulos, 2006/2011). Overall, it is within advisory, town meeting and fairness that students and teachers are able to influence school-wide policy through a direct democratic model and emphasis on critical dialogue and debate.

According to the principal at the time of the research, Vincent Brevetti, this democratic model requires that the student population remain under 200 to be able to provide the type of education that it does, although ideally, it would be set at 150 (interview, March 19, 2007). The rationale for a relatively small student population is to provide a more personalized learning environment so that adults can work closely with students; however, at 150 students, a "critical mass" is maintained that allows for a diversity and exchange of different forms of knowledge. This number is, in fact, smaller than most current small schools that average 400 students. In April 2007, the school population at Prep was 163 students and the number fluctuated between 160 and 183 throughout my fieldwork. While students and alumni repeatedly refer to the importance of the small size of the school community, as well as the aforementioned structures that help re-engage them academically (see Hantzopoulos, 2011), they also indicate the relevance of overall school culture that enables them to learn and grow in meaningful ways. In this sense, small is certainly fundamental, but alone, does not fulfill the critical mission of the school. It is simply one of many tools that permit such an environment to flourish.

METHODOLOGY

As a former teacher at Prep, I was interested in a more in-depth under-standing of how former and current students felt about their experiences at a school that emphasized academics, as well as democratic structures and a culture of core values. By privileging students' perspectives, I agree with Noguera (2006) that:

> Students may not have all the answers to the problems plaguing urban schools. This does not mean that they may not have ideas on improving schools on a wide variety of issues ... [they] may very well have ideas and insights that adults are not privy to, and that could prove to be very helpful to improving schools if adults were willing to listen. (p. 209)

In order to understand more closely students' experiences, I felt a qualita-tive approach, based on ethnographic methods, was best suited for my design. Since qualitative research is rooted in the methods of participant observation, individual and group interviews, and document analysis, I employed all of these methods in my study over the course of two years. I also collected 231 surveys to retrieve demographic data, select interview participants, and obtain cursory anecdotal data about students' experi-ence in the school.

Central to data collection was participant observations, and there were several overlapping phases of this throughout the duration of my study (which began in September 2005 and ended in June 2007). These included school-based participant observation of actors (and my interac-tions with them) within the school and "off-site" participant observation of former and current students in spaces outside the sphere of the school. I recorded and logged daily field-notes about what I observed in the class-room, hallways, and other spaces where students were engaged in school-related activity.

Another key feature of the research process was semi-structured inter-views, which served as a way to obtain information that was "simply not amenable to observation, so that asking people about [the participants] represents the only viable means of finding out about them within a qual-itative research strategy" (Bryman 2006, p. 329). Specifically, I conducted in-depth semi-structured interviews with 20 former students, 6 current students, and 14 faculty members. I employed a semistructured inter-viewing method because it allowed me to gain more flexibly legitimate access to the world-views of participants, and not lose sight of the specific needs of my study (Bryman, 2006).

I also conducted five focus group discussions with current students who were not interviewed individually but indicated on the survey that they were willing to participate. These focus groups assisted in obtaining perspectives that I did not get through my interviews (Fontana & Frey, 1998), particularly as many students were accustomed to group discussions, one of the central pedagogical practices in the school. In that sense, focus group discussions emulated the way that naturalistic phenomena normally occurred in the school. By triangulating the study through the usage of multiple methods, I was able to increase the internal reliability and validity of the study (Maxwell, 2005).

Finally, I engaged in a dually inductive and deductive process of data interpretation. Every 2 weeks, I reviewed my field-notes and transcriptions to capture the themes emerging from the data as I was in the process of collection. Every 2 months, I re-read my notes and memos to both develop data displays that modeled the developing analysis and search for negative cases. Sometimes, this forced me to recode units of data and revise the codes accordingly. When I wrote up my findings post-field-work, I had already interpreted and analyzed much of the data.

While my role as a former teacher at the school may raise questions about objectivity, I employed phenomenological approaches to my observations so that I could continually "strange-make," discover phenomena anew, and allow for the emergence of emic concepts (LeCompte & Preissle, 1993; Marshall & Rossman, 1999). Moreover, qualitative research rejects the assumption that true objectivity in any type of research is achievable. In fact, this position as "insider" worked as an advantage, as my previous experience and history with the school made me much more qualified to conduct the ethnographic work that required deep immersion into the culture and phenomenon being studied.

CREATING SCHOOL CULTURE:
CARE, RESPECT AND QUESTIONING

While teachers and administrators might assume to know what practices matter, *students'* perceptions of what matters most to their successes often diverge from this. The following section focuses on specific aspects of the school culture that students identify as central to their academic socialization and sense of belonging in the school. According to the data, students suggest that there is a culture of care manifest in the strong student-teacher relationships; a culture of respect rooted in the school based Core Values; and a culture of questioning and activism, implemented in part through thematic, culturally-relevant and inquiry/project-based curriculum that encourages democratic participation, "collective" critical consciousness, and a commitment to social change. Taken together, these elements of school culture not only contribute to student academic success in school, but also provide students with ways to imagine and create alternative frameworks for engaging in the world and thinking about the future.

Culture of Care: Strong Student-Teacher Relationships and Beyond

As indicated in several other chapters in this volume, relationships are essential to student academic socialization and success in school (see Bartlett & Koyama; De Jesús; Rivera-McCutchen; Shiller; Tyner-Mullings). It is no different at Prep. Resoundingly, former and current students express feeling comfortable at Prep and often described their experiences with peers and teachers as "family-like," welcoming, supportive, and community-oriented. Further, when students talk about teachers as friends or family, it is embedded in a concept of care that is not paternal, but more akin to people with whom they feel comfortable, seek advice, get extra help, and generally converse with about myriad issues. The following passage, written by Joey, a senior, exemplifies this:

> It's hard to find teachers in other high schools that are like Prep because they're very focused on you as an individual, they really want you to excel and it's more of like, let me see—the relationship, yeah to some extent it is teacher/student, but it's more of a family and they really genuinely care about the students so even if you do have an issue it's not like, you know, you have to worry about being reprimanded or you're going to be punished or sent to detention. It's more of like having that open communication as a student, which is really important. (interview, April 12, 2007)

Repeatedly, many students discuss how these relationships contribute to an increased sense of confidence, belonging, and academic success. The majority of current and former students interviewed even suggest that their relationships with their teachers in high school helped them talk to other adults beyond school; in fact, for those alumni in college, they note that their experiences at Prep make professors in college more approachable.

While there is a body of literature on caring and relationships in schools that germinates from liberal feminist perspectives (see Belenky, Clinchy, Goldberger, & Tarule, 1997; Gilligan, 1982; Noddings, 1992), many critics have shed light on how these theories fail to incorporate *cultural* notions of caring. Several scholars (Antorp-Gonzalez & De Jesús, 2005; De Jesús, this volume; Valenzuela, 1999) demonstrate, through ethnographic work with Latino youth, that sometimes teachers' notions of caring clash with those of their students and, thus, argue for more *authentic* forms of caring that align with familial and cultural expectations.

These theorists suggest that high expectations for students, in an authentic caring environment, lead to increased confidence and academic achievement among Latino students (Antrop-Gonzalez & De Jesús, 2005; Rodriguez & Conchas, 2008).

Similarly, findings from this study suggests that Prep teachers adopt more of a critical care model in relationship to their students, though these students are not exclusively Latino and come from diverse ethnic, racial and socioeconomic backgrounds. Bajaj (2009) extends this notion of culturally-based caring to context-based caring, suggesting that studies of caring have been "context-blind." She urges greater consideration of the "larger social, economic, and political structures that surround schools" to comprehend what happens within them (p. 21). While students at Prep come from a variety of settings, many face social and economic hardships (i.e., incarcerated parents or siblings, homelessness, foster care, responsibility for raising siblings, and necessary outside employment) that are often overlooked by schools. Though these examples are not the case for every student, many students at Prep share the experience of feeling uncared for in their previous schools, making schooling a marginalizing rather than inclusive experience. This is particularly the case for transfer students. For instance, Nelson, an alumnus, compares and contrasts Prep with his old school (as well as public schools in general) in the anecdotal portion of his survey:

> Public schools are a mess. Public schools more often lend themselves to creating mindless students who are taught only to memorize facts from state-mandated learning "materials." The teachers don't care, punishment is more important than learning, and the social structure within the schools is based on class/race and often creates life-long psychological scars. In short, I hated my old school and most of the people within it; I learned nothing there except how to hate, and maybe a few facts about World War II. (survey, n.d.)

Nelson's description evokes some of the critiques that public schools emphasize standardization over creativity, punishment over learning, and ultimately, reproduce some of the hegemonic social structures in society at large. His narrative about Prep, written in the same survey, is remarkably different:

> Attending Prep was like getting to live in a free country after living for many years in a not-so-free country. Prep works on a different model. While still adhering to state standards, Prep somehow (whether through the spirit of the teachers or from the diversity of the students, or the emphasis on community) manages to teach and inspire within the mess of public education. The difference between Prep and other schools is so obvious to me—

because I experienced it—that I have trouble describing it. If not for Prep I would never have gone to college; I would never have been afforded a different point of view; I would have never have enjoyed education; I would never have sought to better myself.

This passage from Nelson is full of hope and potential. While he presents ambiguity about how Prep "works on a different model," he actually does in fact suggest concrete reasons that are resonant with an authentic care framework that makes school enjoyable and inspires him to go on to college, among other things. While there may be other factors that contribute to these outcomes, he depicts an almost opposite scenario from his previous school, where teachers "don't care," suggesting that at Prep, there is intentionality in a counterpractice that simultaneously adheres to "school standards."

Lisa also describes in her survey a scenario in her old school (a Catholic school) that indicates that she was on the verge of dropping out. Her mother chose the Catholic school over her local public school, despite struggling to pay the tuition. While she always considered herself a good student, Lisa struggled in this environment:

I left [School X] because I felt like the primary focus of the school was to mold everyone of us into people that they wanted us to be. There was no room for self-expression and individuality. Classroom lessons focused around lecturing. There was no form of interactive learning such as group discussions. There were constant forms of disciplinary actions practiced against petty incidences [sic]. Like for example, the first day of my sophomore year I did not have the money for my books... Because I didn't have the money right when they wanted and refused to acknowledge my financial situation, I was sent to detention. Detention at my school was not a time to do extra assignments or homework like most schools do. We had to stand and face the board until they decided we can go. That day I was there for an hour. It was ridiculous! I was punished for something that was beyond my control. During junior year I was beginning to lose interest in going to school. I stopped going and did not care about my work. This was so out of the norm for me because all my life prior to that moment I was an excellent student. I was failing one class after the other as time passed. I did not want to dropout of school. (survey, n.d.)

Like Nelson, she emphasizes, in more detail, excessive punishment at her previous school; yet, she also describes how her experience in that school killed her desire to learn. Moreover, she feels that the school failed to recognize her family's financial hardships, thereby not caring about her particular economic context, further leading to her alienation. Her description of Prep contrasts greatly:

Transferring to Prep was the best decision I made for myself during my high school career. I saw myself as being more than that [a dropout] and it was at that moment I realized that my future is in my hands. I called several high schools and Prep was the only school that would accept students at any point during their high school career. I was a 2nd semester junior. I loved Prep! I loved all my classes and I was encouraged to have a voice in the classroom. Prep teachers believed in their students regardless who they were and where they came from. We were seen as individuals and embraced for it. Classroom lessons were held in group discussions which helped me retain what I was being taught. I can honestly say that I learned way more at Prep than I did at [School X]. My education up until Prep seems like one big blur. Prep also made it important that its students would be in touch with the world around them by taking out sometime once a week to talk about current events in big group discussions called quads. Prep opened up my eyes to the world around. Because of prep I was able to form an idea of what I wanted to do in life. I had realized how much I loved writing and having the opportunity to have a voice, and that's when I thought studying journalism in college was something I was going to do.

Lisa is now a college graduate with a degree in Communications and Media Studies. In her description of Prep, she underscores many of the themes and structures that emerged in my research that helped define her experience at Prep, including the type of pedagogy and classes, an emphasis on voice and current events, and belief in the ability of all students. Most importantly, she writes about being re-engaged academically, describing how she was on the verge of "dropping out" and how she was pulled back in. Authentic caring, therefore, is not simply about demonstrating care, but also about rethinking school structures that foster an environment that believes in the potential and worth of students and their abilities.

Moreover, students consistently cite feeling acknowledged by teachers as more than just students, contributing to a sense that there is less of an authoritative and hierarchical structure than that which usually defines student-teacher relationships. For instance, Franz, an alumnus, wrote, "The teacher/student boundaries were blurred, and the teachers learned as much from the students as the students did from them" (survey, n.d.). Additionally, in interviews, focus groups and surveys, students repeatedly describe teachers at Prep as "down-to-earth" and "open" to sharing their experiences, reinforcing notions that teachers perceive students as "equals." According to Selma, an alumna, this equalized status serves as a "source of hope and inspiration" for her because she feels validated as a human being (January 23, 2007).

While many scholars (Bartlett, 2005; Oyler & Backer, 1997) have critiqued the ways that egalitarian relationships between students and teachers are ultimately conceptualized and enacted in schools (describing many of their manifestations as limiting, "soft," and too lenient), this study suggests that students and teachers and Prep endeavor to share authority, rather than one group solely possessing or abdicating it. For instance, Dalia, an alumna, recalls the environment at the school as one that "was wonderful because there was no structure or apartheid, if I can use that word, between teachers, students, everyone interacted with each other, everyone looked at one another as equals and it created a true sense of democracy within a school which is quite rare" (survey, n.d). While Dalia echoes the unique student-teacher relationships described by students in earlier passages, she also suggests that there were fewer hierarchies among students themselves. Though this may initially seem insignificant, it actually speaks to how the school emphasizes the worth of all students, and contributes to what many students refer to as a culture of respect that they describe as lacking in other environments. Moreover, these perceptions reveal that one group's status is not necessarily elevated over another's.

Culture of Respect: Engaging the School Core Values

Related to the culture of care that manifests in and through the various school relationships, many students articulate the importance of the core values[9] in helping to create a culture that is fundamental to students' academic and social well-being at school. For instance, Sammy, an alumnus, explains that the core value of respect for the intellect contributes to a sense of belonging in the school:

> Well, I mean, in terms of respect for the intellect, like, there's a lot of really intellectual stuff going on at Prep. Like, a lot of really good classes with things that might not be discussed in other classes in other schools. And respect to [sic] everybody's level of intellect, you know, just something ... there's something for everybody to feel smart about.... I think the fact that the teachers didn't judge people because of stuff, like, trickled down to the students; so, the students were less judgmental of each other. And then people would accept ... I don't know because it's hard to ... there's a lot of people who are, like, have similar interests and can get along well. But they won't ever know it unless it's in the right circumstances, you know. And I think Prep is the right circumstances for a lot of people who wouldn't normally realize that they have stuff in common, to find out that they have things in common. It was very accepting and very, you know, like I said, nonjudgmental. (interview, April 28, 2007)

Linking the sentiment that the classes are inclusive and intellectual, Sammy suggests this affects how students interacted with each other. By being in a community that, as he describes, accepts the individual (and her intellect and thoughts), Sammy posits that students feel less alienated and actually, more connected to their peers and teachers than they would have previously imagined. Similarly, Sebastien, a current student, points out:

> You know, I feel like if people come to this school they will actually feel a part of it, instead of just feel like they are entering a building for a few hours where they have no choice but to go and just leave afterwards.... I know a lot of people who stay after school, including myself, just to be around and 'cause I enjoy being in this school so much. I think people will feel a part of something rather than just going to school, you know. It's a community and a school, that's what I think people would like most about it because the teachers are so inviting as people ... very welcoming. So, I really think that about the educational level too ... I feel like people will learn and being that the school is small you know, like, teachers will keep up with people and they will know people on a deeper level ... instead of having thousands of students in one school when you have a few hundred, I think that's actually better for students. (interview, May 2, 2007)

While Sebastien explicitly connects "smallness" as a way to be known on a deeper level, he also discusses being part of a community rather than just a school. Thus, students are keenly conscious of the explicit social mission of the school, as well as the obvious academic one. In Sebastien's case, these two missions are inextricably linked, contributing to an expectation that school is not just about "academics," but also a site for democratic engagement and a culture that is infused with respect.

Students also feel that the Prep core values contribute to an environment that both emphasizes tolerance and cooperation and creates safety and less violence. For example, Luis, an alumnus, states:

> I hear kids [in other schools] that say they get into fights all the time, but, you know, since Prep is so small, you knew everybody's name, and you know ... you had the core values, everybody, you know, ultimately got along with each other. (interview, March 13, 2007)

Like Sebastien, Luis underscores the role of smallness; however, he also identifies the core values that serve as a benchmark by which to negotiate behaviors. Similarly, Joshua, who attended a small middle school, echoes Luis' sentiment about the lack of fighting at Prep, but also adds that issues tend to get resolved nonviolently:

> if I went to my old school, there might not be fights inside but whenever you got outside somebody was talking about somebody that's gonna fight. Here, there are no fights. Everybody's cool if there is a problem. If there is a fight

> it's resolved in like two days. There are no problems. It's not like, okay we
> have to go get guns and knives—none of that. (interview, March 22, 2007)

Joshua suggests that the lack of physical violence is not merely a result of
problems being sidelined for later, but rather, indicative of a more healthy
school culture in which issues are dealt with and confronted through communication. This observation mirrors Sammy's earlier comment that
teachers' interactions with the students "trickled down" to create an environment of tolerance and respect towards each other. Reneka affirms this
by stating:

> They [other schools] have a lot of fights. I think the only reason they have
> fights is because the teachers can't communicate with the student; it seems
> like the teachers are scared of the students. As long as they communicate
> like the teachers at Prep did, every high school in New York should be fine.
> But, they don't communicate, they treat the kids like just any other number
> and the kids feel that, that's why they take attitudes on the teachers, or they
> just want to fight all the time, they're aggressive. (interview, March 12, 2007)

Though there were two fights during my year of fieldwork, most students
still describe Prep as a school in which violence rarely occurred. Overall,
students generally feel that the school is safe and there is an expectation
of congeniality. More importantly, students repeatedly describe a
resounding culture of respect that goes beyond superficial niceties. As
Matthew, a graduating senior, suggests:

> I think that what I learned from this school is just about people in general
> and how people are with one another. Despite all of the problems that
> everyone has with one another in this school, you know how everybody talks
> about each other. But we're all stuck together though, no matter what hap-
> pens its crazy—what somebody told you that that person said this about you,
> —we always remain friends. That goes for everybody; we're stuck together.
> When it came down to it, we all have each other's back and I think that's a
> beautiful thing. We're all growing to be brothers and sisters in some kind of
> way; we're all close, it's crazy … I'm gonna miss this school, … I had a good
> experience in this school with people and friends and teachers and stuff like
> that. I don't think I will get this experience again towards people. (focus
> group, May 18, 2007)

While Matthew invokes some of the familial themes treated earlier, he also
remarkably describes how there was a general sense of conviviality among
everyone, despite issues that arise among people, decreasing any escala-
tion of tensions. He does not negate that there are quibbles or gossip, yet
he expresses how at Prep, people transcend these because of the expectations of respect.

This welcoming and tolerant atmosphere that transpires in the school is not random, but thoughtfully integrated through a core values framework. While other intentional mechanisms and structures play a role in creating this environment (see Hantzopoulos, 2011), the core values certainly contribute to establishing the school culture, which ultimately supports the academic aspects of the school.

A Culture of Questioning: Curricula, Coursework and Critical Consciousness[10]

Another central way in which students describe their academic engagement at Prep is based on the overall curriculum. In particular, they repeatedly emphasize the theme-based, in-depth investigatory nature of their classes and feel that not only does this engage them in their learning, but also exposes them to new ways of thinking about the world and the way it works. While it is impossible to gauge whether or not schools can actually be transformative, many students articulate that the classes at Prep, as well as the other non-academic structures mentioned earlier like relationships and a culture of respect, facilitate their critical consciousness.[11] Current and former students note that their classes often deconstruct dominant narratives by using a multiplicity of sources. For instance, Dalia, in her alumna survey wrote that:

> teaching, not through textbooks, not through mainstream education, but through actual artifacts, and pieces, and writings, and every single class I took from art class to music class or history, everything, just, the depth of it and understanding the topic was what I needed. (n.d.)

In this passage, Dalia understands the limitations of textbooks as sites for perpetuating singular views of history. As Kuzmic (2000) and Kaomea (2000) elucidate in their work, textbooks also maintain dominant cultural, racialized and gendered values and norms to obfuscate the ways in which marginalized populations have contributed to societies and have resisted dominant ideologies. By working with and deconstructing these dominant narratives in their classes at Prep, students described how they begin to view "the world" differently, or as Kevin, an alumnus, describes, "not accept something at face value" (December 20, 2006).

Many students describe the curricula as being culturally and social relevant to their lives. Lisa, an alumna who is Puerto Rican, shares her astonishment at having a course on Caribbean history that emphasized Puerto Rico, and states:

> I felt like...coming here it was a part of my history. Like, I was learning about myself so it was interesting. I feel like in another school you don't really have that advantage. So it's pretty ... I guess ... more rounded, the education here. (interview, March 27, 2007)

Not only does she suggest that this experience gave her a more complete education, but she also explains that it "made me want to further learn ... learn more about the issues that are going on in Puerto Rico," increasing her commitment to activism around Puerto Rican issues. As a student who previously describes herself as one on the verge of dropping out, Lisa truly benefitted from such an approach to curriculum. This runs concordant with how, in general, students describe learning more (about themselves, their skills, and content knowledge) from theme and project-based classes; for students who have been previously unsuccessful or disengaged from school, the relevant nature of classes are a way to re-socialize them academically.

Related to this, students also suggest that this type of approach helped them examine their own role in society, so that historicized knowledge and contemporary events are reinterpreted based on their personal experience. For instance, Lexus describes in his survey that "This school made me want to learn about what is going on around the world beyond NYC. It opened my eyes to issues going on around the world." This suggests that he became "aware" of something that was either unbeknownst or uninteresting to him before, and was pushed to learn beyond what he previously deemed his personal sphere of interest. Similarly, Elvis, in his survey, echoes this by stating, "the school challenged me to explore the world and current events. To be open-minded and think about these issues." Statements like these repeatedly came up in interviews and surveys, suggesting that the students felt equipped with critical thinking skills that both allowed them to continually question what was presented to them as truth about the world and see how their own role in society fit into this. As Garrold, an alumnus states in his survey:

> Well as everyone knew me to be, I was very "young" coming into Prep. I had a young mind and was very closed about certain aspects of today's life. Prep helped change me into becoming a man and it gave my mind an opportunity to grow and look at certain situations different. In Prep, class discussions, Advisory and quads help broaden my mind and helped me to become a deeper thinker in any conversation or situation in life. (n.d.)

Some alumni and students describe this process of analysis as one that did not simply encourage them to interrogate taken-for-granted assumptions about "the world," but also made them question their own particular histories and narratives. One alumna, Rebecca, highlights how being at Prep made her view Jamaica, her ancestral country, in a different way, such that she "noticed disparities between the rich and the poor. I was there for 11 days and saw *so* much [and before] I just did not have that view of Jamaica (interview, January 5, 2007).[12] In this sense, Rebecca credits her experience at the school as one that not only led her to think about *the* world differently, but specifically as one that led her to think about *her* world differently.

Other alumni and students explain that the type of critical thinking encouraged at the school propelled them into activism or made them more committed to enacting social change. For example, Luis, an alumnus explains:

> I started to see that ... I can influence the world just as much as people influence me ... I didn't think that when I first came here. I thought, I'm just, you know, an ant in a colony ... playing a role. You know, but I know that I can actually do stuff now to influence other people and to know make life better for others. (March 13, 2007)

In fact, Luis later describes that the school compelled him to want to go into teaching as an act of social change to study education at Hunter College.

Related to this, students and alumni often feel hope that they can transform their society based on their experiences at Prep. Queenia, an alumna, describes how when she went with classmates to City Hall to read letters to officials in opposition to high-stakes testing, she realized that she could affect change:

> you hear about people doing these amazing things, these protests and these campaigns and what not and just taking up these causes that they feel strongly for and you never realize that those people are the same people as you. *There's nothing about them that's extraordinary, except that they choose to be extraordinary people.*[13] (interview, May 6, 2007)

In this excerpt, Queenia describes how this encouragement made her feel that she *could* affect change in her community and be more like the people she admired. Others, like Abigail, an alumna studying in Costa Rica during my fieldwork, specifically credit Prep in a survey for making "me a more socially and politically conscious person and drive me to want to be an active participant in the global community" and in particular, for catalyzing her interest in her current work on immigrant rights issues (n.d.). These perceptions are concordant with the ways in which many students, current and former, feel that they can both have a voice and stake in their communities, and in some cases, work actively towards affecting change, locally and globally.

CULTURE CLASHES:
NAVIGATING DEMOCRACY ON UNDEMOCRATIC TERRAIN

While students describe how their experiences at Prep helped them feel cared for, respected, and contributed to cultivating their critical thinking skills and commitment to activism, and that these experiences contribute to their academic success in school, some also describe brushing up against 'realities" that challenged the frameworks and experiences they had at Prep. For instance, Antoinette, an alumna studying abroad in Jerusalem, writes in her survey about her experience at Prep:

> Prep reinvigorated a love of learning for me [after transferring from a highly competitive NYC, specialized private high school]. The teachers encouraged me to look at the world around me, ask questions, and initiate positive change. One of the most important lessons that I learned was that activism did not have to be only big issues that you hear about on TV or marching with signs, but could be as small as helping someone in the neighborhood, or making the school look nicer. By making activism possible, Prep instilled in me the need to always be working towards positive change. Living now in Jerusalem I struggle with this, as it is hard for me to walk to Arab neighborhoods and see poverty and discrimination, but be unable to help without putting myself in danger. I am sure, though, if I look, I will find ways to work in small ways. (n.d.)

Antoinette describes the difficulty of being an agent of change when larger societal forces prevent her from even engaging in the world in the way that she previously imagined she could. Since this excerpt is from a survey and not an interview, I cannot probe what she means by "danger." Nonetheless, what this does convey is that she feels there are real obstacles to her sense of agency when she is confronted with larger structural inequities.

Rebecca, who earlier discusses her experience in Jamaica, faced a similar dilemma and commented that while Prep raised her awareness of social issues, it also "sheltered [her] from other institutions where [her] voice may not have been heard (survey, n.d.). Like Antoinette, Rebecca describes feeling inhibited by external structures and institutions that limit her "voice." This comment about "sheltering," however, reveals an interesting paradox. When I asked her about this in an interview, Rebecca describes her college as a "rich White school." She explains that as an African American female student from NYC, she struggles to find a place where her voice is legitimized and heard. Yet, she also states that being silenced allows her to understand what else "needed to be changed." While she is critical about how Prep sheltered her, in some ways, the reality of being silenced at the post-Prep institution has compelled her even more fervently to find her public voice. One might also wonder if she had never been in a place where her voice mattered (at Prep), she might not feel so compelled to fight for her voice (and other voices) to be heard at her new college.

In addition, alumni describe the intergenerational, diverse, and convivial atmosphere at Prep as something that is hard to replicate elsewhere. According to some alumni, this leads to huge disappointment with their new institutions and makes them unsure about how to integrate themselves into the larger environment. For instance, Dalia, describes how she feels shocked at college when she cannot connect with other students:

> I was kind of thrown into the real world and went to a school where I didn't really know anyone, and it was a commuter school so it was really hard to meet people. So my first freshman year in college I absolutely detested the school I was in, even though I'm still in it now, I feel remotely better about it, a little bit, but I, it was very bizarre for me cause I just went from a school that had so much warmth, and liveliness, to a school that didn't. It almost felt like being at [the mainstream school] again, not Humanities Prep, but a very, rigid environment, and I was like (sic) "Isn't Prep prepping me for college ... it's not!" (interview, February 15, 2007)

This sentiment expressed by Dalia was not uncommon among alumni interviewed. In fact, many often lamented the lack of diversity and community they experienced in their academic life post-Prep.

Despite what Dalia notes above, she also explains that she negotiated this tension by becoming involved in Arab American clubs and networks at her school and beyond. In fact, she is currently "active" in her community, and is making a documentary about the fetishization of Arab American culture in mainstream American culture called "Arab Craze." Dalia also concludes,

> But you know, it did actually (prepare me for college), the way we interacted with one another, whether it was with students or teachers at Prep, being in college long enough and being a part of organizations, and functions, and classes you start to see how that really preps you for college.

Thus, she links her experience at Prep to the sense of activism she found in her community.

In these cases, Rebecca and Dalia sought out particular groups in which they *did* have a voice, despite not finding these inherently in their post-secondary institutions. Rebecca, for instance, describes joining an African American women's community-service oriented sorority at another school (because it did not exist at her home institution) and Dalia is incredibly active in her community. Both alumna joined and became active in groups or societies that were related to their race or gender, perhaps as a place to initiate change and also to have a voice in an otherwise racist or sexist environment. This involvement in groups suggests that students do not lose hope for change and find new and creative ways to mediate these tensions.

It is also important to note however, that students clearly do not live in a vacuum while attending Prep. There are other societal factors that students have to contend with on a daily basis, many of which are in conflict with the type of community values that exist at the school. Nonetheless, their description of life post-Prep accentuates that students may have expected something different from their college institutions because of their experiences at Prep.

IMPLICATIONS FOR CRITICAL SMALL SCHOOLS MOVEMENT

At Prep, smallness is ultimately not what defines students' academic achievement. While current and former students appreciate and value the smallness of the school, and recognize it as an essential feature of the design, they also identify important aspects of the school culture that contribute to their academic success. In particular, they suggest that the culture of care that is infused through strong student-teacher relationships, the culture of respect that is transmitted through the core values framework and the culture of questioning that is promulgated through a curriculum that is thematic, culturally-relevant, and project and inquiry-based, collectively helps lay the groundwork for their academic (re)socialization. Moreover, this study shows that course work that allows for contestation is vital not only for the cultivation of voice, but also for student academic engagement. This is particularly poignant for those students who have previously felt marginalized in other schools, though just as valid for those that have always experienced "success" academically.

In this sense, schools like Prep and others in this volume provide keen insight into the inner workings of what Fine, Weis, and Powell (1997) deem " 'integrated' school[s] ... one[s] that self-consciously creates intellectual and social engagements across racial and ethnic groups" (p. 1). By exploring the ways that students made meaning of their experiences at Prep, this chapter sheds light on how contexts of diversity and democracy in schools might also partially generate youth leadership, agency, democratic participation and a commitment to social change. While some students note a disconnect between their high school experience and that which they experienced in other institutions, they still seem equipped to negotiate these tensions in ways that allowed them to stay true to their values.

Attention must be paid, however, to how critical small schools prepare students for dealing with the complexities of democracy, voice, and sense of belonging when they leave their respective school sites. Though students found ways to circumvent the clashes they faced when they left Prep, there was a sense that Prep was an idealized "bubble" that could not be replicated in the real world. Thus, it is imperative for those committed to creating space for youth agency and participation to carefully consider ways in which students can be ready to take on challenges beyond the sphere of schooling. This requires a conscious effort to continually link school experiences with those of the real world. At Prep in particular, they have now instituted an Alumni Day at which former students come back and talk about their post-secondary experiences with current students. Included in these discussions are not just conversations about academics, but also some of the emotional and social pressures New York City students often face when they leave the city. This type of activity can only be informative for Prep students and students who attend other critical small schools.

While there are likely a myriad of other approaches to forge these connections, another more explicit one might be to incorporate opportunities for students to participate in off-site community based internships with local social justice-oriented nonprofit organizations as some of the schools in this volume did. This could include consistent interaction with local activists, as well as space for reflection and community action. While these opportunities sometimes present themselves at Prep through their Community Action Internship program, this is not a mandatory requirement for students so many do not take part. Perhaps more consistent attention to providing these types of opportunities might provide students with more realistic experiences beyond the scope of the school, in which their agency is challenged more directly. Since many former students describe difficulty negotiating their "Prep ideals" with external realities, those that work in these organizations provide insight and models for how to respond to such challenges. In this sense, the foundation that is laid at these critical schools can move towards helping students cope with the complexities of enacting social change beyond the sphere of their school.

Despite these challenges, students and alumni at Prep feel overwhelming positive about their experience at the school. While it is in the spirit of the original movement to reflect critically on the struggles of enacting social and educational change, educators and school reformers should take heed of the triumphs as well. Particularly in this time of top-down educational reform, it is more important than ever for the critical small schools movement to maintain its commitment to the types of pedagogies, practices and cultures that were born out of the original movement. In this vein, what students tell us is the most instructive lesson of all.

NOTES

1. "Dropping out" is the common nomenclature to describe the behaviors and actions of students who do not graduate from high school. More recent ethnographic work argues that it is not the behavior or actions of students that results in their nonmatriculation; rather, it is the treatment of students *by* schools that results in the students getting "pushed out" of schools (see, e.g., Eubanks, Parish, and Smith, D. (1997) and Fine (1991).

2. New Visions for Public Schools is a nonprofit organization that financially supported, though large philanthropic foundations, a large number of new small schools in NYC.

3. In another article (Hantzopoulos, 2011), I demonstrate the inlfluence of school wide intentional democratic spaces (town meeting, advisory, the fairness committee) at Prep on the academic socialization. These structures are not dealt with as explicitly in this chapter.

4. The city rate is often contested because it does not always take into account when students leave school to enroll in a GED program (Gootman, 2006). Thus, city dropout rates are considered much higher than 19.9%. In fact, because the city statistics of measurement obfuscate the actual number of dropouts, Advocates for Children and the Public Advocate of the City of New York (2002) conducted a study that looked at "discharge" rates of high school students as a more accurate measurement. What they discovered was that in 2000-2001, over 55,000 students were discharged; this exceeded the number of the entire 2001 graduating class of 33,250 NYC students.

5. Math is the exception to this, as Prep often used a more traditional and hierarchically structured math curriculum that required students to master a particular skill prior to enrolling in the next course.

6. Outside evaluators are invited by teachers and parents in the school and represent people who are not formal teachers in the school.

7. In 2000, the school replaced weekly whole school town meetings with weekly meetings known as Quads. As the school grew in size, it no longer was feasible to meet as a whole school community every week. Instead, in Quads, four rotating advisories meet for the same purpose as previous Town Meetings. After each rotation, the school would meet for one week in a Town Meeting, and then would go back to the Quad schedule.

8. Restorative justice models focus more on the relationships among "victims" and "violators," as opposed to retributive justice, which emphasizes interpretation of strict legal code.

9. The core values are respect for humanity, diversity, the intellect, and truth and commitment to peace, justice, and democracy.

10. For another detailed account of this section, please see Hantzopoulos (2011).

11. Critical consciousness refers to process by which people come to understand their social worlds and the nature of oppression and subsequently take action to transform it (see Freire, 1972/2003).

12. Italics mine.
13. Italics mine

REFERENCES

Antorp-Gonzalez, R., & De Jesús, A. (2005). Toward a theory of critical care in urban small school reform: Examining structures and pedagogies of caring in two Latino community-based schools. *International Journal of Qualitative Studies in Education*, *19*(4), 409-433.

Bartlett, L. (2005). Dialogue, knowledge, and teacher-student relations: Freirean pedagogy in theory and practice. *Comparative Education Review*, *49*(3), 1-21.

Bajaj, M. (2009). Why context matters: The material conditions of caring in Zambia. *International Journal of Qualitative Studies in Education*, *22*(4), 379-398.

Belenky, M., Clinchy, B., Goldberger, N., & Tarule, J. (1997). *Women's ways of knowing: The development of self, voice, and mind.* New York, NY: Basic Books.

Bryman, A. (2006). *Interviewing in qualitative research. Social science methods.* New York, NY: Oxford.

Eubanks, E.,, Parish, R. & Smith, D. (1997). Changing the discourse in schools. In P. Hall (Ed.), *Race, ethnicity, and multiculturalism. Policy and practice.* Missouri Symposium on Research and Educational Policy: Garland Reference Library of Social Science.

Fine, M. (1991). *Framing dropouts: Notes on the politics of an urban high school.* Albany, NY: State University of New York.

Fine, M., Weis, L., & Powell, L. (1997). Communities of difference : A critical look at desegregated spaces created for and by youth. *Harvard Educational Review*, *67*(2), 247-284.

Fontana, A., & Frey (1998). Interview: The art of science. In Norman K. Denzin & Yvonna S. Lincoln (Eds.), *Collecting and interpreting qualitative methods* (pp. 47-78), London: SAGE.

Freire, P. (2003). The pedagogy of the oppressed. New York: Continuum. (Original work published 1972)

Gilligan, C. (1982). *In a different voice: Psychological theory and women's development.* Cambridge, MA: Harvard University Press.

Gootman, E. (2006, October 22). Study takes a sharp look at the city's failing Students. *The New York Times.* Retrieved from www.nytimes.org

Hantzopoulos, M. (2006/2011). Deepening democracy: Rethinking discipline in schools. (Reprint with permission from *Rethinking Schools* in *Schools: Studies in Education.* University of Chicago Press. Spring 2011, Vol. 8(1), 112-116).

Hantzopoulos, M. (2009). Transformative schooling in restrictive times: Engaging teacher participation in small school reform during an era of standardization. In F. Vavrus & L. Bartlett (Eds.). *Comparatively knowing: Vertical case study research in comparative and development education* (pp. 111-126). New York, NY: Palgrave.

Hantzopoulos, M. (2011). Institutionalizing critical peace education in public schools: A case for comprehensive implementation. Special Issue of *Journal of Peace Education*, *8*(3), 225-242.

Humanities Preparatory Mission Statement. (n.d.). retrieved April 12, 2010, from www.humanitiesprep.org

Kaomea, J. (2000). A Curriculum of Aloha? Colonialism and tourism in Hawai'i's elementary textbooks Colonialism and tourism in Hawai'i's elementary textbooks. *Curriculum Inquiry, 30*(3), 319-344.

Kuzmic, J. (2000). Textbooks, knowledge and masculinity: examining patriarchy from within. In N. Lesko (Ed.), *Masculinities at school* (p. 105-126). Thousand Oaks, CA: SAGE.

LeCompte, M., & Preissle, J. (1993). *Ethnography and qualitative design in educational research*. San Diego, CA: Academic Press.

Marshall, C., & Rossman, G. (1999). *Designing qualitative research*. Thousand Oaks, CA: SAGE.

Maxwell, J. (2005). *Qualitative research design: an interpretative approach*. Thousand Oaks, CA: SAGE.

Meier, D. (2004). NCLB and democracy. In D. Meier & G. Wood (Eds.), *Many Children Left Behind* (pp. 66-78). Boston, MA:vBeacon.

Noddings, N. (1992). *The challenge to care in schools: An alternative approach to education*. New York, NY: Teachers College.

Noguera, P. A. (2006). How listening to students can help schools improve. *Theory Into Practice, 46*(3), 205-211.

Oyler, C., & Becker, J. (1997). Teaching beyond the progressive—traditional dichotomy: Sharing authority and sharing vulnerability. *Curriculum Inquiry, 27*(4), 453-467.

Performance Assessment, (n.d.). Retrieved December 12, 2007, from www .performanceassessment.org

Rodriguez, L., & Conchas, G. (2008). *Small schools and urban youth: Using the power of school culture to engage students*. Thousand Oaks, CA: SAGE.

The Public Advocate for the City of New York & Advocates for Children. (2002). *Pushing out at-risk students: An analysis of high school discharge figures*. New York, NY: Author.

Valenzuela, A. (1999). *Subtractive schooling: US-Mexican youth and the politics of caring*. Ithaca, NY: SUNY.

ABOUT THE AUTHORS

THE EDITORS

Maria Hantzopoulos is an assistant professor of education at Vassar College, where she is the coordinator of the Adolescent Education Certification Program and a participating faculty member in the programs in Women's Studies and Urban Studies. She teaches a variety of courses related to methodology, sociology of education, educational reform, and peace and justice studies. Before coming to Vassar, Dr. Hantzopoulos supervised pre-service undergraduate and graduate student teachers at Columbia University's Barnard and Teachers Colleges and worked as a staff developer with middle and high school teachers. She also taught humanities and social studies for 10 years at Humanities Preparatory Academy, and worked for 3 years as a dialogue facilitator at Seeds of Peace International Camp. Additionally, she has been on the planning team of several small new high schools in NYC and served as the youth leadership development coordinator at ASPIRA of New York for 3 years. Dr. Hantzopoulos remains active with many NGOs and non-profits on curriculum writing, advocacy, and policy. Her current research interests and projects involve critical media literacy, restorative justice in schools, peace and human rights education, the education of immigrant youth, and urban educational reform. Her work has appeared in a variety of publications, including the *Journal of Peace Education, Schools: Studies in Education,* and *Rethinking Schools*. She completed her doctorate in 2008 at Teachers College, Columbia University in the Department of International and Transcultural Studies and is a long time resident of Queens where she lives with her husbandand two children.

Alia R. Tyner-Mullings is currently an assistant professor of sociology at The New Community College at the City University of New York. As a founding faculty member, she has helped to design and develop the curriculum, assessment and student services for The New Community College, CUNY's first new college in 40 years. The school opens in the Fall of 2012 in midtown Manhattan. She has taught courses to both graduate and undergraduate students in sociology, statistics, the sociology of education and race and education. Dr. Tyner-Mullings' interest in critical small schools began while attending CPE and CPESS from 6-17 years of age. Upon visiting a school in another country, she came to realize how her schools differed from the mainstream. Dr. Tyner-Mullings received a degree in English at Oberlin College before teaching mathematics and creative writing at Humanities Preparatory Academy. After teaching for 2 years, Dr. Tyner-Mullings matriculated at the CUNY, Graduate School and University Center where she earned a doctorate in sociology through her dissertation on CPESS and its structure, outcomes and transformation. Upon finishing her doctorate, she was a post-doctoral fellow at Teachers College, Columbia University in the Sociology and Education Program. Before joining the faculty at the New Community College at CUNY, Dr. Tyner-Mullings taught at the historically black college, Morgan State University in Baltimore, Maryland. Dr. Tyner-Mullings currently sits on assessment committees for two critical small schools and has worked as a statistical and academic consultant for several colleges and universities. Her present research interests include the sociology of education, with a focus on equity and urban educational reform; the sociology of communities, the sociology of sports and cultural studies. Dr. Tyner-Mullings is in the process of publishing a sociological writing textbook with Dr. Angelique Harris as well as a book focusing on her research on Central Park East Secondary School and its relevance in current educational policy.

THE AUTHORS

Nora Ahmed is currently researching the viability of implementing student-run legal information clinics in public high schools in New York City as part of her honors thesis for the Faculty of Law at McGill University. In addition to researching garbage as a metaphor for the waste that war creates in Mali, West Africa, teaching ESL students in France, and learning Spanish in Guatemala, Ms. Ahmed visited schools in South India in order to gain a more comprehensive understanding of education equity and affirmative action. As a law student, Ms. Ahmed interned for the State Department of the United States, the Drug Law Reform Project of the

American Civil Liberties Union, and Paul, Weiss, Rifkind, Wharton & Garrison LLP. During the four years that preceded law school, Ms. Ahmed taught high school English in the South Bronx at Pablo Neruda Academy for Architecture and World Studies.

Lesley Bartlett is an anthropologist and associate professor in the Comparative and International Education Program at Teachers College, Columbia University. Her research and teaching interests include sociocultural and multilingual studies of literacy, teacher education, and social inequality and schooling. She is the coauthor, with Ofelia Garcia, of *Additive Schooling in Subtractive Times: Bilingual Education and Dominican Immigrant Youth in the Heights*, the author of *The Word and the World: The Cultural Politics of Literacy in Brazil*, and the coeditor (with Frances Vavrus) of *Critical Approaches to Comparative Education: Vertical Cases Studies from Africa, Europe, the Middle East, and the Americas*. Dr. Bartlett's work has also been published in a wide variety of journals, including *Teachers College Record*, *International Journal of Qualitative Studies in Education*, *Comparative Education Review*, and *Anthropology and Education Quarterly*.

Liza Bearman spent many years as a high school teacher and administrator in Los Angeles and New York City, followed by years as a staff developer and literacy coach for new small secondary schools in New York City. She also served as a Small School and Leadership Study tour facilitator with Stanford University's School Redesign Network and has been active with the Coalition of Essential School for years, frequently presenting at their Fall Forums and Summer Institutes. After her time in New York, Dr. Bearman was a regional director for a national small school development organization (a member of the Association for High School Innovation) that focused on creating schools rooted in personalized project-based learning. Currently, Dr. Bearman develops and implements programs for the Collective Voices Foundation in Los Angeles, a nonprofit organization serving underresourced children and schools. She is also a school change facilitator and curriculum coach at two high schools located in Los Angeles County Probation Camps and an adjunct assistant professor in the Rossier School of Education at the University of Southern California.
  Liza received her bachelors degree from the University of Wisconsin-Madison, and her master of arts (MA), master's of education (EdM) and doctor of education (EdD) degrees from Columbia University's Teachers College.

Janice Bloom has been involved in urban school reform in New York City for the past 15 years, as a teacher, staff developer, researcher and professor of educational studies. After starting her career as a teacher in New

York City public high schools, she earned a doctorate in Urban Education from the CUNY Graduate Center. She has since done extensive professional development work in high schools around college access, inquiry teaching and curriculum design, and implementation of small school structures. At the university level, her teaching and research at Eugene Lang College/The New School focused on issues of access to higher education, social class, and urban schooling. Her recent publications include "Social Class Resources and Widening the Road to College" (ASHE/Lumina Critical Essay Series, 2008) and "(Mis)Reading Social Class in the Journey Towards College: Youth Development in Urban America" (Teachers College Record, 2007). From 2009-2011, Dr. Bloom worked as the co-director of the College Knowledge project at the Institute for Student Achievement; she is currently one of the co-directors of the New York City based organization College Access: Research & Action.

Anthony De Jesús is an assistant professor at City University of New York (CUNY) Hunter College School of Social Work in New York City where he teaches courses on research methods, epistemology and schools. His research focuses primarily on addressing the social and cultural barriers which prevent Latino and African American students from accessing post secondary educational experiences and successfully transitioning to higher education. Dr. De Jesús' professional interests include community and school-based social work practice, the history of Puerto Rican/Latino education organizing/activism for school reform and representation and the sociology of education.

Jay Feldman is currently a senior research associate at MPR Associates in Berkeley California. In his almost 20 years of experience, Dr. Feldman has conducted research on children and adolescents in school and out-of-school settings and on school change, policy, and teacher practice as well as providing technical assistance to K-12 schools. Prior to coming to MPR, he was the director of research for the Coalition of Essential Schools National office where he evaluated a national 60-school professional learning community that supported the creation of almost 30 new schools developed as start-ups or through the conversion of large comprehensive high schools to independent small schools. As codirector of research and evaluation at the Center for Collaborative Education in Boston, MA, he conducted research on the practices of the Boston Pilot School Network and the Turning Points Middle School reform model. He is the author of the book *Choosing Small: The Essential Guide to Successful High School Conversion*, with Lisette Lopez and Kathy Simon. He received his EdM at the Harvard Graduate School of Education and his PhD in Developmental Psychology at Boston College.

Martha Foote is director of research for the New York Performance Standards Consortium, a coalition of critical small high schools that supports the use of performance-based assessments. A graduate of Swarthmore College and Bank Street College of Education, she completed her PhD in teaching, curriculum and change at the University of Rochester, where she worked as a researcher for a Spencer-funded international study on change in high schools. A teacher for 12 years, Dr. Foote has parlayed her teaching experience into the research world. Her studies on school reform and assessment have been published in *Phi Delta Kappan* and *Educational Administration Quarterly*.

Jill P. Koyama, an anthropologist, is an assistant professor in the Department of Educational Leadership and Policy in the Graduate School of Education, State University of New York at Buffalo. Her research is situated across three interrelated strands of inquiry: the productive assemblage of policy, the complexities of immigrant and bilingual education policy, and the controversies of globalizing education. Dr. Koyama's recent book, *Making Failure Pay: For-Profit Tutoring, High-Stakes Testing, and Public Schools* was published by The University of Chicago Press in 2010 and her work has appeared in several journals, including *Anthropology and Education Quarterly*, *Teachers College Record*, and *International Journal of Bilingual Education and Bilingualism*.

Anne O'Dwyer is the dean of academic affairs at Bard College at Simon's Rock. She began her transition into higher education administration at Simon's Rock while on the faculty, serving as head of the division of Social Studies, chair of the Faculty Senate, and Faculty Lead on the College's re-accreditation. She subsequently moved into administration, first as associate dean of academic affairs, and then serving as dean of academic affairs since July 2010. Dr. O'Dwyer's focus as an administrator has been on student retention, assessment and the development of new academic programs and initiatives. She was a professor of psychology at the college for over ten years. Her research interests include the consequences of interpersonal and intergroup conflict on individuals' sense of self and identity; most recently, she has been exploring the sociocognitive bases of anger. She received her PhD in Social Psychology from Boston College in 1996 and began her tenure at Simon's Rock shortly after.

Rosa L. Rivera-McCutchen earned her doctorate in teaching and learning at New York University, and is currently an assistant professor in the Educational Leadership Program at City University of New York (CUNY) Lehman College. Prior to joining the Lehman faculty, she was an instructor in the Scaffolded Apprenticeship Model program, an educational leadership and comprehensive school improvement initiative at CUNY Baruch College. Dr. Rivera-McCutchen has worked as an educational consultant, supporting professional development in various NYC small schools, as well as conducted numerous program evaluations. She began her career in education teaching Humanities and History for several years at Wings Academy high school in the Bronx, after which she served as the first operations director of DonorsChoose.org, an educational nonprofit organization founded by a Wings' colleague. Dr. Rivera-McCutchen currently lives in the Bronx with her husband and three small children.

Jessica T. Shiller is an assistant professor of education in the Department of Instructional Leadership and Professional Development at Towson University in Maryland. Her research and teaching focuses on urban schools, school reform efforts, and the teaching and learning of low income youth of color. Shiller began teaching high school social studies teacher in a small school in New York City Public Schools after getting a master's degree from Teachers College, Columbia University in 1995. In 2007, she completed her PhD from New York University where she conducted research on the development of the small schools in the South Bronx. She spent 3 years teaching at Lehman College, City University of New York before moving to Towson.

INDEX

CPSIA information can be obtained at www.ICGtesting.com
Printed in the USA
LVOW071506240113

317120LV00004B/255/P

9 781617 356834